Faith and the Intifada

Palestinian Christian Voices

Edited by

Naim S. Ateek
Marc H. Ellis
Rosemary Radford Ruether

Maryknoll, New York 10545

The Catholic Foreign Mission Society of America (Maryknoll) recruits and trains people for overseas missionary service. Through Orbis Books, Maryknoll aims to foster the international dialogue that is essential to mission. The books published, however, reflect the opinions of their authors and are not meant to represent the official position of the society.

Manufactured in the United States of America

Library of Congress Cataloging-in-Publication Data

Faith and the Intifada : Palestinian Christian voices / edited by Naim
Ateek, Marc H. Ellis, Rosemary Radford Ruether.
p. cm.
Includes bibliographical references.
ISBN 0-88344-808-4 (pbk.)
1. Jewish-Arab relations—Congresses. 2. Christians—Palestine—
Congresses. 3. Jewish-Arab relations—Religious aspects—
Christianity—Congresses. 4. Intifada, 1987- —Congresses.
5. Liberation theology—Congresses. I. Ateek, Naim Stifan, 1937- .
II. Ellis, Marc H. III. Ruether, Rosemary Radford.
DS119.7.F315 1991
956.95'3044—dc20 91-44736
CIP

Contents

PART 5
INTERNATIONAL RESPONSES TO THE QUEST FOR PALESTINIAN THEOLOGY

Foreword

Welcome

SAMIA KHOURY

In the Holy Land, the cradle of the three monotheistic faiths, it is only natural that theology and religion should be at the center of our lives. At the same time, we have been struggling for liberation in our troubled land since time immemorial. But for us this is the first time that liberation and theology have come together on the same platform.

Religion has played a major role in the struggle of the indigenous people of this land. In the name of religion wars have been waged and under the pretext of religion violations of human rights continue to be justified. Religion has been used, abused, misinterpreted, and misunderstood. So much has been done in the name of God that his image has become distorted, so much so that we find ourselves struggling to hold on to our faith, or putting it aside. As Palestinian Christians we often feel embarrassed by our faith, because it is related so closely to the faith of our oppressors and their supporters.

The Christian faith, which we so proudly offered to the whole world as a single unit, has often come back to us fragmented and in the form of religious colonization. It has been used to justify the many injustices inflicted upon us. And to add insult to injury we are always asked how and when we were converted to Christianity. We have always been Christians; but in our struggle for liberation we are together as Palestinians, Christians, and Muslims alike. There is a mentality of colonization and occupation that has tried to split our people on the basis of religion. Why do the security police at the bridge [the Allenby Bridge, the border checkpoint between Jordan and the occupied West Bank] ask me whether I am Christian or Muslim? What does that have to do with his obsession with security other than to create confusion and mistrust amongst us Palestinians? Luckily most of us are aware of this ploy.

Yet as Christians we cannot help but wonder: could all this suffering be blessed by the same God whom we know to be the God of love, peace, and hope? How does this faith relate to all the injustice that surrounds us? Can we truly turn the other cheek or love our enemy in this situation? What does Christian love even mean? To be submissive and to succumb to the forces that dehumanize us, or to be angry, rebel, and do something about it? I suppose if we were true Christians our faith would help us find the right answers, but we are not Christians by faith alone. Faith without action is dead. It is our deeds and our work with the poor, the oppressed, and the marginalized that will determine whether we are true Christians.

This conference is held at a time when the Palestinian-Israeli conflict is at a crossroads. We had hoped that the peace plan offered by the Palestinian National Council (PNC) on November 15, 1988, in Algiers would have been welcomed by the Israeli government. Since the establishment of the state of Israel in 1948 it has sought peace but claimed there was no one to talk to about peace. Now that there is a party to talk to, it has become clear that peace is not really on the agenda of the Israeli government at all. In spite of the concessions made by the PNC for the sake of peace and an end to suffering, the Israeli government has completely ignored the Palestinian peace plan and instead come up with its own initiative, the so-called election plan, a plan that seems to be leading nowhere. The prime minister who initiated this plan has no intention of negotiating with the Palestinians, most specifically the PLO which is our representative, which means no peace, as peace has to be negotiated between enemies.

As the Intifada goes into its third year, it has become increasingly clear that it has helped the Palestinians regain their dignity, and that the iron-fist policy of the military has failed to deter our young men and women from struggling and resisting occupation, a right of all people living under occupation. The prime minister's intransigence was demonstrated by his willingness to see the government collapse rather than making concessions and accepting the new reality that the Palestinians are his only negotiating partner for peace. He will have to answer to many Israeli parents whose young sons are becoming dehumanized and demoralized as they continue to play the role of occupiers and oppressors against all Jewish ethical and religious values.

"What doth the Lord require of thee but to do justly, to love mercy and walk humbly with thy God?"

We could not have chosen a better place than Tantur for a conference on liberation theology—midway between Bethlehem and Jerusalem, midway between the birthplace of our Lord Jesus Christ and the place of his crucifixion and resurrection. May the spirit of incarnation and sacrifice, and the hope of the resurrection guide us in our deliberations.

Preface

The Conference and the Book

ROSEMARY RADFORD RUETHER

This book represents, in part, papers that were given at the First International Symposium on Palestinian Liberation Theology at Tantur, between Bethlehem and Jerusalem, during March 10-17, 1990.

The conference itself was two years in the planning, and several workshops were held around Israel and Occupied Palestine to prepare for it. The conference was not an end in itself, but was seen as part of a process by which Palestinian Christians across all historical traditions established a conversation about their own theology, contextualized in their national struggle for liberation.

As Father Naim Ateek makes clear in his opening remarks, a Palestinian theology of liberation had become necessary, not simply because Palestinians were engaged in a struggle for national liberation, for this had been the case since the time of the British Mandate and the Balfour Declaration after World War I. But this struggle was seen as a secular struggle, a struggle against colonialism and for a secular democratic state where Palestinians of all religions had equal civil rights.

A specifically theological reflection had become necessary because Israeli and Diaspora Jews and also Western Christians were evoking the Bible and theological themes from the Jewish and Christian religions to claim a divinely-mandated right of the Jews to the land. After the 1967 war and the occupation of East Jerusalem, the West Bank, and Gaza, these religious claims became more extreme and were applied to these occupied territories. Palestinian rights were disregarded altogether by these religious Zionists.

Palestinian Christians had a particular need to formulate a reply to these biblical and theological claims, since such claims came from the scripture they held in common with these opponents. This misuse of the Jewish and Christian scriptures by religious Zionism also left the impression in the minds of many Muslims in the Middle East that these were representative Christian teachings, and thus Middle Eastern Christians themselves were implicated in such teachings. Middle Eastern Christians also had to take the lead in protesting to the Western Christian churches the use of the Bible and the name of God to promote injustice.

It was no easy task to develop a common theological conversation among Palestinian Christians. The Christian community in the Holy Land has been tragically victimized by the very veneration in which this region has been held by Christians around the world. Every historical Christian tradition, from Old Catholics and Orthodox to Roman Catholics to every form of Protestantism, has aspired to have its titular community in Jerusalem and in the Holy Land. The indigenous churches have been continually fragmented by this ecclesiastical imperialism, dominated by foreign clergy and funding.

Indigenous Christians, particularly in the last forty years, have had an increasingly difficult time maintaining their presence in their own land. The pressures to emigrate from the Israelis have particularly affected Palestinian Christians with their greater opportunities for education and ties with the West. Thus, as Don Wagner shows in his chapter in this book, there is real danger that Palestinian indigenous Christianity will dwindle to the point that only dead stones, but not a living church, will testify to their historic presence in the land of the birth of Jesus.

This fragmentation across all the historical divisions of church history, together with pressures to emigrate, made the task of creating a base for a Palestinian theology of liberation especially challenging. Yet this book also testifies to the success of that process. As one reads the chapters of this book, one has a sense of a common Arab Palestinian Christian voice. The fact that the authors range across denominations—Mennonite, Quaker, Lutheran and Presbyterian, Anglican, Roman Catholic, Melkite and Greek Orthodox—is discovered only by reading the brief biographies of the contributors. In the actual conference both the Greek Catholic seminary choir and the Armenian church choir provided music for the worship services.

Thus one might say the first task of this conversation on Palestinian liberation theology was to generate a common sense of being the church of Palestine, the indigenous Palestinian local church. As Geries Khoury emphasizes in his chapter, Palestinians must develop an ecclesiology of the local church to overcome this historic fragmentation and to speak with one voice as Palestinian Christians. It is only in that context that it then becomes possible to discuss a Palestinian theology of liberation that responds to and expresses the national struggle for liberation. Here Palestinian Christians speak as part of a united Palestinian people across the three monotheistic faiths, Christian, Jewish, and Muslim.

This conference hoped not only to bring together Palestinian Christians, but also to assemble international representatives of liberation theologies around the world to reflect with them and to learn from them. Palestinians felt the need to learn from the experiences that Latin Americans, Asians, and Africans had already had in developing indigenous liberation theologies in the context of their historical cultures and struggles for justice. Palestinians were also aware that many liberation theologians around the world were oblivious to Palestinian Christians and to the Palestinian struggle. They thoughtlessly used themes of "exodus" and "promised land" with little sense of the negative use of such biblical themes to oppress and colonize the Palestinians.

Thus the Palestinians also hoped to conscienticize the world community of liberation theologians, to make them aware of the negative underside of many biblical themes, when these are used in an exclusivist, ethnocentric sense as a theology of conquest.

Invitations went out to liberation theologians around the world, to Latin America, North America, Europe, Africa, and Asia. Unfortunately, most liberation theologians were not prepared to put the Palestinian issue on their agenda. No Latin American theologian came, although many showed initial interest. Africa and Asia were better represented with Malusi Mpumlwana from South Africa, Emmanuel Kandusi from Zimbabwe, Shirley Wijesinghe from Sri Lanka, and Myrna Arceo from the Philippines. (Unfortunately, of these four only Myrna Arceo sent a paper for the book.) Europe was represented only by Ireland in the person of Dr. Ann Louise Gilligan. Thus in this book the section on international response is much more North American than was the original hope.

However, the first purpose of the conference, which was to gather a representative dialogue among Palestinian Christians, was well expressed at the conference and even more so in this book, since several Palestinian Christian leaders, such as Father Elias Chacour and Canon Riah Abu El-Assal, who had participated in the planning of the conference, were not able to make the actual conference itself. However, they contributed papers, which are part of this publication.

As is the case with liberation theology generally, Palestinian liberation theology is reflection on praxis. Therefore it begins by analyzing the situation of oppression and the struggle for liberation. For Palestinians this situation of oppression is Israeli occupation, and the struggle for liberation is the Intifada, the organized uprising against occupation which has been conducted with great suffering, primarily as a nonviolent struggle, since December 1987. Thus many of the articles in this book take the form of analyzing this situation of struggle.

Dr. Hanan Ashrawi and Dr. Salim Tamari, both of Bir Zeit University, provide political and sociological analyses. Dr. Jad Isaac of Bethlehem University delineates the struggle for the land and the maintenance of a Palestinian agriculture, the crucial basis of Palestinian economic and cultural survival. Sameeh Ghnadreh contributes a discussion of the distinct social and political situation of the Palestinians within Israel, primarily in the

Galilee, who are Israeli citizens, but suffer under second-class citizenship and continual encroachment upon their remaining land. These are the remnant of that Palestinian community that was driven out during the 1948 war when the Israelis pushed out a million Palestinians and destroyed some 450 villages, confiscating more that 80 percent of the land that had been held by Palestinians.[1]

Many of the other papers in this collection are primarily sociological in nature. They represent the voice of the Palestinian experience, articulating its sufferings and also the hopes that the Intifada has brought to a silenced people the world seemed to have relegated to the dustbin. It is in this context of the articulation of the Palestinian experience of struggle that these authors then dare to venture a theological word, a word about the connection between faith and the Intifada, and also a word about what the role of a Palestinian church must become.

Although the sufferings of Palestinians after two and a half years of organized uprising were extreme in March of 1990, this situation has significantly worsened in the ensuing eighteen months, particularly during the Gulf War of January to March 1991 and its aftermath. The Israeli government and military took the opportunity afforded by world sympathy and diversion of attention during this war to wage an all-out economic war against the Palestinians in the Occupied Territories.

A million and a half people in the Occupied Territories were kept under continual curfew for six to nine weeks. The Palestinian economy was devastated. Crops and animals died because Palestinians were not allowed out of their homes to tend them. Unemployment soared to 50 percent, the medical and education situation deteriorated further, and many Palestinians, particularly in Gaza and in the refugee camps, faced starvation. After the war was over it was evident that the Israeli government did not intend to return even to the conditions before the war, but rather to impose travel restrictions and continual curfews that would make daily life for Palestinians close to impossible. At the same time there was a new stage of land confiscation, the rapid building of new settlements and expansion of old ones, so that now some 60 percent of the West Bank and 40 percent of Gaza have been confiscated, not to mention the almost total control of water.[2]

Clearly the Israeli government wishes to create so many "facts on the ground" that any political settlement that would trade land for peace would become impossible. Nor were the Palestinian communities within Israel exempt from this pressure. The Galilee also saw new expansion of Jewish settlements, squeezing still further the diminished land available to the three-quarters of a million Palestinians who live in Israel. Hundreds of thousands of immigrants from the Soviet Union were being rushed into Israel to provide a demographic base for the take-over of all Palestine by Israeli settlement.

Soviet immigrants also were victimized in this process because many had been partly coerced to come to Israel by deliberate blocking of their opportunities to immigrate to other countries, particularly to the United States, which many would have preferred. Many of the new immigrants found that the planning for their arrival was so poor that they were both homeless and jobless in Israel. Israeli newspapers reported numerous Soviet women being sent into the streets as prostitutes to make a living.[3] Despite feeble protests, it is primarily American money that continues to subsidize this Zionist project of squeezing out Palestinians and replacing them with Jews, a process in which Palestinians are the first victims but many of the Jewish immigrants are unjustly treated as well.

This book on Palestinian theology is thus offered to the American and English reading public at a critical time, a time which, as Jewish theologian Marc Ellis has warned, may see the end of the Palestinian community in historic Palestine. This will go down in history as one of the great crimes of Western colonialism, along with the extermination of indigenous people in so many other parts of the world. It is a particularly egregious crime because it has been one in which Western Christians have collaborated with Jews, and both have exploited the memory of past injustice and the mandates of religious faith to cover it up and carry it out.

Yet there is still time for repentance. There is still time for an Israeli community of conscience to grow in Israel. During the Intifada thousands of Israeli Jews crossed the "Green line" that divided Israel from the Occupied Territories, got to know Palestinian people for the first time, and entered into movements of solidarity. The Israeli Peace Movement began to be a movement *with* Palestinians, rather than simply a movement that referred to Palestinians *in absentia*.

As Michel Warschawski of the Alternative Information Center has made clear, this new stage of the Israeli Peace Movement faded during the Gulf War primarily because it was not deep enough. It was still based primarily on seeing the Palestinian as enemy rather than as a neighbor whom one wishes to live with as a fellow human being.[4] Yet the seeds were planted, and it is very much up to the world community to help support and nurture these hopeful beginnings of a new community of Palestinians and Israeli Jews who have determined to create the conditions of authentic justice and peace.

These conditions begin when the Palestinians are recognized not as stereotypical enemy, not simply as victims, but as a people with a great heart. This people has extended the hand of friendship to Israeli Jews and is ready to find a basis of genuine justice and peace, based on an affirmation of the rights of both people to share the land they both love.

But the Palestinians—Muslim and Christian—and the Israeli peace community cannot create this change by themselves. The world community must finally say "*Yesh Gevul*" ("Enough!") to subsidizing land confiscation, settlements, and the destruction of the Palestinian community, and yes to an international peace conference under the United Nations. The chapters of this book represent this Palestinian hand of peace with justice extended to the world. The time for an adequate response has grown very short!

NOTES

1. See Michael Palumbo, *The Palestinian Catastrophe* (London: Faber & Faber, 1987).

2. For detailed information on these human rights violations, see the reports of the Database Project on Palestinian Human Rights, January-May 1991, P.O. Box 20479, Jerusalem, or 4753 N. Broadway, Suite 930, Chicago, IL 60640.

3. Reports on these problems with Soviet immigration are found in the 1990 and 1991 issues of Israeli peace newsletters, such as *The Other Israel*, P.O. Box 956, Tel Aviv, 61008 and *News From Within*, P.O. Box 24278, Jerusalem, Israel.

4. Michel Warschawski is founder of the Alternative Information Center in Jerusalem, and *News From Within*. His critique of the Israeli Peace Movement can be found in his talk to the Eighth United Nations North American Regional NGO Symposium on the Question of Palestine, Montreal, Canada, 28-30 June 1991, available from NACC, 1747 Connecticut Avenue, N.W., Washington, D.C. 20009.

Acknowledgments

Particular thanks go to Kathy Bergen, who did much of the work in organizing the conference that led to this volume. Also to Elaine Zoughbi, who was given the task of collecting the Palestinian papers after the conference and who did the initial editing. Thanks also to Sami Ghattas, who designed the conference emblem that appears as the logo of this book. Bob Carroll, Linda Koops, and Helen Hauldren did noble work in retyping the edited papers.

Introduction

The Emergence of a Palestinian Christian Theology

NAIM S. ATEEK

In this brief introduction I would like to present an outline of some of the ideas that have been key in the creation of a Palestinian theology of liberation. This, I hope, will help situate the content of this book and provide the necessary background to the emerging Palestinian theology in its historical and theological context.

To begin with, it is important to emphasize that the year 1967 has been perceived by many Palestinians as a watershed in both the political and religious spheres. The occupation of the West Bank and the Gaza Strip, along with other parts of Syria and Egypt in such a swift way, was attributed by most Jews and many Western Christians to God's purposeful and powerful intervention on the side of Israel and against the Arabs. Thus the events of 1967, their aftermath, and the ensuing years of establishing a firmer control over the Palestinians and the entrenching of the occupation—all of these have given prominence to the new critical importance of the religious factor in the conflict. One can even notice in Israel after 1967 a gradual shift from a secular form of Zionism to a religious form of Zionism.

Many of the early Zionists were not at all religious. Indeed some of them, like Ben Gurion, were atheists. They did not choose Palestine because of religious consideration. What was paramount in their minds was to find a solution for Jews away from anti-Semitism and assimilation. In fact, the early Zionists entertained the idea of choosing countries other than Palestine for the creation of a home for Jews. The country of Palestine entered later into Zionist thinking and was first promoted by a few Western Christians who were, indeed, the first Christian Zionists. By 1948, therefore, the religious factor in the conflict was not totally absent from the minds of many Jews and Western Christians. The occupation of the West Bank, including East Jerusalem, more than the occupation of any of the other Occupied Territories, however, gave a new religious impetus to many Jews and Western Christians after the war of 1967.

With this background in mind, one can observe four developments since 1967 in both Israel and abroad, among Jews and Western Christians. For our purpose I would like to summarize them briefly, though not necessarily chronologically, pointing out the thrust of their basic positions without entering into details.

First was the rise of Jewish religious fundamentalism. The 1967 occupation of the West Bank, including East Jerusalem, created much euphoria for Jews. They had "liberated" Judea and Samaria, the area that witnessed a great part of their history. Thus the emergence of the *Gush Emunim* ("block of faithful"), sometime later, signalled the beginning of a deep-rooted religious claim to the whole of the land. For this religious group the victory of the 1967 war was a very clear indication of the faithfulness of God to the Jewish people and a vindication of the rightness of the state of Israel. It killed and dissipated any religious rejection of the state. God had unequivocally and dramatically shown his unwavering support of the state. God was fulfilling his promises to the Jewish people. Therefore, it was against God's Law, the Torah, to give up one inch of the biblically promised land. In fact, the emphasis for this group was to work for the achievement of a Greater Israel, which would include even wider territories. The "liberated" land of Judea and Samaria must, therefore, be settled. The Palestinians initially might be allowed to live on the land, but for certain, the land is the eternal possession of the Jewish people.

Since 1967 new religious groups have emerged within Israel. Some have gained political clout and have influenced many of the policies of the government. The religious claim to the land has become, therefore, very prominent and dominant.

Second was the rise of Western Christian fundamentalism. This is the Christian counterpart of Jewish fundamentalism. Western Christians saw the victory of the state of Israel against all the Arab countries in 1967 as a miracle from God. This, for most of them, was the second stage in God's plan in achieving his purposes for the Jewish people and for the world. God brought the Jewish people back to Palestine in 1948. Now he showed his faithfulness to them by giving them East Jerusalem, where they should rebuild their Temple as a prelude for the Second Coming of Christ. Prophecy was being fulfilled before their very eyes. It was incumbent on these Christians to support the state of Israel. Since God was certainly on the side of the Jews, so should they be. There are more than sixty million Christian fundamentalists in the United States, many of whom espouse such a theological attitude toward Jews and the state of Israel. Their support has been substantial in many different aspects. No questions regarding morality or justice are being asked by them. For these Christian fundamentalists, the state of Israel has a God-given right to keep the Occupied Territories. Tough luck for the Palestinians!

The third and fourth trends draw more on the liberal groups on the Jewish and Christian sides. On the Jewish side there was the development of Holocaust theology. After 1967 a theology that reflected on the Jewish Holocaust in Europe under the Nazis began to be elaborated. But this theology was not only about these past events. It also carried an implicit or explicit message about Israel and the Jewish future. It suggested that the Jews faced such a threat today, that the 1967 war, if it had been won by the Arabs, would have been another Holocaust of the Jews.

We know, however, that the war of 1967 was exactly the opposite in reality. There was no real war from the Arab side, but only a preemptive strike on the Arab armies from the Israelis. The fact that so much land—the whole of the West Bank, Gaza, the Sinai, and the Golan Heights—was overrun in six days shows that there was no real battle coming from the Arab side. Rather, the Palestinians in the West Bank and Gaza were overrun and occupied without even a fight.

The conquest of the West Bank and Gaza led Holocaust theologians to speak of the interconnection between the Holocaust and Jewish empowerment. Jewish empowerment as a way of answering the Holocaust of the past and preventing any new Holocaust became a central theme of their theological thought, as Marc Ellis has shown in his book *Toward a Jewish Theology of Liberation.*

On the Christian side, there also arose a theological counterpart to Jewish Holocaust theology. Liberal Christian scholars, such as Paul van Buren, felt they must take responsibility for the Western Christian role in bringing about the Holocaust. They had to repent of this past Christian fault toward the Jews. The result was a second type of Christian Zionist theology that aligned itself with Jewish political empowerment and political aspirations.

These "liberal" Christian Zionist theologians began to develop a theology of the state of Israel as something divinely ordained and a redemptive act of God in history. They believed that Christians should support this state unconditionally, both because of the Holocaust and because Christianity owes its relation to God to the Jewish people. For these Christian Holocaust theologians the Palestinians did not exist at all. They did not even notice their Palestinian Christian brothers and sisters.

These two sets of religious responses to the 1967 conquest—Jewish and Christian fundamentalism, and Jewish and Christian Holocaust theology—suddenly brought the question of the religious basis for support for the state of Israel into prominence. For us Palestinian Christians this was a particular challenge. Western Christians and many religious Jews were using the same Bible as we, but claiming to take from it a revelation from God that justified the conquest of our land and the extermination of our people. This demanded a religious response from us, both biblical and theological, even though before that time the struggle of Palestinians for their national rights had not seemed to us to be a religious question, but rather a political and a human question. It was out of this challenge that the need arose for a Palestinian Christian theological response, a Palestinian theology of liberation.

On the local scene, this Palestinian theology of liberation was influenced by four distinct elements or factors. First, there was the pastoral aspect. Some of us Palestinian clergy were working with our people at the grassroots and listening to their cries. We found ourselves needing to give them help and respond, not only to their physical sufferings, but also to the way these sufferings were being aggravated by the religious argument in the political conflict. Where is God in all of this? Why does God allow the confiscation of our land? Why does God allow the occupation and oppression of our people? We needed to work out a Palestinian theology of liberation as a pastoral response to many such questions.

The second aspect was the indigenous factor. Foreign expatriate clergy have for a long time controlled our churches. But now it was necessary for the indigenous Palestinian clergy, the Palestinian Christians who grow from the soil of this country, to make a response. It is we, as Palestinian Christians, who have to define the meaning of this land to us in response to these theological and biblical claims, for it is our lives and also our faith which is threatened.

Third, there is the biblical question. Many of our Palestinian Christians wanted to abandon the Bible, particularly the Old Testament, which was being used against them. They wanted to have nothing to do with this scripture. They did not want to have it read in church to them. But as Christians we cannot do theology outside the Bible or apart from the Bible. The Bible is central to our faith. So it was essential to work out our Palestinian Christian reading of the Bible, this Bible that was being used against us to deprive us of our land and our rights, this Bible which is also our Bible. We needed to find in the Bible the God of justice, the God who is concerned with the oppressed, who is concerned with the Palestinians as the oppressed of this land.

Finally, there is the theological factor. We needed to understand how Christ is related to this historical process. What is our understanding of the incarnation, of God's involvement in history through the coming of Christ into the world? How do we relate the coming of Christ to the Jewish people and to the Christian church? How do we understand, as Palestinian Christians, the coming of Christ as an answer to claims of messianic fulfillment which are being used by Jews and by Western Christians to oppress and destroy us?

These four factors, in interaction with the political reality, made a Palestinian theology of liberation necessary. We could not avoid it. A Palestinian theology of liberation had to emerge out of this context, and only Palestinian Christians could do it. We had to make a response, both for ourselves and for our own faith, and also in relation to the world outside.

What are the central issues of this theology? I will mention some of them. At the heart of this theology of liberation is the question of God. How do we understand God? There is a special problem of theodicy for us Palestinians. How can one justify what God is said to be doing? Has God become an enemy to the Palestinians, the adversary of Palestinian aspirations to liberation? When it is said that God gave our lands to the Jewish people, and so the Israelis have a right to come and take it today, what kind of a God are we really talking about? For us, we were sure that such a God was a false God. This was not the God of the Bible, the God of justice, mercy, peace, the God whom we have come to know in Jesus Christ, the true God of justice.

We also had a problem with the Bible, as I have indicated. The Bible is being used by both Jews and Western Christians to silence us, to make us invisible, to turn us into the negated antithesis of God's "chosen people." How can we interpret the Bible so that it becomes a redemptive message for us, for all people, but not in a way that sets one people against another, as was happening with the Jewish religious Zionists and some Western Christian fundamentalists' use of the Bible?

We also had to ask about the question of power. Israel was using power in a terrible way to oppress us, and these Jewish and Christian people were celebrating this kind of Israeli power as something redemptive and from God. What is just and unjust power? What do we mean by peace? We hear people calling for peace, but their definition of peace is one that excludes us. Can this be peace? How are violence and nonviolence related to true peace and justice? These are all key questions for our Palestinian theology of liberation.

As Palestinian Christians we needed to deal with the realities of hatred and bitterness and how these could be truly answered by forgiveness and love, but in a way that is based on truth and justice and that leads to real peace, not just to our silencing and surrender. We also needed to find the role of the church in this process, the local Palestinian church. How can our Palestinian church become involved in the struggle for peace and justice in this land?

These are the crying issues that gave birth to the discussions that have been taking place over the last few years and led to the calling of the first conference in Jerusalem between Palestinian Christians and a number of international theologians. We Palestinian Christians are beginning to find our own voice, to define our Palestinian theology of liberation. Small and weak and divided as we are, I believe that we have a crucial role to play in breaking apart what confronts us these days in false theology, false reading of the Bible, and a false concept of God.

We are committed to speak the truth against this false theology prevalent in some circles in Israel and abroad. We are desperately in need of finding a theology of liberation for ourselves that will also be a theology of peace and reconciliation for the peoples of this land, for Israelis and Palestinians as two peoples of this land. But first of all, we must continue to talk together as Palestinian Christians in order to find our own way of replying to this conflict and the misuse of religion in this conflict. This is the task that we have set for ourselves.

PART 1

THE PALESTINIAN REALITY

1

The Intifada: Political Analysis

HANAN ASHRAWI

My stress here is on the political rather than the historical. The pursuit of knowledge is part of the essence of the Intifada itself, in the sense that knowledge in itself is both a burden and a responsibility.

Whenever I speak, especially when I travel a lot, my daughter asks me about the results of my speeches. She says, "You go out and you tell people the truth, and you tell them what's happening, and I'm sure once people know, once people have that knowledge, once people know the truth, then we shall be free."

How do you explain to your child that, in the case of the Palestinians, truth alone is not enough to set you free? That truth has to be translated into clear, political, actual, concrete steps; into positions of human courage and daring and commitment; into a full program of peace and reconciliation. Actually, peace is a much more difficult pursuit than conflict and war. It's an extremely arduous task, and it doesn't take place as a result of inertia or by default or an absence of war; it has to be pursued very actively.

Most people, when they understand that we come from families that go back centuries, are amazed. They're not aware of the truth of the Palestinian people or of the age of this nation. We are also the product of two thousand years of continuous Christian presence in Palestine. This fact has to be kept in mind: Palestinians are an ancient and proud nation. We are not an accident of history.

At one point Palestinian nationhood and Israeli statehood were mutually exclusive. The affirmation of one meant the denial or the negation of the other. At one point Palestinian statehood and Palestinian legitimacy was the exact opposite of Israeli or Zionist ideology.

Now we have come to the realization, as Palestinians, that we have come to terms with the distinction between the idea of a homeland and that of a state. We have come to terms with the distinction between the dream of reviving historical Palestine and the reality of its partition. We have come to terms with the difference between historical truth and our responsibility toward achieving a secure and peaceful future. And we have come to terms with the difference between the boundaries of national self-definition, and actual, concrete, geographical boundaries.

Given the choice between an endless cycle of violence and conflict on the one hand, and a peaceful settlement and solution on the other, based on compromise and pragmatism, we have opted for peace, reconciliation, and relative justice. This wasn't a sudden revelation; this wasn't an epiphany in our history; this wasn't a Jovian bolt from the skies. It came as a result of a very painful, painstaking, long process of political analysis, of discussion and often argument, self-education, and self-criticism. This dates back perhaps to the beginning of the issue, but it dates back primarily to 1974, when the idea of the two-state solution was presented as an option for the first time by Palestinians for discussion among Palestinians. This solution has become part of, or the objective of, the Palestinian peace initiative.

There are two landmarks in contemporary Palestinian politics. The first is December 1987, the beginning of the Intifada itself, and the second is November 1988, the PNC (Palestine National Congress) resolutions in Algiers. I would like to focus on the Intifada, because it is the human substance of the political program. This is the human dimension of peace. It is very hard for us to talk about the Intifada in this passionless discourse, because it is our lives, it is our future, it's the future of our children, it is our daily reality. The Intifada is not just a detailed list of statistics pertaining to human suffering and loss of life, to killings and beatings and house demolitions and uprooting of trees and thousands of people imprisoned. No words can really encompass the pain of a whole nation just as no words can encompass or describe the exhilaration and self-confidence of a nation on its way toward statehood or self-realization, once it has made up its mind that human right may triumph over military might.

The Intifada is the accession of dignity and self-respect among the Palestinians and also among the Arabs as a whole. It is a voice of the people in expressing its will to assert its own right to freedom and self-determination over against military subjugation. This is a process of acceleration and intensification and the natural progression of the history of our national development and resistance. Therefore, it is part of the continuum. It is a significant phase, but it is also a result of the cumulative struggle of Palestinian people everywhere, not the least of which is the luminous, heroic, and painful struggle of the Palestinians in the refugee camps in Lebanon, which must never be forgotten.

The Intifada is a quantum leap, if you will; it is a qualitative change in the history of resistance, especially when you look at the incremental experiences we have had, particularly in 1974 and 1981, the earlier Intifadas, which did not have the scope, the dimension, or the continuity of the present Intifada. As such, it is a massive, collective, and comprehensive popular movement of resistance to and rejection of Israeli occupation, with all its imposed imperatives and norms and distorted realities, and an affirmation of the Palestinian will, identity, rights, and national legitimacy. It's an authentic utterance; it is the voice of the people and an actualization of our historical rights and aspirations. As such, it has forged national unity on the ground, has practiced democracy and pluralism as a concrete reality, not only as an intellectual or political desirability, but as a system that actually works, that is viable, and that is capable of achieving results.

We have the example of the National Unified Leadership, which has negated all the earlier norms of authority and power and responsibilities that existed in traditional societies and emphasized the whole idea of democratic emergent leadership from the people. It has refocused attention on the Palestinian people and the Palestinian society itself on its own land as the authentic base of struggle and confrontation in the equation of occupier versus occupied, rather than on the Palestinians in exile. It has restored again the proper perspective on the Arab-Israeli conflict by zeroing in on the Palestinian issue as the central core in a sort of outward emanating energy.

If there is to be any solution to the Arab-Israeli conflict, it has to start with the Israeli-Palestinian conflict, and has to address the Palestinian issue, not through oblique or external channels or directions, but by addressing the central issues that deal with Palestinian nationhood and self-determination. The Intifada has succeeded in wrenching the Palestinian question from its course of armed struggle and has redirected it toward political struggle. Hence it has brought to the fore the viability and necessity of a negotiated settlement and has led to the articulation of a political program, which started in 1974, but which was actually formulated in 1988 in Algiers. The Intifada's activities have also enhanced and substantiated the PLO legitimacy, because it formed in a way a popular referendum, an active referendum for the PLO, and has imbued our leadership with the authority and authenticity of a constituency and a social base.

The Intifada has redressed a situation of asymmetry and disequilibrium in the equation of occupier versus occupied, military violence versus human will and dedication to freedom, by asserting the moral ascendancy and the political responsibility and maturity of the Palestinians. In this confrontation between might and right we have faced the monster and discovered that we are stronger, and this emerging self-confidence is also part of the mood and the spirit of the Intifada. As such, we see it as a state of mind, as well as a state of being, and a concrete political reality. It has its own self-generating and self-sustaining momentum and motivation, because it is the motivation of a people coming to grips with its own reality and its own history and destiny.

The Intifada has three dimensions. The first dimension is the level of overt resistance and confrontation. These are the visible, dramatic activities of defiance seen on television. This has served several purposes. It has exposed the underbelly of the Israeli occupation. It has made the occupation visible to the world, but mainly to the Israelis themselves. It has also become a natural and logical reaction to an abnormal and imposed situation. When you have a situation of oppression, of military oppression, domination, and occupation, the will of the people has to be expressed in resistance, and this is the most visible form of resistance: sit-ins, marches, strikes. It has also succeeded in capturing world attention, world consciousness, but we still maintain that it has not captured the world's conscience yet.

There is also a level of demythologization. The Intifada demythologized the misperceptions and misconceptions of a beleaguered Israel; the myth of Israel as David versus Goliath, for instance, and Israel as a democratic state which can afford to fragment democracy, applying it one place and withdrawing it from another. It has demythologized the so-called idea of the benign occupation because, as we all know, occupation in all its forms is always malign and destructive. It has also exposed the myth of the nonexistent Palestinians. I will not go through the metamorphoses we have undergone, from nonexistent to different types of life, whether two-legged vermin, or grasshoppers, or dogs, or whatever, to the abstraction of becoming even a demographic problem in Israel.

The Intifada has shown the human substance of the Palestinians as a people, as a nation. For the first time it has made Israel confront its own reality as occupier; the fact of its being an occupier, rather than a caretaker, or a malign sort of supervisor over a civilian population. Israel has come face to face, for the first time, with the consequences of its actions, and they are now asking the right questions. For the first time in Israel, peace has become an item on the agenda. The Palestinian question and Palestinian legitimacy have become items on the political agenda. This did not exist before the Intifada.

The second dimension of the Intifada is that of social transformation and nation building. In essence, it is a disengagement from the occupation and a process of delegitimization of the occupation and legitimizing the Palestinian will, building alternative institutions.

The third dimension is the political dimension, which cannot in any way be separated from the PNC resolutions, because the human will of the Palestinians, of the Intifada, has given guidance to the political program that was articulated in Algiers in 1988.

It is very clear at this stage that we as Palestinians are not a vindictive nation. We do not harbor bitterness, hatred, or nourish them in the dark, and then translate them into political programs, distorted, destructive, based on slogans, and hardened positions of revenge. We have espoused the positive politics of peace, of reconciliation, of national construction, of expansive affirmation of human value, and we have eschewed the politics of hatred, of revenge, of convoluted internalized entrenchment, and pathological obstinacy now very characteristic of the Israeli government.

We are a healthy nation. The Intifada is not a sign of despair. Actually, it is a sign of hope, of self-confidence. It is a sign of the empowerment of the people, which has led in other places to the release of Nelson Mandela; in other places it has led to whole changes in governments. In Palestine it has to lead to freedom, to the end of the occupation, and to statehood.

Now the political program is based on three major principles. First of all, there is the principle of partition, through United Nations Resolution 181, which accepted the partition of Palestine into two states. This is the basis of acceptance of a two-state solution. The second principle is the acceptance of Resolutions 242 and 338 *in conjunction with self-determination for the Palestinians*, because 242 and 338 do not deal with the Palestinians as a nation, but rather with the Arab states only and with the issue of the refugees. We view ourselves as a whole nation, whether under occupation or in exile, and, therefore, 242 and 338 must be related to national self-determination. The third is the denunciation of terrorism in every form, including state terror. All these provisions can be implemented through the mechanism of an international conference. These basically were the resolutions that we affirmed by the PNC in Algiers.

Now, underlying this, are the basic principles of self-determination and statehood, the legitimacy of our own voice, of our own will, and therefore of our own representational leadership, which is the PLO, and the mechanism of the international conference. This is the significant move toward a commitment to a peaceful resolution to the conflict. But peace cannot be achieved at any price. Peace also has to be based on mutuality, on reciprocity, on mutual legitimacy. Peace cannot be achieved by coercion, or by subjugation, or by capitulation. Peace has to preserve the dignity of both peoples and the rights of both peoples.

Now we feel that peace is not only possible, but it is probable and obtainable. We have a unique opportunity to achieve peace. The objective conditions have come together among the Palestinians to make peace possible. However, peace cannot be left and should not be left to the discretion of the Israeli government, to the priorities of the Israelis, who are the occupier. The Israeli veto on peace is capable of demolishing it. Shamir's detachment and rejectionism should not be the bottom line on peace.

I would like to move on to the immediate pitfalls and dangers we face in the Intifada. The Intifada, as the voice, as the empowerment of the people, has to be maintained if there is to be a human substance to the political process. First, there is a process of desensitization and inurement through redundancy and routinization, getting used to the continual loss of Palestinian rights and life. This is very serious to us because it reverts back to the double standard that was generally employed when evaluating Palestinian lives as opposed to other lives.

There is a gradual neutralization of the horror and a devaluation of the moral currency of Israel which threatens to lead us back to the invisibility of the Palestinians or to the abstraction of Palestinians into numbers. It has become acceptable for people now to hear about one, two, three Palestinians killed. We are back to numbers. The whole moral repugnancy of the situation has been removed from it through redundancy, particularly through the whole policy of closed areas and military seizures, which imposed a media blackout. Therefore you do not get the real situation, you do not get reality, you do not get the truth. You get the abstractions of the truth.

The immediate pitfall is in reducing the Intifada to a card in a political game and therefore, again, removing the human substance and base of the peace process or reducing it to a status quo with which Israel can comfortably exist. And this has been consistently Israel's attempt. This is especially true in view of the censorship, the blackout policy, and the state of siege.

The second major pitfall is reestablishing Israeli perceptual and linguistic dominance, and misrepresenting, misinterpreting, and distorting reality. We are seeing the reemergence of cheap catch-words such as the "inter-fada" or the "revival of terrorism," cheap labels like that. Now, historically, Israel has succeeded in its own diction, its own terms of reference on international public opinion. As Edward Said has said, we have been denied our right to narrate, directly and clearly, our own story and our own rights. We must not allow Israel again to take over, to patronize, to confiscate our own voice, our own right to narrate, to impose its own diction, its own visions, its own perceptions on dealing with the issues and on the way Palestinians are perceived. Stereotyping and prejudice have worked for a long time in removing the Palestinians from world vision, but they should not be imposed again.

More insidious, perhaps, is the imposing and unconsciously adopting Israel's priorities in formulating the peace agenda and discourse. Frankly speaking, it is not the security of Israel that is my main concern as a Palestinian. It is the future of my own people that is my main concern. This language is untrue, it is hypocritical, and it should not be adopted by Palestinians. We are not trying to safeguard Israel's security. Our main motivation, let us be honest, is the safety and security of our own people, especially now under occupation, and the future of our children. I am not worried about the sensitive psyches of the Israeli soldiers and the brutalization of their emotional well-being as they beat up our children or kill them. I'm worried about my own children. I am worried about our Palestinians who are being beaten, about the victims who are being killed. This is my main concern. We must not have an extreme sympathetic leap whereby the priorities of the enemies—and we still are enemies—become my priorities. Let us be honest and express our priorities clearly. Without honesty, I do not think we'll get anywhere.

What we need, both peoples at this stage, is a willing suspension of disbelief, if I may borrow a literary term. We cannot afford to wait until we establish mutual trust, until we finish the whole process of confidence-building measures, because, by that time, there might be no Palestinian community or society left in Palestine. It seems to me that, side-by-side, simultaneously, along parallel tracks, there should be a clear, responsible, serious political process moving along with confidence-building measures. But the greatest source of security and confidence is a genuine peace, a peace within international guarantees and legitimacy.

The third pitfall is Israel's regaining the offensive and initiative in manipulating tactical and procedural directions. This it has succeeded in doing by setting the international agenda on the way people deal with the Palestinian-Israeli conflict and primarily in setting American foreign policy. Israel, as a client-state, has actually succeeded in formulating the foreign policy of its patron, a major power. Now, when the United States is beginning to show signs of rebellion by making a few statements, I understand there's a move in Congress to declare that Jerusalem is the unified capital of Israel. So, in many ways, the freedom of the United States to formulate its own foreign policy is quite limited, depending on Israel's priorities.

A fear in Israel is marginalizing Israeli opposition through either the absorption or the neutralization of the Labor Party or the fragmentation of the Left, until there is the impression that there is no alternative to peace except the coalition government or this present government. This has led to the present crisis in the government, to this polarization, to this sense of either/or when it comes to Israeli politics.

The fourth pitfall is the perpetuation of Israel's policy of creating facts, facing us with faits accomplis, which might render meaningless and irrelevant any political discourse or settlement. This is especially true in the escalation of the Iron Fist policy, in view of what I said earlier about the inurement and desensitization to the loss of Palestinian lives, and in the closed-areas policy, whereby Israel in the dark is literally getting away with murder. Also Israel is again establishing "facts" in the very thorny issue of Soviet Jewish immigration. It is establishing "facts" by promoting Soviet Jewish immigration to the Occupied Territories, including East Jerusalem, and this is a definite undermining and destruction of the peace process.

In the current political climate we can sum up three major headings and areas of danger. First of all, there is the danger of the confiscation of the Palestinian voice and will, what I call the hijacking of the Palestinian utterance, especially through the veto and the control of our representation. In the past much of our history was shaped by voices and forces outside our own volition; that is why we are particularly wary of any attempt and repetition of that mistake. The Palestinians have to be in control of their own utterances, of their own will. We speak out for ourselves, and there can be no confiscation of our voice. This is capable of short-circuiting the peace process entirely.

The second mistake is one which has often been committed historically in attempting to solve the Palestinian-Israeli question. This is the mistake of allowing other governments to represent us. Nobody can deliver peace on our behalf. We are the only people who can deliver peace on our own behalf. And we, for the first time in our history, have a national consensus and overwhelming majority committing ourselves to peace.

The PLO is our legitimate representative and interlocutor. There is no reason to look for alternative leadership or to create spurious leaderships. No Palestinian delegation for negotiations or for dialogue will move or can claim any legitimacy or credibility without this dual empowerment by the PLO and by the Palestinian people. Therefore, it is the PLO that has to designate the delegation and has openly to announce them. There needs to be a clear definition of roles. Either you are playing the role of a neutral peacemaker, or you are party to the conflict. The United States sometimes has difficulty in absorbing that. We view the United States as party to the conflict, especially in its continuous history of being the sole and major supporter of Israel. Therefore, if it seeks to play the role of a peace broker, it has to exhibit neutrality; it has to exhibit more even-handedness; it has to empower the United States-PLO dialogue.

Again, no one can usurp the role of our leadership by representation, and we have to make the distinction between legitimacy and recognition of Israel. The whole world may recognize Israel, but the only people who can give Israel legitimacy are the Palestinians, because we are the aggrieved party. Israel was created on our land. And we will choose when, and how, and if to give Israel legitimacy. Nobody can legitimize Israel except the Palestinians. This has to be made clear, and I think this is becoming clear to the Israelis.

Too, we must be on the lookout for the derailment of the peace process through diversions, digressions, side issues, evasive tactics, detours that might lead to dead-ends through sidestepping the central issues. We are seeing an increasing obsession with technical and procedural issues, rather than with the principles that would make concrete progress possible. We are also seeing a dedication to a sense of motion without direction, which might lead into the wrong direction. We are seeing, in this case, a reduction in the peace process, a reduction that can lead us to the quagmire of details and technicalities where we lose sight of the basic objective. We must understand that the PLO itself has a highly politicized and critical constituency. Instead of pressing on the point of least resistance, it seems to me that the United States and the world have to address the real source of rejectionism and entrenchment, which is Israel, not the PLO.

The third and last danger is the diminution in the scope and substance of the peace process. We have witnessed a geometric regression in the peace process. There has been a serialized compromise. We have the Palestinian peace initiative of November 1988, and after that, we had the belated and minuscule response of the Shamir government, what we call the Shamir plan. And Shamir's minuscule response was actually taken by the world as if, all of a sudden, Israel had created or invented the term elections, as if democracy is now creating a renaissance in Israel. It is claimed that the Palestinians are going to elect representatives, under occupation, in free and democratic elections, when the whole people, the Palestinians, are neither free nor enjoying their democratic rights.

Then you get a compromise between these two positions, the first being of historical magnitude to us, and the second this very minor reaction to it. You have the Egyptian ten points, which missed two major issues: the self-determination issue for the Palestinians and the role of the PLO as our representative, but included many of the technical points. Then, as a compromise between that compromise and the Israeli position, we end up with Baker's five points. And, after Baker's five points, we end up with Israel's six provisos and conditions and so on. Perhaps in the twenty-first century we will be able to start some kind of dialogue.

Let's look at where we are now. There are moves toward negative selectivity, toward excessive isolationism and localization, toward preconditions, and toward stress on technicalities and legalities without the political framework or the context. However, if we look at the Palestinian reaction we find that it is characterized by flexibility, by maturity, by a willingness to deal with the imperatives of the moment. The Palestinians have accepted the principles of elections, but within the framework of linkage, and with a clear objective and with the principle of dialogue. This means dialogue without undermining the legitimacy of the Palestinian voice and will. Dialogue has to be through Palestinian leadership; it has to be based on an open agenda, not a closed agenda; it has to be a part of the mechanism toward the international conference. Because we certainly know that the conflict has international and Arab dimensions, and real security comes from international legitimacy and peace.

We stand now in an Israeli government crisis, based on one issue that was raised in order to have preparations for preliminary discussions for a tri-party meeting in Washington. There the Israelis, the Americans, and the Egyptians will discuss the formation of the Palestinian delegation, so that the Palestinian delegation may be formed in order to have a dialogue between the Palestinians and the Israelis, so that this dialogue may lead to the preparation for elections, and for what? Elections for what? For autonomy? The Intifada and the Palestinian political program have proven that autonomy, in whatever guise, whether under Camp David or other, is a non-option.

Now, again, we must be careful that the whole issue is not hijacked, is not sidetracked into issues that are dead-ends, into directions that are dead-ends. Negotiations have to take place within a state of equilibrium based on mutuality and symmetry. They have to take place between legitimate representatives. They have to have substance, be capable of realizing and achieving settlements, and take place without negating the legitimacy or the power base of either party. Negotiations must have a purpose, not to buy time, or as a rationalization for rejectionism, but a genuine commitment to the achievement of peace. As Palestinians we must constantly resist obfuscation of the real issue and constantly focus the discussion on that issue, which is genuine national self-determination.

2

The Intifada: Sociological Perspective

SALIM TAMARI

There have been three crucial transformations of consciousness during the Intifada. First is the involvement of youthful elements, unhindered by the established norms of political conduct set by political parties existing before the Intifada, not least in street action, in strike committees, and in daily confrontation with the Israeli army. These confrontations have affected the relationships between youthful elements and their immediate environment, with their families and their peers.

The second transformation deals with the new forms of communal organization at the neighborhood and community level, which have created new forms of solidarity and perhaps dissidence.

The third, and perhaps most interesting, is the emergence of religious fundamentalism as a popular movement with mass appeal in the northern districts of the West Bank, but most importantly in Gaza, and increasing in the main urban areas of Palestine. Fundamentalism, as opposed to traditional religious consciousness, is an urban phenomenon and has very weak roots in the countryside.

Of the first of these developments—youthful involvement—the most crucial feature is the challenge to traditional authority. I think the image of young Palestinians using their slingshots against the Israeli army has been the most persistent image of youthful rebellion printed throughout the mass media in the Western world. In the countryside the rule of the *muktars* (traditional community chiefs), which was already eroding in the last fifteen years, was suddenly brought to an end through the mass mobilization of young people in the various factions of the underground movement. Established families and their leading figures had little to contribute to a revolutionary movement that questioned not only the legitimacy of occupation, but also the legitimacy of an established hierarchy based on lineage.

Regardless of what we say, the Intifada has not only been a nightmare to the Israelis, but has threatened deeply established patterns of behavior and deference to authority within our own community. This has to be faced and discussed. The marks and procedures and stature formerly associated with elders have now been replaced with prison records and party affiliations by young people asserting their own identity. If you have not been imprisoned, somehow your patriotic attachment is questioned or questionable.

In the cities the weakening of parental control has been accompanied by new assertiveness by women against traditional forms of seclusion and domination. Since the national struggle dictated new norms of behavior in the streets, so the norms of conduct expected from young men, in deferment to elders, and women, modesty in formal conduct, were often suspended. Staying out late at night, spending days out of the parental home, not having to explain behavior, these were increasing and grudgingly imposed on traditional parents. The number of marriage unions concluded with little notice and often against parental consent multiplied, and, in many cases, these were marriages taking place across class and religious lines, a phenomenon rare or even unthinkable before the Intifada.

Obviously this has not been a consistent pattern, and one of the contradictions of social change during the last two and one-half years has been not only the explosion of the domains of freedom by the young, but also a retrogressive attitude which has seized many traditional families and led them to impose new restrictions on their offspring, especially their daughters.

One of the things we have monitored from the records of religious courts is the substantive decline in the average age of marriage for women. The decline has been from an average of 18 1/2 to 17, which is a decline in a record of improvement in the last thirty or forty years. This record has to be explained, and the explanation, in the absence of any scientific research, is subject to speculation and guesswork. But my explanation, my interpretation, is that in many cases traditional families, fearful for the safety of their daughters not only in the countryside but in cities, fearing that they may be exposed to imprisonment, or attack, or violation by Israeli soldiers, and feeling that their increased politicization will bring them into contact with young men, tend to marry them off at an earlier age.

Another explanation, not so retrogressive, has to do with the fact that during the Intifada—and this is a considerable achievement—the demonstrative manner in which families concluded marriage unions, with a lot of splendor and immense expenses that burdened the budgets of young men and their families, has been practically abolished. The *maher*, the bride price, has also gone down because of pressure by the political activists and leaders of the Intifada. This was a historical opportunity for many young men and women to marry before things changed. So that is another explanation for what may have happened.

On the side of retrogression, one should mention increased use of the veil and increased practice of seclusion of women, which must be seen side by side with the increased freedom accorded to women during the Intifada. So what we have is really double contradictory and countervailing trends, as you would expect in any social revolution. Because I believe this is a social revolution with limited objectives, we should watch and monitor these contradictory trends and assess them for what they are.

The second major change in consciousness is the one borne by the immense amount of organization at the local level, especially at the community and neighborhood level. Most significant in these trends are forms of solidarity, which make many neighborhoods share the burden imposed by the Israelis on individuals in their communities. Especially during the first year, and most recently in the classic rebellion exhibited especially by the town of Beit Sahour, a new spirit has prevailed, which we have not seen before. It is true that forms of resistance have been heightening in the last twenty-two years, but the Intifada was a quantum leap, a new phase, a qualitative transformation in terms of communal and local solidarities.

The most important of these developments is the manner in which this new consciousness of neighborhood and communal solidarity institutionalized itself through the creation of organizations, groups, patterns, and economic strategies of sustaining the people, recognizing that Israeli oppression is going to go on for a long time. Therefore, not only did the leadership have to be realistic in putting demands on the people, but the people had to know that, in order to sustain this rebellion, they have to organize in a manner which can take the oppression that has been imposed piecemeal over a long period of time.

These economic strategies, which were generated at the local level, were not always successful. For example, cooperatives and domestic industries, or home industries, as they were known, were often amateurish attempts to recall or reinstitute traditional forms of food preservation, marketing surplus, and basic levels of industrialization of food products; some lacked both the necessary technology and the necessary marketing skills required to bring fruition. However, from these mistakes new confidence emerged as well as a political stamina that would not have been there had it not been for these experiments in local organization. Thus, economic strategies of survival and sustenance during the Intifada may have failed technically, but the attempts succeeded in bringing new forms of political consciousness and political solidarity that would not have been there had people not concentrated on specific, concrete ways of tackling their dilemma.

The third form of consciousness—fundamentalism—is, I think, important both because of the promise it raises and also because of the pitfalls it engenders for our society. The national movement of Palestine in the last three quarters of the century at least, certainly since the First World

War, has been a secular movement. The contribution of the Arab Christian communities to the secularism of the Arab Palestinian national movement has been substantial. There is a clear explanation for this major contribution for a national religious minority among the Palestinians, who constitute less than 10 percent of the population now, and, at their height, constituted not more than 16 or 17 percent of the people. Within the decline of the Ottoman control over Palestine and greater Syria, Christians looked for a form of independence that would guarantee their civil freedoms, link them with their Muslim brothers and sisters, and guarantee their legal equality and national identity within the whole people. Secular Arab nationalism was the only possible form which would guarantee both civic freedom for the Christian minorities and would be the bridge uniting them with their Muslim brothers and sisters.

That secular trend of thought began in the 1850s, 1860s, and 1870s as a heretical or dissident minority vision of what the future or the Arab East would look like, voiced by people like Schibli Shumayyil, Jurji Zaydan, and other graduates of the Syrian Protestant College, which later became the American University in Beirut. Later in Palestine, with the great intellectual figures like Khalil Sakakini, Christians became dominant figures in the intellectual formulation of Palestinian nationalist thought and also in Syrian nationalist thought and in Arab nationalist thought generally. Christian figures in this movement were very visible; their intellectual contribution was very weighted.

By the Second World War this intellectual current, by stressing the secularism of the Arab nationalist movement rather than its religious dimension—although there was always a temptation to go back to the Muslim roots of Arab nationalism—had a decisive influence through the emergence in Syria of the Baathist party, the Syrian nationalist party, and in Egypt and North Africa the emergence of Nasserism as the new main form of Arab nationalism. This was true generally in the Middle East, as well as among the Palestinians.

Israeli occupation challenged the dominance of this form of nationalism and its secular component. I believe that the explanation of this challenge lies in the inability of Arab socialism and of Arab nationalism to create the necessary normative and ethical guides of conduct, which would equip people to deal with their future in times of crisis. This has been the greatest challenge, at the intellectual level, Israel has posed for us.

Having been caught unawares, the nationalist movement reverted to Islam by asserting the authenticity of national culture without trying to create alternative modes of behavior. Now this explanation may be too cryptic and definitely needs elaboration, but I believe that this is the weak point where the Muslim fundamentalist currents were able to penetrate the gaps in the cultural and intellectual thinking of the Arab nationalist movement and the Palestinian nationalist movement, which is, after all, part of this larger unit. This was very visible to those of us who taught the last fifteen years in local universities and saw the persistent emergence of the fundamentalist currents, with their concrete answers to concrete issues. I must stress that I speak here for people who identified always with secularism and saw religion not as a form of emancipation, but as a form of disease for our country. I use this form not without care, but knowing fully that religious fratricide and religious fanaticism has always been lurking as a main danger for the future of the Arab national community. One can see these problems in the situation in Egypt and in the emergence of the Muslim Brothers in the last fifteen years as a major political force in Syria, and lately in Jordan.

These pathological aspects of religion were compounded by the insistence of the fundamentalist groups on imposing social legislation, not only on their co-confessionals, but also on religious minorities. This became the situation in Iran and in Sudan. Therefore, the struggle for a separation of religion and state was also a struggle against religious fanaticism and against the new modernist fundamentalist interpretation of religion by the Muslim Brothers and the Khomeinis. I must also add to this picture certain Christian currents in our midst, although these were much weaker and tended to be more defensive.

One of the biggest challenges that the Intifada poses for us is not only to operationalize and draw new strategies and tactics to meet the Israeli challenge, but also to create an intellectual, political, ideological debate that will answer the normative needs for the Palestinian community without falling into the pitfall of fundamentalism and fanaticism. So far, I believe, there has been a partial victory for the secular forces.

Unfortunately, in some regions like Gaza, the fundamentalist movements were able to impose forms of dress codes and forms of behavior for women that have defeated years of struggle by Palestinian women to establish their own independence and assert their dignity in the Palestinian community. But the battle is far from being lost. A few months ago the Unified Command in one of their main leaflets (no. 40, I believe) defended the independence of women in asserting their own dress code and their own forms of behavior, and attacked the chauvinist and authoritarian positions of the fundamentalists. This is an important step forward.

This came at a time when there was a feeling in the nationalist movement that perhaps you must humor your protagonist because inherently the people are conservative; this is the way the Unified Leadership seemed to have been thinking. But, there is a limit to how far you can go in this kind of thinking. A clean break had to be made, and it was made in circular no. 40.

I think now we are at a new stage. This challenge imposes on us new forms of thinking, new strategies of political action, and ultimately the necessity to make links between political forms of struggle and the sociocultural prerequisites of emancipation. These two forms of struggle must not be separated. Today there is consciousness about the need to link them so that when the day of salvation comes, Palestine will achieve political as well as social freedoms.

3

The Arab Masses in Israel

SAMEEH GHNADREH

The Arab masses in Israel are a part of the Arab Palestinian people and, at the same time, are a national minority in Israel. They are the remnants of the Arab Palestinian people that remained in that portion of its homeland which became known as Israel after that state was created subsequent to the war of 1948.

Here we are not addressing ourselves to the Palestinian people living under occupation from June 1967 in the West Bank and Gaza, but to the Arab national minority inside Israel, those people who carry Israeli identity cards and who some call "Israeli Arabs" or "Israeli Arab citizens."

The special status of this national minority derives from this fact: it is part of the Arab Palestinian people, yet it carries the Israeli identity as citizens of the state of Israel. It is a national minority in its own homeland. These people have not immigrated into a land in which they became a minority, but they have refused to emigrate and withstood the waves of forced expulsion of their own people in 1948 which reduced them from the dominant majority to a small minority. They woke up one day to find 780,000 of their fellow citizens expelled from that area that became Israel and found themselves a national minority in their homeland, where they had always been a majority.

The state of Israel had promised in its "Declaration of Independence," which continues to be an official document to this day, to treat all the citizens of Israel on the basis of equality without any discrimination based on race or religion, yet this promise was merely ink on paper. The basic features of official Israeli policy toward this national minority can be summarized in one word: apartheid, a policy of racist persecution and national discrimination in all areas of life. The major features of this policy are as follows:

a. Forced emigration.

b. Confiscation of Arab land and destruction of Arab agriculture.

c. Destruction of industries and domination of work and the marketplace.

d. Forced national ignorance.

Theodore Herzl, the spiritual father and founder of Zionism, spoke about "settling a people without a land into a land without a people." Yet the land was not empty; it was full of an Arab Palestinian people. This gave rise to the Zionist slogan "the largest amount of land possible with the least amount of people on it."

According to the partition resolution issued by the General Assembly of the United Nations on November 29, 1947, which formed the basis for the creation of the state of Israel, there was to be two states, an Arab state and a Jewish state. It was intended that the Jewish state have 495,000 Jews and 490,000 Arabs, while the Arab state was to have 725,000 Arabs and 10,000 Jews. Jerusalem itself was to become international with 105,000 Arabs and 100,000 Jews.

Yet Israel was, in fact, extended over a larger area than the one appointed by the said partition resolution. Even after that, the whole area of the Triangle was added to it on April 3, 1949. Yet the Arab Palestinian people have been prevented from erecting their own state until this day. The conditions of war were utilized to throw out the Palestinians from their own homeland, including that portion which was slated for the creation of the state of Israel according to the partition resolution. In addition, massacres were committed in order to spread terror and to enable the process of forced eviction (such as the massacre of Deir Yasein on September 4, 1948). In this manner, 780,000 Palestinians, out of 940,000 who originally were residing in the area slated for the state of Israel, were deported and only 160,000 remained (some sources speak of only 146,000 remaining). In addition, 478 Palestinian towns and villages were destroyed out of a total 585. Jewish settlements and cities were created in place of Arab ones. Their names have been altered, or new names given to them, such as Ahidout in place of Al Burwa, Kafa Beischat in place of Al Bassa, Tsipoury in place of Safourya, Faroud in place of Fradya, Kufer Anan and Saigeve in place of Mea'ar, and Beit Sha'an in place of Beisan, Roushpena in place of Al Jaa'ouna, Afouleh in place of Al Fouleh, Keriat Shmouneh in place of Al Khalsa, Beit Dajoun in place of Beit Dajan, Heteem in place of Hiteen, Gish and Heziev in place of Al Zeib, Shdout Yam in place of Quesarieh, etc., etc.

Not only were Jewish settlements set up in place of Arab towns, but public national parks and entertainment places were built up on the ruins of Arab villages, like the park of Kvar Hahourish in place of Ma'loul, and the Lavia Park in place of Lubiya, and so on. One of the early leaders of Israel, Ketsi Nelson, said, "My conscience is completely at peace with respect to the legality of deportations because one thousand enemies outside the house are easier than one inside it."

This policy of expulsion continues to this day but by other means, especially after the failure of the Kufur Qasem massacre on October 8, 1956 to create a panic in the area of the Triangle and a resultant flight of its population. Yesha'yahou Ben Forat had admitted, "The first truth is that there is no Zionism without settlement, and no Jewish state without the removal of the Arabs and the confiscation of their lands and fencing it." Ahroun Yareive, the former Israeli head of Military Intelligence and Minister of Communications, revealed the existence of government plans "to utilize the existence of a state of war in order to deport 700 to 800 thousand Arabs. . . . These ideas are not only discussed but the means of their implementation is prepared."

However, that which succeeded in the conditions prevailing in 1948-1949 is no longer easy or suitable today. That is why the Israeli authorities have been careful since that time to deepen and solidify the policy of national discrimination—stealing Arab land, strangling Arab agriculture and industry, dominating workplaces and the market, and pursuing a deliberate policy of lack of education—with the view of making life intolerable for Arabs, thus creating their (voluntary) emigration. The policy also aims at isolating them in their cities and villages as third-class citizens, after Eastern Oriental Jews (who are Israel's second-class population), without permitting them to develop normally or to have any influence over the life of the country. At the same time, the attempt has been made to separate them from the rest of the Arab Palestinian people and to treat them, not as a people, but as a small minority composed of different denominations: Muslims, Christians, and Jews. The authorities imposed military rule upon them from December 12, 1948, until 1966 in order to carry out this program. The Koening Document, which was an official racist document exposed by the Al Hamishmar paper on September 7, 1976, described the features of this policy under the title "Memorandum for Treatment of Israeli Arabs." This document clearly declared that the mere existence of Arabs in the country and their normal reproduction create a demographic danger to the state. It makes a number of recommendations for reinforcing the discrimination against them in order to further isolate them and deport them.

BASIC FEATURES IN A PANORAMA OF DISCRIMINATION AND PERSECUTION

Official racist declarations and positions: Several Israeli ministers have repeated at different times and on different occasions apartheid statements that have become a clear reflection of the racism which permeates the thought of Israeli officials when it comes to its Arab citizens. Among these were the statements, "The only good Arab is a dead Arab," "The Arabs are a cancer in the body of the State," "We are willing to pay the taxi fare for any Arab who leaves," and "We want to make Arabs into just drugged cockroaches in a bottle." . . .

Land confiscation: The number of Arabs in Israel over the past forty-two years has quadrupled, while their landownership has been reduced by two-thirds. They comprise today about 17 percent of the entire population, but they own less than 4 percent of the land. In the Galilee they constitute more than 50 percent of the population but only own 9 percent of the land. Out of the 956,000 acres the Arabs owned in Israel in 1948, today they own no more than 323,000 acres, of which approximately 179,000 acres are agricultural. The share of each individual in land in Aum Al Fahem went from 2 acres to .2 acres; in Tibeh, from 2 acres to .15 acres; in Teereh from almost 3 acres to .15 acres; in Arabeh from 10 acres to .2 acres; in Ain Mahel from 3 acres to .15 acres; and in Asefia from 4.5 acres to .2 acres.

The land area of the city of Nazareth in 1948 was 3,336 acres, and its population was fifteen thousand people. Today the population has risen to fifty-five thousand people, but the land area has been reduced to 1,668 acres.

In addition, the extensive Islamic Waqf properties (religiously owned properties held communally) were abolished, and new laws were passed enabling the confiscation of land for state and security purposes. Also, the Project for the Judaization of the Galilee was passed and the lands of the Bedouins in the Negev were expropriated. After all these laws, Arabs today only own 111,000 acres—less than .2 acres for the individual—out of which thousands of acres are reserved for public building and utilities, as well as for the Muslim and Christian religious buildings. Deir Hanna, which had a population of five hundred, owned over 4,400 acres in 1948. Today it only owns 1,100 acres, even though its population has increased to fifty-five thousand. Sakhneen also has today only 3,800 acres out of an original 21,000 acres. This story could be repeated for village after village.

Industry: Neither the government nor the Histadrut has built or encouraged the building of any factory in the Arab sector. Quite the contrary, it created continual difficulties for existing Arab factories until it forced them into bankruptcy and closed them. In the whole city of Nazareth, which has existed from the times of Christ, there is not a single factory, while in the newly created Upper Nazareth, a Jewish city built in the late 1950s on land belonging to the city of Nazareth as part of the Project for the Judaization of the Galilee, there are 160 factories and a major industrial area. The government refuses to grant any Arab town the classification of a development town, which would make it eligible for additional funding, tax benefits, and exemptions industrialists and investors can employ when they build their factories in a particular area.

Agriculture: Prior to 1948 more than 80 percent of the Arab work force lived from agriculture. Now, because of land confiscation and the strangulation of Arab agriculture, more than 77 percent of Arab breadwinners are daily wage earners, and the number of workers in agriculture in Arab towns is now less than 10 percent.

It must be noted that the share of irrigation water for Arab agriculture is only 1 percent of the amount that is delegated to Jewish agriculture. Only 5 percent of the Arab land is irrigated, while half of the Jewish land is irrigated.

The official government policy has effectively destroyed the basic Arab agriculture products, such as tobacco, vegetables, citrus, and wheat. The only branch that is mostly available to Arabs is olives, whose produce is accumulated in the homes or bought by the state for very cheap prices, while the state itself imports oil from Spain and Italy.

Arab workers: Arabs work primarily in the "black jobs." These are the jobs that are more physically taxing and lower paying. Arabs are the last to be hired and the first to be fired. The percentage of Arabs working in free trades, academic, scientific, educational, technical, and administrative careers do not exceed 19.5 percent whereas 50.4 percent work as laborers. Arab workers in construction and its subdivisions, masonry, transportation, and in non-professional work number 26 percent (29.3 percent for Jews) and 6 percent in office jobs (19.5 percent for Jews).

Based on the above it is no surprise that the average wages of the Arab worker is 60 percent of the average of his Jewish colleague in the same category. Over half accept wages that are less than half the general average of wages. Arabs constitute 55.5 percent of the holders of the tenth and last degree of income—the level of poverty (remember, Arabs constitute only 17 percent of the population). Unemployment in the Arab sector reaches 22 percent while the national average is 8 percent.

Housing: Neither the government nor the Histadrut has undertaken any housing project in the Arab sector except for several scores of apartments in Nazareth. Official government corporations and the Histadrut corporation refuse to sell or even rent any residential apartment it builds to Arabs, using as an excuse that they only allow those who serve in the army to rent or buy their apartments. Twenty-four percent of Arab families live in a housing ratio of over three individuals to the room, as opposed to 1 percent of Jewish families who suffer the same level of crowding. As a result of the confiscation of land and the refusal to expand municipal boundaries of Arab cities and villages, Arabs live in extremely overcrowded conditions. They have been forced into building illegally and without license, which results in the problem of house demolition by the Israeli government. Today there are over seven thousand houses at risk of destruction, in addition to forty Bedouins and village collections of housing not recognized officially as villages. To illustrate this problem we can say that the total population of Upper Nazareth is less than half the population of the city of Nazareth, but the land area of the Jewish Nazareth is over 2,100 acres, while the land area of the Arab Nazareth municipality is not quite 1,700 acres.

Education: Because of the large number of children in Arab families, the number of Arab children in elementary schools is about 20 percent the number of Jewish students. However, the dropout rate among them, because of the backwardness of their schools, ranges between 20 percent and 30 percent (4.5 percent among Jews). No more than 50 percent manage to finish the secondary schools (80 percent among Jews), and the rate in higher institutes and universities is only 6 percent.

The average number of students in the Arab classroom is thirty-five (the average in the Jewish classroom is twenty-five). In order to reach a fair ratio between the number of Arab teachers for the number of students with the number of Jewish teachers, Arab schools would need four thousand additional jobs, since there is one teacher to every twenty-eight Arab students as opposed to one teacher for every nineteen Jewish students. The entire Arab population of seven hundred thousand has only two industrial schools. The professional branches only take 20 percent of Arab students who study technological and professional courses (60 percent among the Jews).

In addition to the backwardness of the Arab schools, and the lack of laboratories, libraries, playgrounds, and yards, there is also the phenomenon of rented classrooms. There are over two thousand rooms rented here and there for teaching purposes in the Arab sector. In Nazareth, for example, fully 161 rooms are rented for educational purposes. (This is the equivalent of eight full schools. The situation would be worse if not for the private Christian schools.) There is not a single kindergarten or nursery school in the Arab sector, but 62 percent of Jewish children enjoy government sponsored kindergarten. Out of 980 top jobs in the Educational Ministry, only 3.26 percent are held by Arabs.

In addition to all the above, the very curriculum that is mandated for Arab schools is aimed at national ignorance and at stripping Arabs from their heritage, national honor, progressive literature, and ancient history. The aim was clearly spelled out by a former educational consultant in the Ministry of Education, Mr. Lubrani, who said that the goal is to "turn Arabs into hewers of wood and drawers of water."

Health conditions: Ninety percent of the Arab population are insured with the Histadrut Copat Holim, a national health scheme. About 15 percent of all participants in this scheme are Arabs, but only 3.7 percent of its employees and 2 percent of its doctors are Arabs. Only 7.9 percent of the clinics are in Arab areas. Arabs have no regional clinics (forty-six such regional clinics serve the Jews) and not a single dental clinic (seventy-nine dental clinics serve the Jews).

There is one doctor for every sixteen hundred persons in the Jewish sector, but only one per twenty-nine hundred in the Arab sectors, and in some areas, like Ain Mahel or Ararah or Beineh, the ratio reaches one per four thousand people. The number of infant fatalities during the first month is 12.3 per thousand (8.3 per thousand among the Jews). Infant mortality between 1 month and 1 year is 10.3 per thousand for Arabs (only 3.5 per thousand for Jews).

The majority of Arab clinics are lacking in specialist doctors or night services. Neither the government nor the Histadrut has built a single hospital in the Arab areas. On the contrary, it creates obstacles to the existing private Christian hospitals, of which there are three in Nazareth.

In addition, the majority of Arab towns and villages suffer from the absence of sewage networks and from old water networks. There are no more than seven semi-complete sewage networks in over one hundred Arab towns and villages.

Social Services: Offices for social services for Arabs only exist in eleven towns and villages. Each of these offices serves a whole number of villages with a very small number of employees. For example, in the regional Tiberias office (for Jews) there is one employee for every seven thousand citizens; in contrast, there is one employee for every eleven thousand people in the Nazareth office. All together the Arab sector receives only 10 percent of the positions and jobs that it deserves. By comparing the Arab town of Aum Al Fahem with the Jewish town Oryahuda, which has roughly the same population, the former has only seven jobs for social work while the latter has twenty-three jobs.

Out of 450 jobs that were designated for young people in difficult economic situations, only twenty-five have been given to Arab youths. Arab social workers must handle about three hundred files, while their Jewish colleagues handle no more than fifty files. In Shfa Amer 2.5 jobs exist to serve twenty-five thousand individuals, while in the Jewish Nazareth Alit, fifteen jobs are designated for an equal population. The budget allocated to an Arab office barely reaches 20 percent of the budget allocated to a Jewish office, despite the fact that the social situation of the Arab population is far worse.

In addition, it is quite disturbing to see the lack of clubs, therapy centers, rehabilitation, entertainment, and counseling centers in the Arab sector. There is not a single institution for Arab juvenile delinquents, who then end up in prison.

Histadrut Services: Arab members constitute 10 percent of the total membership of the Histadrut Labor Union. Yet there are only three elected union councils in the Arab sectors and only one regional council. This means that 21 percent of the Arab workers in Histadrut enjoy belonging to an elected council and 12 percent belong to a mixed council, but the 63 percent remaining do not enjoy any union representation whatsoever, despite the fact the Histadrut regulations specify the right of every Arab town to elect its own labor council as long as it has seventeen hundred or more laborers who belong to the Histadrut. There is an elected labor council in the Jewish Kfar Youna (1,614 members), Ben Yahoud (1,634 members), and Tilmond (1,985 members), while there are no elected union councils in such Arab villages as Kufur Qare'a (2,024 members), Kufur Yaseif (2,033 members), Yafet Al Nasera (2,502 members), Al Teireh (2,298 members), Qulanswa (2,184 members), and so on.

The importance of the Histadrut representation is evident when we consider that the Histadrut controls about 25 percent of the entire economy of the country. Yet it has not set up a single factory or undertaken a single housing project in the Arab sector. The few Arab labor committees receive only 33 percent of their share of the budget and 20 percent of the jobs that are offered to equivalent Jewish union committees. For example, the budget per member in the Nazareth Labor Committee in 1985 was 11.6 shekels per member, in contrast with 34.25 shekels per member in Megdalha Aimick, 39 shekels in Keriat Shmoneh, and 84.89 shekels in Telmond. There are thirteen jobs in the Labor Committee of Nazareth and Ain Mahel, serving 18,640 members, in contrast to nineteen positions in the upper Nazareth Labor Committee, which serves eleven thousand members.

To this day, the Histadrut refuses to allow Arab agricultural workers to join its agricultural center. Therefore, it does not offer them any assistance, support, or agricultural counselling, nor does it care to market their products. Similarly it only sets up and supports a very small number of clubs or sports rooms in the Arab sectors. For example, in Nazareth the Histadrut set up a single club, a single nursery, and a soccer team (Hapo'ael), while in Upper Nazareth it set up a major central club, six neighborhood clubs, two women's clubs under the Me'amat Organization, twelve nurseries, two soccer teams, two basketball teams, a swimming team, a team for table tennis, two teams for bicycling, and a team for wrestling. In addition, it built modern institutions for child care and summer camps for children in Upper Nazareth.

Arab local councils: Fewer than half the Arab towns and villages enjoy locally elected municipal bodies—56 towns out of 137. To this day not a single town planning scheme has been finally approved for any of these local committees, and the Arab local authorities only have influence over less than one-third of the total area of land that should fall under their jurisdiction. The rest is kept as a reserve for future confiscation; it is not allowed to be used for building, despite the major population crises in Arab towns. The total budget for Arab local councils in 1986 was 3.3 percent of the total budget for Jewish local councils, even though they served 12 percent of the entire population. Generally, an Arab local council enjoys 30 percent of the amount given to its Jewish counterpart, in regular budgets, less than 5 percent of the development budget granted to its Jewish counterpart, and 20 percent of the jobs.

The budget of Upper Nazareth is 16.96 shekels per person, in contrast to 7.1 shekels per person in Nazareth. In the Jewish town there is one employee for every fifty-nine citizens, in contrast with one for every 127 citizens in the Arab Nazareth. The Jewish city gets 260 percent more grants than Nazareth.

The following table will help us with this comparison:

Village or settlement	*Population in 1985*	*Size of budget in 1984*
Beit Jin (Arabs)	6,000	39,748
Zakhron Ya'cove	5,100	137,740
Iksal (Arabs)	5,900	40,148
Yourham	6,100	293,592
Abu Snan (Arabs)	6,500	41,094
Hashour	6,600	226,869
Al Tybeh (Arabs)	18,500	240,897
Yaqney	18,200	506,147
Tamara (Arabs)	14,300	109,827
Beit Shan	13,200	339,686
Jadedeh (Arabs)	4,300	38,889
Bar Yacove	4,700	146,740
Kaboul (Arabs)	5,200	25,387
Upper Yaknam	5,500	171,062

It is clear that the Arab municipalities and local councils are unable to provide necessary services to their citizens or to undertake sewage networks, build clubs, pave roads, construct schools, and provide other basic services. The entire economic, social, and legal system of Israel is based on systematic discrimination between one privileged population, Jewish, and a second, Arab, which is barely tolerated and which the Israeli government regards as scarcely having the right to dwell in the region of its historic homeland at all.

4

Agriculture in the West Bank and Gaza

Status and Prospects of Development

JAD ISAAC

Agriculture is considered to be the most important productive sector in the economy of the West Bank and Gaza, contributing about 35 percent to the Gross National Product of the Occupied Territories and providing employment for about one-third of the labor force inside these areas. Plant production, especially vegetables and citrus in the irrigated areas of the West Bank and Gaza, and olives in the rain-fed areas of the West Bank, is the backbone of agricultural production in these areas, while animal production constitutes about one-third of the total agricultural production in these areas.

During the past twenty years the agricultural sector in the West Bank and Gaza has witnessed a series of changes reflecting changes in the political scene. In the early years of occupation the political emphasis in the Occupied Territories focused on liberation and the ending of the occupation. Yet, for the average Palestinian, economic necessity took precedence over nationalist considerations. Steadfastness, a popular slogan for resistance to the occupation, implies a passive role in the developmental process taking shape in the Palestinian community. There were those who felt that in the presence of occupation and in the absence of a national authority, no real development could take place. But development for the sake of steadfastness, coined by the Arab Thought Forum in Jerusalem, became an acceptable strategy that could provide a practical alternative for Palestinians under prolonged occupation.

In these early years of occupation the Israeli authorities launched a massive campaign via the Department of Agriculture for developing the agricultural sector, especially in the Jericho area. This came to a halt in the mid-seventies as a result of pressures from the Israeli farmers and changes in the policies toward the Occupied Territories. A PLO-Jordanian joint committee was established to channel funds to the Palestinian people under occupation to help them remain steadfast. At the same time a number of private, Western voluntary agencies and nongovernmental organizations started working in the occupied Arab territories to improve the quality of life.

By the late seventies and early eighties the work of the PLO-Jordanian fund and the various PVOs (Private Voluntary Organizations) and NGOs (Nongovernmental Organizations) had encouraged a mentality of "dependence on external organizations" among a good percentage of the Palestinian population in the occupied Arab territories. The attitude of "What can we do while we are under occupation?" and "Things can only improve when we have our own state" became the norm in the West Bank.

I believe that 1982 marked a turning point in the Palestinian attitude toward occupation and, for that matter, toward self-understanding. A new leadership emerged, characterized by motivation, commitment, self-confidence, self-reliance, with no illusion of support for the national Palestinian aspirations by the various parties in the Middle East conflict. In a very short time grassroots organizations based on this new Palestinianism attained the support of many people, despite harassment and suppression.

These conditions, combined with the failure of various peace initiatives to end the occupation, resulted in the popular uprising against the occupying Israeli authorities. Following the onset of the Intifada, there was a considerable shift toward backyard farming as a survival strategy for the Palestinian population in the face of increasing conditions of hardship and oppression. This manifested itself in the form of growing vegetables and fruits at home, in addition to maintaining and breeding a small number of farm animals.

The Intifada has established the base and environment for economic change; the evolution of its economic strategies would naturally include the analysis and planning of not only short-term but also medium- and long-term economic and social policies and plans. The current strategies of the Intifada have significantly and necessarily relied on survival mechanisms and organizations for self-sufficiency. But the future Palestinian state has the resources for vibrant economic growth, and social sectors will therefore need to evolve during the period of transition as well as with the implementation of statehood.

It is in this context that the following considerations are presented to shed light on options, opportunities, and needs Palestinians will be facing in the development of the agricultural sector.

THE LAND

Land is the crux of the Palestinian-Israeli conflict, and at the same time it is the basis of agricultural production. The total area of the West Bank, including Jerusalem, is about 1.3 million acres of which 419,810 acres (32 percent) are cultivated. The total area of the Gaza Strip is 81,000 acres of which 38,835 acres are cultivated (48 percent). In the West Bank 23,000 acres are under irrigation, representing 5.5 percent of the cultivated area, while in Gaza there are 24,000 acres under irrigation, representing 61.8 percent of the cultivated areas. In Israel, 49.1 percent of the cultivated land is under irrigation.

The main constraint facing Palestinian agriculturalists has been land confiscation by the Israeli authorities. At present, more than 60 percent of the land in the West Bank and 40 percent of the land in Gaza is under Israeli control.

While the land is the center of the political conflict and thus cannot be resolved by agriculturalists, yet it is vital here to explore the potential of land development in the occupied Palestinian territories.

Analyzing the variations in land usage in the West Bank and Gaza indicates a substantial potential of increasing the cultivated areas through land reclamation, especially in the Bethlehem, Ramallah, and Hebron districts. This has been estimated at 445,000 acres of which 222,000 acres could be cultivated with trees and other crops, 111,000 acres to be used for forest trees and the other 111,000 acres for grazing. Depending upon the topography of the land, reclamation may be simple, that is, removal of rocks and creating contours at a cost of approximately $540 per acre, or complex, which requires heavy machinery and could cost approximately $1,100 per acre. The topsoil and the slope will determine the type of crops to be used.

Pasture plants do well on 12 inches of topsoil, while field crops require 12-20 inches. Fruit trees vary in their topsoil requirement: 20 inches for figs and olives, 23 inches for grapes, 27 inches for almonds, apricots, peaches, plums, and 31 inches for apples. Land reclamation would increase the production base for agriculture, and it would also provide an opportunity for creating developmental nuclei in these areas, which are essentially needed with statehood. One should point here to the results of a study which showed that housing 110,000 inhabitants in an area of 78 square miles provides 13,300 direct jobs in agriculture, 4,500 jobs in production services, and 2,760 job opportunities in administrative and public services.

It is anticipated that the cost of reclaiming 445,000 acres will be in the range of $400 million. It is understood that very little can be done in land reclamation under the present political circumstances, but planning and preparations for such a project should be initiated now, including data collection, technical training, managerial skills, and support structures in the areas of extension, pasture plants, land conservation, agricultural systems, policies, and so forth.

An important characteristic of potential concern in agricultural development in the occupied Palestinian lands is a ratio of land ownership to tenancy and low-size holdings, which hinders the investment in mechanization into these areas.

About 50 percent of the farmers in the West Bank have fewer than 4.5 acres. In Gaza there is a higher percentage of larger landownership because of the nature of crops in this area, where two-thirds of the cultivated land consists of orchards. Agricultural cooperatives could play a major role in promoting the introduction of mechanization, yet the track record of the existing cooperatives has so far been disappointing.

WATER

Water is considered to be the most crucial factor in the development of agriculture in the Middle East in general and the West Bank and Gaza in particular. The annual water potential of the West Bank is about 600 million cubic meters. (Note: a cubic meter of water is approximately 264 gallons: 600 million cubic meters of water is only slightly less than the amount of water in Lake Michigan in the United States.) This water comes from three main water aquifers, the Northwestern and Northeastern basins, which are shared with Israel, and the Southeastern basin, which does not affect Israel's water supply.

Immediately following the occupation of the West Bank and Gaza, Israel took control of the water resources in these areas. Drilling of wells was prohibited and many existing wells were closed. At present, the Palestinian population in the West Bank is allowed to utilize only 115 million cubic meters annually. The Israeli settlements are utilizing 40-50 million cubic meters annually, and the rest, which comes to 25 percent of Israel's water expenditures, is used inside the "green line" (in Israel).

Not only is there an imbalance in the distribution and consumption of water between Palestinians and Israelis, but the pricing of water is also discriminatory. Jewish settlers pay 7.5 and 11.5 cents per cubic meter for agricultural and domestic use respectively. Palestinian farmers, on the other hand, pay 35 cents for each cubic meter of water whether it is for agricultural or domestic use. Palestinian municipalities charge an even higher rate for water, ranging between 50 to 80 cents per cubic meter.

The Gaza Strip has a water potential of 80 million cubic meters annually, of which the Palestinians are using 60 million cubic meters annually. There is an overpumping of water in the Gaza Strip reaching 120-140 million cubic meters per year. This has caused an increase in the salinity of the aquifers, which in turn is endangering the agricultural sector in Gaza.

In summary, the Palestinians are now using 5.8 percent of the water potential of geographic Palestine. Whether based on population or size, the Palestinians are entitled to no less than 25 percent of the water resources, which means that there is a potential of increasing the irrigated areas by at least fourfold. However, it should be pointed out that in the long term, water consumption for domestic use will increase and therefore, water conservation and management will be a priority in the Palestinian agenda for development. There is a need to examine carefully from a Palestinian perspective the potential of increasing the water resources in the West Bank and Gaza through projects like the Turkish pipeline, the Med-Dead channel, desalinization of sea water, and so on. For the Bethlehem area there is a potential of utilizing the deep water aquifer in Herodion. This aquifer cannot be replenished and, at the same time, it is being depleted annually as a result of the continental drift. In short, the water issue will have a high priority on the agenda of the politicians. It is becoming increasingly evident that the Israeli water and regional security interests are interrelated, making this issue a very difficult one.

PLANT PRODUCTION

Despite the small size of the West Bank and Gaza, these areas enjoy a diversity of climatological regions that makes it possible to grow almost anything all year round. Economic considerations have been the prime factor determining the type of plant production in the various areas. Intensive farming prevails in the irrigated areas of the West Bank, where vegetables are the major crop, followed by citrus. In Gaza, citrus is still the major crop, followed by vegetables.

Plant production in rain-fed areas in the West Bank is divided among vegetables (5.6 percent), field crops (32.9 percent), olives (45.4 percent), and other fruit trees (16.1 percent). In view of the low landownership in the West Bank and Gaza and the subsequent difficulty in introducing mechanization in those areas, there has been a gradual decline in the areas of field crops, and many farmers have resorted to planting fruit trees.

Irrigated cultivation in the West Bank and Gaza is well developed but continues to encounter the following production constraints:

1. The increasing cost of purchased inputs, which are mostly imported from Israel. Last year the purchased agricultural inputs for the West Bank and Gaza, which include seeds, irrigation equipment, fertilizers, pesticides, and plastic, came to $68.5 million and $22.7 million respectively, while the agricultural GDP were $221 million and $46.5 million respectively.

2. Surplus production and lack of marketing outlets. This phenomenon seems to be prevailing in irrigated areas due to lack of planning and the absence of central government.

3. Technical problems, such as the white flies, which have damaged large areas of crops, especially tomatoes, due to the spread of viral diseases. Other problems are the sudden yellowing of citrus trees and the red spiders, which are damaging the watermelon crops. In 1988 frost also caused serious damage to the Jordan Valley and Gaza cultivation.

As for rain-fed farming, there has been a shift toward fruit trees, mainly olives, which may be attributed to the following:

1. Profitability. It is estimated that on average, one acre of land in rain-fed areas has a net annual revenue of $89 if planted with wheat, while this revenue will be $135 for olives, and may easily reach $450 for other fruits, such as apricots, plums, or peaches.

2. Fruit production other than olives is labor intensive compared to field crops, which depend heavily on mechanization. This fact renders fruit production in the Occupied Territories, especially under a situation of prolonged occupation, to be a source of employment for a good number of Palestinian farmers and may reduce their temptation to join the Israeli labor market.

3. The planting of trees by itself may help partially in reducing the Israeli appetite for confiscating Arab land on the grounds that the land is not cultivated.

4. Planting fruit trees in marginal land requires much less effort and investment than other crops when it comes to land reclamation, and this factor is of prime importance to Palestinians.

Following the onset of the Intifada, many Palestinians went back to their lands as a survival strategy to combat the increasing conditions of oppression and hardship and as a self-reliance mechanism to express the internal strength of the Palestinian population and its determination to get rid of the occupation. While no figures are officially available to substantiate this claim, it is estimated that during the last two years more than 500,000 fruit trees have been planted in the West Bank and Gaza.

Whether for national feelings or economic or even ecological factors, every effort should be made to capitalize on rain-fed farming, which faces the following major problems:

1. This sector has unfortunately been neglected for the past twenty-two years with the closure of experimental stations and deficient public extension services. Introducing new resistant varieties and modern agricultural practices can easily increase the production in rain-fed areas. A classic example is the trellising of grape vines, which can increase the grape production by eightfold. In fact, only 10 percent of the grape vines in the West Bank are presently trellised.

2. Fluctuations in production due to changes in annual rainfall. Olives in particular are affected by rotation; one year, like 1986, the West Bank produced 150,000 tons of olives, compared with 8,400 tons in 1987. Considering the international growing demand for olive oil, this physiological periodicity may be solved through technological practices.

3. Marketing constraints due to the one-way traffic of goods between the Occupied Territories and Israel; seasonability; and restrictions on export.

4. Lack of diversity in produce.

5. Lack of expertise in pest control, especially against things like phylloxera, which is threatening large areas of grapes in the Hebron area, and the apple and peach borers, which have seriously reduced the areas of these trees in the highlands.

ANIMAL PRODUCTION

Livestock development is a prerequisite for the agricultural development in the occupied Palestinian territories. While this sector has the advantage of being less dependent on resources such as water and land, yet it has been facing other types of difficulties and constraints.

With the Intifada, there has been a shift toward small-scale animal production enterprises ranging from five hundred to one thousand chickens, or twenty to thirty lambs/goats or five to ten cows as self-employment enterprises. Obtaining accurate official statistics regarding the numbers of the various farm animals in the West Bank and Gaza at present is rather difficult. However, it is estimated that at present, there are more than twenty-two thousand cows, six hundred thousand laying hens, and seven hundred thousand sheep and goats in the West Bank and Gaza.

The main problems facing livestock production in the West Bank and Gaza may be summarized as follows:

1. The increasing cost of animal feed, which continues to be the crucial factor affecting the profitability of animal production projects. It is estimated that feed costs constitute more than 50 percent of the total production costs in animal husbandry. During the past two years the prices of animal feed have soared, and this has seriously affected the profitability of animal production units in the West Bank and Gaza. An example is the price of barley, which used to cost $100 per ton just before the Intifada; its cost now is $220 per ton. The situation is, in fact, worse because the currency used is the Jordanian dinar, which was and perhaps still is the dominant currency in the Occupied Territories. Before the Intifada a ton of barley used to cost 32 dinars while now it sells for 176 dinars.

2. The decreasing grazing potential. For the past twenty-two years the Israeli authorities have been progressively confiscating or closing large areas in the West Bank and Gaza which were formerly used for grazing. Official figures show that more than 52 percent of the total land area in the West Bank and Gaza is under Israeli control (as of October 1989).

As a result, the limited areas available for grazing before the 1967 war have been progressively depleted of their grazing potential, especially in the Eastern highlands and the Jordan Valley. The low production of rain-fed areas have forced many Palestinians to abandon their fields and work as laborers in Israel, and this has contributed to the increased desertification of marginal lands. At present, grazing can at its best satisfy less than 15 percent of the total feed needs for animals in the West Bank and Gaza. Consequently, the majority of animal production units are essentially based on intensive management, and this practice will have to continue in the foreseeable future.

3. The deficient veterinarian services, especially the governmental ones. A classic example is the cancellation of the artificial insemination services a few years ago. Brucellosis is becoming endemic in the West Bank and is threatening the livestock in this area.

4. The traditional way of management.

5. Dependency on Israel for stock. Israel has repeatedly denied the Palestinians the right to produce their own stock hybrids as a deliberate

policy to control livestock development in the West Bank and Gaza. The hatchery project of the UNDP, for example, was cancelled, and the few existing hatcheries were ordered to close their operations.

It should be pointed out that bee-keeping in the West Bank and Gaza is a growing field. Rabbit breeding also has gone up during the past few years as a cheap source of protein in rural areas. Fish farming is still in its infancy here, but this branch may prove to be feasible, especially in the Ghur and Gaza areas.

Considering the number of livestock in the West Bank and Gaza, it follows that there is a need to supply at least 150,000 tons of feed for the local market per year at an estimated annual cost of 50 million dollars. The total production of concentrates in the West Bank and Gaza is about 25,000 tons per year.

There are ten feed factories in the West Bank and Gaza that have a total production of thirty thousand tons of feed per year. Most of the raw materials required for these factories are imported. Accordingly, the overall feed produced locally satisfies less than 10 percent of the cattle and sheep feed and less than 15 percent of the chicken feed demand. This renders animal production in the West Bank and Gaza quite dependent on Israel or imports for providing animal feed.

Increasing pasture areas and pasture management, together with diversification of field crops, including the promotion of growing feed concentrates, such as barley, vetch, and so on, may help to alleviate some of these problems. In addition, there should be an attempt to utilize more efficiently the large quantities of farm byproducts in producing animal feed. Due to intensive farming in the West Bank and Gaza, there is a surplus of agricultural produce and farm byproducts that can be easily incorporated in feed rations, such as poultry waste, banana leaves, olive pulp, citrus peels, and surplus fruits and vegetables.

MARKETING AND EXPORT

While the West Bank and Gaza have the potential to be nearly self-reliant in their food needs, this is presently not the case. Of the total vegetable and fruit production in the West Bank and Gaza, it is estimated that 62 percent is used for local consumption, while 38 percent is considered to be a surplus which has to be either processed or exported. On the other hand, Palestinians are depending on imports for their food and feed crops. As a result, the West Bank and Gaza have a surplus of agricultural imports over agricultural exports estimated at $23.8 million for 1985. Plant production in the West Bank and Gaza faces serious problems due to controlled marketing and lack of diversification. Palestinian produce is not permitted to be marketed in Israel, while Israeli produce enjoys free marketing in the West Bank and Gaza. Export of agricultural produce to neighboring Arab states and Europe faces many obstacles. Heavy losses for Palestinian farmers due to these constraints and restrictions have become part of their lives.

As mentioned earlier, pure economic considerations have taken precedence over national food security in determining the type of plantation. In the absence of a national agricultural planning commission, the decision has been left to individual farmers, and in many cases, this has led to chaos. Attempts to establish an agricultural council have so far been unsuccessful.

As a result of the Intifada, there is a growing attitude among the Palestinians toward self-reliance. Yet, due to the absence of a central national authority and for other reasons, it is unlikely to achieve self-sufficiency, but decreased reliance is becoming the norm. One should remember here that Israel produces 95 percent of its food needs. While the current activities of self-reliance should be continued, in the future emphasis should be directed toward the production of high value cash crops, especially in irrigated areas, with particular attention given to market opportunities. Given the best circumstance, self-sufficiency in legumes and cereals is unlikely to be economically sound.

The agricultural exports from the West Bank and Gaza in 1985 came to $78.3 million while Israel's agricultural exports in 1988 were $600 million. There is a great potential of increasing agricultural exports from the Occupied Territories especially following the approval of the Israeli authorities to export directly to the EEC countries. It is rather unfortunate that last year's test case of exports was less than successful, especially with oranges. It should be reiterated here that marketing fresh produce is not an easy thing. One should never count on good will or sympathy in Western markets. Quality and competitiveness are the name of the game. Exporting surpluses is definitely not the right approach for competing in the international market. Competitiveness requires product-specific production and marketing for export.

AGRO-INDUSTRIES

The industrial sector in general and the agro-industries in particular have lagged behind the other productive sectors in the West Bank and Gaza, contributing less than 7 percent to the total GNP of these areas. The main agro-industries in the West Bank and Gaza are the following: four beverage production plants, four distilleries and wineries, two cigarette companies, four microdairies, one tomato-canning plant, two citrus-packing plants, three snack factories, and two pasta plants. Except for the citrus plants, two wineries, and the microdairies, the raw materials used in these industries are imported. The local tobacco companies prefer to import their tobacco, while the local tobacco is sold to the Israeli companies. The locally grown durum wheat, ideal for pastas, is used for making bread, while the pasta factories import flour from Israel.

The Intifada has created the interest in establishing agro-industries for processing surplus fruits and vegetables. Several proposals have been submitted, including a pea-freezing plant in Ramallah, a tomato-canning plant in Hebron, a citrus juice plant in Gaza, a pickling plant in Tulkarm, and a grape juice plant in Hebron. I strongly believe that this approach is not the right one. A basic food science principle is that the quality of the product is determined by the quality of the input. One simply cannot use table grapes or salad tomatoes for producing juice or tomato puree because of the low percentage of solids and aroma constituents, in addition to the high cost of water evaporation. By the same token, pickling surplus local cucumbers is one thing, while producing pickled cucumbers is something else. Also, freezing local peas planted for fresh consumption is one thing, while producing frozen peas is another. For each kind of processing, there are special varieties that have to be planted in order to get a quality product.

Another factor must also be taken into consideration here. The profitability of agro-industries depends on scale. Canning, for example, is a scale-dependent industry, while bottling is a scale-neutral one. Considering the small size of the local market in the West Bank and Gaza, in addition to the tough competition with Israel and other countries, this issue becomes of paramount importance. I realize the deep national feelings that are motivating us to become self-reliant and the relative ease of channeling external funds for starting such enterprises. I am also aware of the job creation opportunities in agro-industries. But I believe it is only responsible to warn against a quick decision to start a factory here and a factory there before the economic feasibility of each plant is carefully investigated by both technical and economic experts. To sustain the economy during the Intifada, it is urgent and necessary that this process begin soon.

HUMAN RESOURCES

The major target of economic development is the human element and the involvement of the human resources in the productive process, otherwise development will have no meaning. The agricultural sector is providing 26 percent and 16 percent of the local employment in the West Bank and Gaza respectively, while it contributes 20 percent of the total employment in these areas. It should be pointed out here that agriculture in Israel provides only 4.7 percent of the total work force due to mechanization.

While there are more than eighty thousand Palestinians working in the agricultural sector, the percentage of agricultural engineers and technicians working in this sector is marginal. It is often reiterated that Palestinians are rich in human resources, and this factor will undoubtedly be the major force which will drive Palestine into prosperity and progress. Yet, there appears to be a disproportion between academicians and technicians, especially in the field of agriculture. While, for example, there are about two thousand physicians in the West Bank and Gaza currently working in their field, there are fewer than five hundred agricultural engineers and fifty veterinarians with more than 50 percent of them working outside their field of specialty. Agricultural technocrats to be conduits for transferring appropriate technology to and from the farm will be needed in agricultural education, research, extension, and policy.

Nevertheless, one should give credit first to the Palestinian farmer and second to the agricultural grassroots organizations for their active role in transferring new agricultural technology. Palestinian farmers have proved to be true entrepreneurs by successfully adopting the new technologies in agriculture, especially in the irrigated areas, and for adapting them to their needs and conditions.

THE AGRICULTURAL INFRASTRUCTURE

There is not much to say about the agricultural infrastructure in the West Bank and Gaza. As mentioned earlier, the policy of the Israeli authorities has been to obstruct any developmental process in the Occupied Territories. The experimental stations are not functioning. The 1985 budget for agricultural research in these stations was $1,400. The credit scheme was cancelled immediately following the 1967 occupation. Between 1975 and 1987 personnel working in the agricultural departments on the West Bank declined by 50 percent, from 95 to 47 administrators and from 267 to 146 extension workers. There are about 230 agricultural cooperatives operating in these areas, together with some PVOs and NGOs, but their role is considered marginal.

Realizing the deficiency in the governmental services, Palestinian grass-root organizations were established as an alternative to provide the necessary services to the Palestinian farmer in the fields of extension, credit, and applied research. I believe that their work is deeply acknowledged by the farming community.

In conclusion, I have tried to shed light on the agricultural sector in the West Bank and Gaza, highlighting the major constraints and identifying the broad guidelines for its development. This sector is and shall continue to be a major productive sector in the Palestinian economy, and therefore there is an urgent need to provide support structures for developing this sector to meet the future needs of the Palestinian state. Preparations for these structures could and should be started now, and the existing institutions in the West Bank and Gaza are definitely well-qualified to assume this role. The two most important factors that will help the Palestinians in achieving their national aspirations and their economic development goals are the two magic words: cooperation and coordination.

5

Holy Land Christians and Survival

DON WAGNER

Everywhere one looks in the Middle East today, Christians are leaving in large numbers. The civil war in Lebanon, raging since late 1974, has led to the exodus of over one million Christians. A civil war and excruciating famine in Sudan, often caused by demonic "politics of food," have led to migration and starvation among the Christian majority in the south that has not been calculated. Egypt's grinding poverty and phenomenal population explosion, where one million new babies are added every six months, has seen Coptic Christians leave in massive numbers to find jobs and freedom. Chaldean and Assyrian Christians in northern Iraq were caught in the siege of the Kurds, and their half-million compatriots in Baghdad suffered under United States bombardment, causing up to one-fourth of Iraq's Christians to leave. The Syrian Orthodox church has lost half of its population in the last decade, most of them leaving Syria for France, Australia, and England. "Fear, human suffering, and hopelessness" have caused so many Christians to emigrate that there is profound concern about the very "continuity of Christian presence and witness in this region," according to Gabriel Habib, General Secretary of the Middle East Council of Churches.[1]

EMPTYING THE CHRISTIANS FROM THE HOLY LAND

Perhaps the most graphic illustration of the "emptying of Christianity from the Middle East," as Antiochian Orthodox Bishop Ignatius IV calls it,[2] is in the Holy Land itself. According to the statistics of the British Mandatory Government of Palestine, in 1922 the city of Jerusalem had 28,607 inhabitants, of which 14,699 were Christians (51.4 percent).[3] According to the office of the Anglican Bishop of Jerusalem and the Middle East, the Christian population of Jerusalem was 37,500 in 1948 at the establishment of Israel. But by 1978 the Israeli Bureau of Statistics reported only

10,191 Christians out of 93,509 residents of East Jerusalem (just 9.8 percent). It should be noted that Israel illegally annexed a sizeable portion of the West Bank and declared it part of the expanded Jerusalem, so the area discussed is three times the land area of the 1922 and 1948 city. Today the bishop's office believes the number of Christians is down to seven or eight thousand.

Harder hit than Jerusalem are the Ramallah and Bethlehem areas in the West Bank. In 1948 each community was over 90 percent Christian. Today the population of each community is less than 50 percent Christian. There are more Ramallahites in the Greater Detroit, Michigan, and Jacksonville, Florida, areas than in Ramallah. There are more Christians from Bethlehem living in Chile or Brazil today than there are in Bethlehem. Local leaders acknowledge that Christians have developed a pattern of emigration through the previous fifty years, partly due to their higher incomes and ability to assimilate more easily in the West than the Muslims.

Christian leaders, such as Anglican Bishop Elia Khoury, expelled by Israel to Amman in 1967, state painfully: "I give Christianity ten to fifteen years in Jordan and the West Bank, no more."[4] His comments did not refer to Jerusalem proper. However, the prominent Israeli author Amos Elon recently wrote that Jerusalem may soon become a mere "museum" for tourists, bereft of Christianity as a living religion.[5] I have heard Palestinians use the phrase *museumification of the church* repeatedly in referring to Israel's policies toward Christians during recent years.

One of the primary reasons for the Palestinian Christian emigration is the accelerated economic crisis in the West Bank. In a March 1990 fact-finding mission sponsored by the United Nations affiliated Nongovernmental Organizations that relate to the Division on Palestinian Rights, we were told that unemployment was running close to 50 percent in West Bank cities and 80-90 percent in small villages and refugee camps. During the January 16 to March 4, 1991, Iron Fist curfew (the entire population of the West Bank and Gaza Strip was confined to their homes), the economy, agriculture, and medical systems came to a virtual standstill. In the agriculturally rich Tulkarm district (on the border with central Israel), greenhouses were ruined and citrus was left rotting on the trees. Workers were forbidden to tend or pick their crops. Livestock and chickens starved due to a lack of food and water. This district alone suffered a $5 million loss during the first two months of 1991, a loss from which it will never recover. For the first time in memory, several refugee camps and remote villages went without food in a region that has always been able to feed itself. Thus the politics of food began to affect the entire Palestinian civilian population of two million. The United Nations, recognizing the severity of the situation, condemned Israel's policy, stating that the curfew had nothing to do with security and was unjustifiable under international law.[6] The repeated use of similar intensive periods of curfew and siege has contributed to making life miserable and hopeless, causing many of those with means to leave their ancestral lands.

TARGETING CHRISTIANS

In recent years Palestinian Christian leaders have sensed increased hostilities toward their ministries, institutions, and communities by Israeli military authorities, paid Arab collaborators, and by extremist Jewish settlers. One important case is that of the Greek Orthodox St. John's Hospice, located in the Old City of Jerusalem, adjacent to the Church of the Holy Sepulchre. On Maundy Thursday, 1990, 150 extremist Jewish settlers moved into the Hospice under military protection. Christians felt the maneuver was deliberately timed to insult the Christian community. The settlers covered Christian symbols on the facing of the building with the Israeli flag.

Later that morning, as the Christians held their traditional Maundy Thursday March up the Via Dolorosa, they stopped in front of St. John's Hospice. An Orthodox priest was hoisted up and the Israeli flag was removed. At that precise moment an Israeli soldier fired teargas into the pilgrimage, downing Orthodox Patriarch Diodoros. The crowd dispersed and the military chased several young Palestinians through the narrow streets. Church officials then declared that, for the first time in history, the Church of the Holy Sepulchre would be closed for Easter celebrations.

The Israeli government initially denied any involvement in the activities by the settlers. Within two days of the denial, an Israeli journalist plus Knesset member Yossi Sarid disclosed that the Israeli Ministry of Housing, directed by David Levy (later to become Foreign Minister), had in fact given the settlers $1.9 million for the down payment. It was also revealed that an additional $2.2 million, collected through various channels, was laundered through a Panamanian bank. The sum was paid to an Armenian named Motassian, a known drug dealer and collaborator with the IDF in Jerusalem, who while lacking official authorization by the Orthodox Patriarchate, turned the property deed over to the settlers and fled the country with $4 million. Meanwhile, the Orthodox Patriarch, the only party legally able to act on the St. John's Hospice deed, was unaware of the maneuver. After more than two years of litigation, the settlers remain in the Hospice while the case is delayed in the courts. I have personally witnessed on at least two occasions, mid-August 1990 and March 3, 1991, the settlers rebuilding the internal structure of the facility. The Christian community has been left with a bitter taste toward the intentions of the Israeli government, which continues to steal their property step by step.

In May 1988 the Jerusalem Baptist Church called Rev. Alex Awad, who was born and raised in Jerusalem, to serve as its pastor. Rev. Awad had studied and worked from time to time in the United States, but through most of the 1980s he had served as a faculty member of the Bethlehem Bible College and resident dean of a boys school in Beit Jalla. However, once he received the call to pastor the Jerusalem Baptist Church, Israeli authorities claimed they had discovered "visa irregularities." Palestinian Christians believe this is a direct result of political punishment by association, as Rev. Awad is brother of the well-known Palestinian disciple of nonviolence, Dr. Mubarak Awad, expelled by Israel in June 1988. Rev. Alex has never been active politically, and those who know him have been critical of his apolitical orientation. He has no political record in Israel or the United States, and there is no history of arrest or involvement in actions that could be used to support such an accusation. Meanwhile, the congregation has been without a pastor since 1986, causing significant problems for this struggling Christian church.

CREATING RELIGIOUS TENSION

Despite many Israeli claims to the contrary, there has never been a history of tension between the Christian and Muslim communities in Palestine. The two have generally lived together, participating in each other's holy seasons and respecting differences. The Muslim majority (until 1967, Christians have numbered approximately 18 percent of the population in the West Bank, under 5 percent in the Gaza Strip, and slightly over 20 percent in the Galilee) has always been extremely tolerant of the Christian minority, and the two have shared the fruits of the land and suffered equally from the historical parade of military occupations.

The Gulf War period (August 2, 1990–March 1991) brought new challenges to Christian-Muslim relations. Canon Naim Ateek of St. George's Anglican Cathedral in Jerusalem told me that he had noticed increased tensions between the two communities during this period. "This is a new phenomenon for us," he added. "Christians have until now enjoyed harmonious relationships here because we have had the same fate of suffering in the Holy Land. We fought and died together at the hands of European Crusaders; we suffered under the Turkish and British occupations, and now under Israel. I believe this will be short-lived, but it is a phenomenon that bears watching."[7]

Canon Ateek cited four reasons for the new tensions. First, the Palestinian Muslim community identified for the most part with Iraq. While they opposed Saddam Hussein's invasion and occupation of Kuwait on the same principle as their struggle against Israel's occupation of Palestine, they viewed United States military intervention as a greater evil. Second, many Muslims from the poorer and uneducated sectors saw American and British Christian leaders justifying the war on Christian ethics. This, in turn, fueled anti-Christian sentiment among some of the growing Islamic fundamentalist movements in Palestine. Traditionally, Israel has encouraged Islamic fundamentalists as a means of dividing Palestinians among themselves and facilitating their anti-nationalist tendencies. Third, younger Palestinian Muslims, who grew up with a depleted or nonexistent Christian Palestinian community, had little if any consciousness of the historic unity of Palestinians, whatever their religious convictions. This led to a lack of respect for Palestinian Christians as indigenous Palestinians and caused local Muslims to associate all Christians with Western colonialism. Fourth, Western fundamentalist Christian Zionists, who endorsed every Israeli military policy and indeed participated in illegal land confiscation, supported Jewish settlement activities, and even paid for Soviet Jews to fly to Israel and eventually settle on Palestinian lands, became more visible thanks to the Israeli press and government, which gave coverage to the tiny Christian Zionist community, particularly the International Christian Embassy in Jerusalem.

Most Palestinians believe the Christian-Muslim tensions are manufactured or encouraged as a continuing strategy of the Israeli government, the military authorities, and by the settlers' movement. During one intense period, the brutal "shoot on sight" curfew of January-March 1991, there were thirteen separate incidents of anti-Christian incitement in the Bethlehem–Beit Sahour area. The attacks included arson, physical attacks on clergy, robberies, desecration of church property and of graves. Rumors circulated that it was the work of Muslim fundamentalists, whose numbers are growing in Bethlehem. Nevertheless, local Christian leaders had seen Palestinian Arabs known to be collaborators with the Israeli military in the vicinity of two incidents. Then, on Palm Sunday 1991, two assailants entered the Melkite (Greek Catholic) church and convent in Bethlehem. A priest apprehended one of the robbers, but the other escaped with 32,500 Israeli shekels (approximately $1,750). The thief was a known collaborator, and word was circulated about the incident. Local Christian and Muslim leaders are striving to build closer relations with each other's communities as a result.

PALESTINIAN CHRISTIANS AND THE INTIFADA

Throughout the Israeli occupation there have been anti-Christian policies and incidents; these have steadily increased since 1967. Since the Palestinian Intifada, which began in December 1987, tensions have escalated. On January 22, 1988, the Palestinian Christian heads of churches in Jerusalem issued their first unified statement in over one thousand years. They joined voices in

> taking our stand with truth and justice against all forms of injustice and oppression. We stand with the suffering and the oppressed, we stand with the refugees and the deported, with the distressed and the victims of injustice, we stand with those who mourn and are bereaved, with the hungry and the poor. In accordance with the Word of God through the prophet Isaiah, chapter 1, verse 17: "Learn to do good; seek justice, correct oppression; defend the fatherless, plead for the widow."

The statement went on to call for a week of prayer, January 24-31, 1988, including fasting and self-denial, "identifying ourselves with our brothers and sisters in the camps on the West Bank and in the Gaza Strip." Christians were urged to give tangible support to the poor and continue steadfast in "seeking real peace built on justice . . . which will never be established unless every person's rights are fully respected."[8]

The Israeli censors forbad the Christian leaders from publishing the statement in the Israeli press or Arab media in Israel and the Occupied Territories. By prior arrangement a colleague faxed the statement to me at the Middle East Council of Churches in Cyprus, where our committee immediately transmitted it to every continent and media outlet we could reach. The statement drew considerable support from around the world and demonstrated the integration of the Palestinian Christian leadership and community in the uprising. This and future statements led to the increased anti-Christian attitudes and actions by Israeli Jews.

The Palestinian Intifada has increased the unity of the Palestinian community and accelerated the Christian community's solidarity with Palestinian nationalist leadership. Following the January 1988 statement by the heads of churches, there were additional statements and a series of collective actions. For example, in April 1988 the heads of churches in Jerusalem issued their second unified statement. The second statement condemned the Christian Zionist Congress, scheduled to be held in Jerusalem, as an outside intrusion "that did not represent the concerns of the local Christian community." Other educational and media activities demonstrated in clear terms the total rejection of the Christian Zionist enterprise by local Christians.

The Christian leadership of Jerusalem has been joined by the leaders of other towns and villages, such as Bethlehem, Beit Sahour, and Ramallah, in standing firm against the Israeli occupation while supporting the unified national leadership in its program of nonviolent resistance. Repeated collective as well as individual appeals have continued throughout the Intifada. In March 1991 the clergy of Ramallah appealed to a visiting Anglican delegation, urging its members to impress upon the British government the exact nature of the "shoot on sight curfew," including starvation and extreme human rights abuses throughout the West Bank and Gaza Strip.

These and other leaders have been active in raising these concerns with the major church bodies of the West, especially in Europe and the United States, prompting bishops and lay organizations alike to increase their advocacy of Palestinian peace, justice, and human rights issues.

THE CHALLENGE TO REMAIN STEADFAST

Despite the many pressures to leave their ancestral lands, Palestinian Christians are constantly reminded of their calling to remain rooted in these historic lands. Christian leaders are urging their congregations to remember that they have a unique calling to maintain the Christian witness and presence in the lands where Jesus lived and where the Christian church began on Pentecost. Canon Riah Abu El-Assal, rector of Christ Evangelical Anglican Church in Nazareth, recently challenged us to rethink our understanding of mission and evangelism in the region. "We do not need your missionaries coming here," he said. "We need your help to declare the desperate need for a Christian 'aliya' [an ingathering and return of Palestinian Christians to Palestine]. Only this will save Christianity from extinction in the Holy Land."

Canon Riah cited several steps that Western Christian churches can take in this regard. Spiritual and pastoral sister-church relationships can be established, providing prayer partnerships and mission support for struggling Palestinian congregations. In Beit Sahour, a Christian village, where the entire village resisted paying taxes to Israel because they received no services ("No taxation without representation" was their theme), there will be a need for Western Christian families to adopt a Beit Sahour family. Such a relationship will need of necessity to have an economic support system that is consistent in order to allow these people to survive and remain in their homes. In other places churches can invest in small business loans or development projects to enable people to either return or remain in business in occupied Palestine.

But of utmost importance, Western Christians must be encouraged to advocate through education and political advocacy the necessity of an independent Palestinian state, achieved through negotiations in an international forum. As Canon Riah has said,

> This is the only answer to our problem. It is the *only* answer that can bring long-term security to Palestinians and Jews alike. Only when we are free from military domination will we be able to live with dignity as Christians and create our own state. Go back and tell your elected officials to implement the United Nations resolutions on the Palestinian crisis, just as they did with Kuwait. Then we will believe that Americans are sincerely seeking justice.

NOTES

1. Gabriel Habib, quoted in *Time Magazine*, 23 April 1990.
2. Bishop Ignatius IV, interview with author, November 1986.
3. Bishop Naim Nassar, *Middle East Perspectives*, MECC.
4. Bishop Elia Khoury, interview with author, August 1990.
5. Amos Elon, quoted in *Time Magazine*, 23 April 1990.
6. UNRWA, press statement, 31 January 1991.
7. Canon Naim Ateek, interview with author, 27 February 1991.
8. Statement by the Heads of the Christian Communities in Jerusalem, 22 January 1988.

PART 2

PALESTINIAN CHRISTIAN IDENTITY

6

Bearing the Cross

A Sermon on Isaiah 53:1-12 and Luke 9:23

BASSAM E. BANNOURA

Who has given credence to what we have heard?
And who has seen in it a revelation of Yahweh's arm?
Like a sapling he grew up before him,
like a root in arid ground.
He had no form or charm to attract us,
no beauty to win our hearts;
he was despised, the lowest of men,
a man of sorrows, familiar with suffering,
one from whom, as it were, we averted our gaze,
despised, for whom we had no regard.
Yet ours were the sufferings he was bearing,
ours the sorrows he was carrying,
while we thought of him as someone being punished
and struck with affliction by God;
whereas he was being wounded for our rebellions,
crushed because of our guilt;
the punishment reconciling us fell on him,
and we have been healed by his bruises.
We had all gone astray like sheep,
each taking his own way,
and Yahweh brought the acts of rebellion
of all of us to bear on him.
Ill-treated and afflicted,
he never opened his mouth,
like a lamb led to the slaughter-house,

like a sheep dumb before its shearers
he never opened his mouth.

Forcibly, after sentence, he was taken.
Which of his contemporaries was concerned
at his having been cut off from the land of the living,
at his having been struck dead for his people's rebellion?
He was given a grave with the wicked,
and his tomb is with the rich,
although he had done no violence,
had spoken no deceit.
It was Yahweh's good pleasure to crush him with pain;
if he gives his life as a sin offering,
he will see his offspring and prolong his life,
and through him Yahweh's good pleasure will be done.

After the ordeal he has endured,
he will see the light and be content.
By his knowledge, the upright one, my servant will justify many
by taking their guilt on himself.

Hence I shall give him a portion with the many,
and he will share the booty with the mighty,
for having exposed himself to death
and for being counted as one of the rebellious,
whereas he was bearing the sin of many
and interceding for the rebellious (Is 53:1-12).

Then, speaking to all, he said, "If anyone wants to be a follower of mine, let him renounce himself and take up his cross every day and follow me" (Lk 9:23).

This passage from Isaiah comes from the fourth and longest song about the suffering servant of the Lord in the prophecy of Isaiah. It contains the central theme, not only within the songs of the servant, but in the entire prophecy.

In fact, the entire passage is quoted repeatedly in the New Testament, and it is always referred to as the gospel of the Old Testament. Both Jesus and the apostles used the image of the suffering servant in Isaiah to interpret the meaning of Christ's messianic mission.

My friends, it is Jesus, our living Lord, who is the subject of this passage. And as we read it, we can sense the deep inner experience of anguish and untold suffering our Lord experienced.

From the very beginning of his earthly ministry, Jesus had only one cup, and it was the cup of the cross, and he had only one way, and that was the way of the cross. He was the lamb of God, appointed for slaughter. He came to die, and this was the supreme purpose of his incarnation. The cross was the fulfillment of his mission, and he moved to it with an inflexible determination.

Jesus had never failed to be moved by compassion in the presence of human need and affliction. In the gospel we have many stories which show the depth of sympathy with which the sorrows of this world affected him. Jesus' suffering was not purely physical; it was much deeper than that. It involved his spirit, his soul, and also his body.

But still, to add to his agony, people did not believe in him. He was rejected, and the rhetorical question in Isaiah 53:1 implies that the servant was not believed, and the revelation of God's power through Jesus was not apprehended. He faced increasingly bitter opposition. He suffered disbelief, rejection, and death.

Again, the servant song begins with the question: Who has believed? And even today we still wonder if it could be possible, and why. Jesus did not seek empowerment. He did not threaten anyone. He repeatedly insisted that his kingdom was not of this world. His only crime was in his very nature as the one who has come to redeem humanity.

As Christians in the Holy Land, we learn in our churches and schools why Jesus had to suffer and die on the cross, but we are puzzled when it comes to our own lives. Why should we have to suffer? Why should you and I suffer? It is true that many are ready to suffer and carry the cross for the sake of their beliefs and convictions, but when the causes of human suffering are not known, we start asking questions; I have tens of these questions, and the number is ever increasing.

I always ask myself: Why do my people have to suffer? And what is the meaning of their suffering? These questions become painful when we recall that we are suffering and being persecuted by Israeli Jews, who were victims of persecution for almost fifteen hundred years, especially in Europe. And again, the questions become even more painful when we, as Palestinian Christians, witness millions of Christians in the world, especially in the West, unconditionally supporting the state of Israel and not even recognizing the existence of the Palestinian people, who are still paying for the price of establishing the state of Israel with their blood.

Jesus' death was full of meanings. It was redemptive, and it was to reestablish peace between God and humanity, as St. Paul argues in Ephesians 2. But, when it comes to the killing of almost one thousand persons from the Palestinian people, I wonder whether their death is also redemptive. When I recall names like Jeries Kunkar from Beit Jala, who was killed in cold blood on his way home to his wife and four children, or the death of Iyyad Abu Sa'ada or Fuad Zabagli or Mohammad or Nizar or Hassan or Samira or Fatima . . . I just rage at the arrogance, the hatred, the contempt for life in these Israeli killings of Palestinians, killings that seem to seek our very physical extermination. Yet we must claim the slaying of hundreds of women and men as full of meaning. These deaths are a cry to the face of Israeli power: "Let my people go; let my people be free."

My brothers and sisters, it is my prayer that what we suffer as a nation will not harden our hearts, but keep them tender and ready to forgive. I ask our international friends to pray for both of our nations, the Palestinian and the Israeli, that both would seek justice and peace. Pray that out of tears, bloodshed, and sorrow will come the rejoicing of forgiveness and new life from God, then forgiveness and new life to each other.

In Luke 9:23 Jesus says, "If anyone wants to be a follower of mine, let him renounce himself and take up his cross every day and follow me." Jesus, who carried his cross, wants us to follow his footsteps. He wants us to be faithful to his message and carry the cross daily for his sake, not our own sake.

My friends, it is a radical decision when one denies herself or himself and lives for others, but again, that is exactly what Jesus did and what he is asking his church to do. I am bearing the cross. Yes, I am bearing the cross. My people are bearing the cross. We are crying to God, "Lord, have mercy on us. Lord, liberate and save us. Lord, help us not to be preoccupied with our own present suffering and unable to see the suffering of people in the rest of the world, even the suffering of our enemies."

Isaiah 53 begins with a question, "Who has given credence to what we have heard?" I would like to end with these questions: How many more severe hardships should my people endure? Why should my people not be secure about their future? Is it possible that one day a Palestinian and an Israeli would carry the same cross? I also wonder whether our Christian brothers and sisters will one day help us to bear the cross.

Jesus' suffering was redemptive; his saving work was universal; his love is overwhelming. Lord, help us. Lord, lead us. Lord, comfort us. And Lord, use us for thy glory. Amen.

7

The Intifada and the Palestinian Churches

NADIA ABBOUSHI

The Intifada of the Palestinians is the earthshaking cry of a whole nation suffering from prolonged injustice. It is an unequivocal refusal to continue being constantly misquoted, distorted, marginalized, and silenced by the world. It is a grassroots revolt against a policy of reducing a nation to a minority of second-class citizens or stateless refugees.

For twenty-three years the myth of a moral, liberal occupation has been carefully created and defended by a Zionist distortion of the truth. The state of Israel, portraying itself as the beacon of civilization and democracy in an overwhelmingly backward and even barbaric Arab world, is the myth that has been finally shattered by a new generation of Palestinians who dared to expose the lie. They were not burdened with the guilty conscience of Western crimes of the Holocaust; as Semites themselves, they cannot be branded as anti-Semitic. They realized, however, that they had become historic scapegoats for the crimes that the West has committed against Jewish Europeans.

The Israeli reprisal against the unarmed Palestinians has been harsh and brutal. New methods of punishment are continually devised with mounting intensity and cruelty, disproportionate to the "crimes" committed.

Administrative detention, arbitrary arrests, night raids, and interrogation with severe mental and physical torture have hit homes in every village and town. The young are being hunted and shot in cold blood by Israeli death squads and settlers. Higher education is forbidden, even criminalized, thus crippling a whole new generation of Palestinian minds and draining the land of its brain power. Confiscation of land, monopoly of water resources, uprooting of orchards, and house demolitions are examples of collective punishment. Denial of family reunification, deportation, and the threat of mass transfer have become urgent options for Israel in light of the current mass immigration of Soviet Jews.

All these measures have found legal justification in the laws of occupation, laws which have been condemned by international lawyers and human rights organizations. Out of this condition of powerlessness the Intifada broke out, not as a desperate suicide attempt, but with a new self-consciousness and new self-confidence. It developed through popular awareness rather than academic ideas. This was the beginning of a process of empowerment whose visible outcomes have included:

1. a social transformation leading toward national infrastructure building;
2. legitimization of our representation by the PLO;
3. a new international awareness of Israeli brutality against Palestinians;
4. a Palestinian determination to continue the struggle until independence.

The Christians of Palestine are an integral and vital force in the national struggle for liberation. Their influence has been felt and demonstrated overtly, as in the valiant case of Beit Sahour's nonviolent acts of civil disobedience, and covertly, as individual members of underground local committees lay the new infrastructure for the independent Palestinian State in the various fields of education, agriculture, medicine, industry, and public relations.

However, the institutionalized local churches have been slow to move, fettered by:

1. their concern to preserve the status quo; the sensitive balance of power between the different churches, and their precious control of the holy places;
2. close adherence to symbolic ritualism and hierarchical orders inherited from the past;
3. allegiance to foreign mother churches in Europe and America;
4. maintaining traditional good relations with the political authorities by choosing to be politically uninvolved.

A united church would be a tremendous force in the empowerment of the people. The challenge facing these churches in the age of the Intifada is the formulation of a holistic vision of peace based on justice in the Holy Land. I believe this to be a divine call requiring a genuine comprehension of the historic complexities and a spiritual capacity to transcend the limitations of present politics. The Arab church is called upon to play a prophetic role in Jerusalem. It may not remain silent, for the stones have spoken! There must be an end to acquiescence to evil and a confession of spiritual death. Righteous anger in the face of oppression is the first step toward getting actively involved with God's work in history.

Today the need for the unification of various local churches is urgent. They are called upon to reread the Bible in light of the present crisis and to seek to interpret the events of the day in relation to the new understanding. By joining together in profound contemplation and careful study, they will be inspired to formulate a creative Palestinian theology in the context of the current events between Palestine and Israel. For a long time a grave theological vacuum existed in our churches. This has isolated them from the historical and political reality around them. A comprehensive framework of a Palestinian theology of liberation will put the churches back in the mainstream of events, get them involved in the on-going struggle against oppression, and empower them toward achieving salvation.

Canon Naim Ateek's book *Justice and Only Justice* is the first serious attempt to address the need to define the political dilemma in its theological context. Here is an open invitation for all concerned to fill the vacuum before it is too late. The outcome is sure to be revolutionary and prophetic. Meeting together is also a step toward achieving the goal whereby we communicate with theologians from all over the world who share with us the concern for the establishment of a better world, free from exploitation and racism. It is a serious dialogue in which both parties seek to learn from each other's experiences and hope to be inspired to further action and deeper commitment. In Palestine, the struggle is ours, however, and the solution must arise from the uniqueness of our predicament. The Intifada has taught us to seek salvation from within rather than from outside.

First, central to the Palestinian theology must be an outright renunciation of the biblical justifications for the establishment of a Zionist state in Palestine. Since so much financial support is continuously flowing into Israel from Christian churches in the United States, based on their misguided faith in a divinely ordained Israel, it is therefore imperative for Palestinian churches to de-Zionize the Bible for themselves, as well as for the rest of the world. They must assert their faith in a universal God of justice and mercy, and not in a tribal deity of vengeance and favoritism.

Second, Palestinian churches must continue the process of demythologizing the state of Israel which the Intifada has started. Using all channels available, they must inform the world of the extent and scope of the atrocities committed against the unarmed Palestinian nation (Muslim and Christian) as a matter of Israeli state policy. We believe that pressures from the world community on Israel were instrumental in forcing the authorities to reopen schools on the West Bank after eighteen months of closure. Liberation theology for Palestinians must be quick, bold, and articulate in recognizing injustice, analyzing its causes, and condemning its practices clearly and unequivocally.

Third, a liberation theology for the Palestinians must provide support for all peace-loving Jews who recognize the occupation as a double-edged sword, dehumanizing the occupier while humiliating the occupied. These brave souls were able to see the human face of the Palestinian stone-thrower hidden behind a mask of terrorism, the label which the official state media has created.

Palestinians and the peace camp in Israel have already started the process of reconciliation; liberation theology will be inspired by their dynamism and the genuineness of such efforts. Its vision will empower and sustain them so that they may work together for transformation of an unholy world of injustice.

Finally, Muslim and Christian Palestinians have risen together with one voice against the occupation. Any liberation theology must bless a community consecrated by the blood of its martyrs, who share the belief in human dignity and justice in a Palestinian state. In the Intifada, a living dialogue between Christians and Muslims has become an existential reality. Where traditional theology has failed, liberation theology will succeed if it sheds the fundamentalist arrogance of monopoly over absolute truth.

We shall not allow ignorance, prejudice, and fanaticism to destroy the spirit of communion so beautifully visible in the Intifada, as Christian priests face the soldiers coming to arrest praying youths in the mosques in Ramallah, or as Muslim sheikhs enter the church to pray to the one God with the Christians in Beit Sahour. Liberation theology will take its spark from the Intifada to address the common humanity of Jews, Muslims, and Christians living together in a land made holy only by their absolute commitment to peace and justice.

8

Reclaiming Our Identity and Redefining Ourselves

MUNIR FASHEH

I plan to tell you some stories about growing up as a Christian Arab in this land of Palestine. But first I must say that I have been, as an Arab, as a Palestinian, and as a Christian, trapped since I was born. Either I speak the language of the West, embody its ideology (including its Christianity), and am deformed—but then many would hear me—or I speak in my own voice, about my own experiences, including my indigenous Christian tradition that lived through the ages and was embodied by people like my parents—and risk the possibility that many will not be able to hear or understand me.

The central problem we face as Christian Arabs is exactly this trap: we have been defined by others, by Westerners. Our voice was never sought, was never heard, and was never articulated. We have been denied the value of our experience and robbed of our voice and sense of self-worth. The challenge we face is how to make our voices heard, our conceptions and practices articulated.

This essay will be divided into three parts. In the first part I will describe the problem of being defined by others, through various examples; how I became aware of the problem and how I perceive the challenge we face. In the second part I will describe, again through examples, the basis for reclaiming our identity and redefining ourselves. And in the third part I will discuss the task ahead of us and mention some guidelines concerning strategy and action.

The problem of being defined by others can be exemplified in many ways. My mother, for example, who never left Palestine, was named Jeannie; my aunt's name was Victoria; my sisters are Mary and Linda. Luckily I was born the day before Easter, *Sabt el Nur* ("Saturday of light"), which is actually a Palestinian holiday, and I was called Munir. (*Munir* in Arabic means "something that gives light," referring to that special Saturday.)

Another example, which is symbolic but revealing, is the picture of Christ that was next to my picture hanging on the wall of our home. Christ's picture looked more like the picture of a Dutch or Swedish man than that of a man from this land. I told my father one day that if somebody came into our home who had never seen a picture of Jesus, the person would guess my picture to be the one of Christ, rather than the Dutch-looking man. Christ, probably, looked more like me than the pictures they sell in markets and hang on walls. I hope that one day a Palestinian painter will draw a more likely and more accurate painting of Christ's face. Unfortunately, this question dare not even be asked, because once you start mentioning such questions then you are starting to build a different vision of yourself, of theology, of God, of Christ, and of everything else.

I was born in Jerusalem in 1941. Like most Palestinians, we were driven from our home in 1948. At that time I was seven years old. Our house is about five minutes from Tantur. We still have the legal papers proving our ownership of the house, but since 1948 I have never entered it. In 1967, three weeks after the war, I went to see it. When I knocked on the door a woman came out. I told her that I had been born in the house and would like to see inside. She said in a trembling voice, "We did not take it from you. The government gave it to us. You can go and talk to the government." I said, "I did not come to take it. I just want to see it. I have an emotional attachment to it." We started arguing. She asked whether I was an Arab, and I said I was. She seemed relieved. "You must be mistaken," she said, "because this house belonged to Christians." I said that I was a Christian Arab. "No, no, you can't be," she said. "The Arabs are Muslims, the *fellahin* [peasants]." I insisted that I was a Christian and an Arab, that it was possible to be an Arab and any religion. "No," she said, "you can't be Christian and an Arab." I gave up. "It doesn't matter whether it can be or not, this is our home." By this time we had attracted a crowd. One neighbor intervened and asked my family's name. I told her and she said, "It's true, this is the house of the Fasheh family." Nevertheless, the woman did not let me in.

What was extraordinary was the woman's assumption that she had the right and the knowledge to define me, to tell me who I was, and that I could not be who I was if I did not fit her preconceptions. She had to accept these distortions to keep her sense of herself intact and to avoid facing the fact that she was profiting from the harm done to my family. It is a small comfort to know she had to distort her perception, so that she would not commit evil knowingly and of her own volition.

After the Israeli occupation of the West Bank in 1967 I went for my first Israeli identification card. The Israeli officer asked me, "What are you?" I did not know exactly what he meant so I replied that I was an Arab. "No, no," he said, "I mean are you a Christian or a Muslim?" I asked, "What does this have to do with my I.D.? I mean, why should it be shown on my I.D.?" He replied, "This is how you are defined."

In 1967 I started to perceive what I am, and how I am defined by others. One of the first things that the Israelis erased from textbooks after they occupied the West Bank was any mention of the cooperation between Christian Arabs and Muslim Arabs throughout history. The pretext that they used was anti-Semitism. It is anti-Semitic (in the language I was hearing) to love one another. Of course there is anti-Semitism in Europe and in many countries that persecuted Jews; it is not that I am blind to that. In Palestine there is no anti-Semitism for the simple fact that we are all Semites. Some Israelis and Westerners, however, often choose to define the world in a way that suits their purposes.

There is a Chinese proverb, probably over three thousand years old, which says, "Whoever defines the terms, wins the argument." This is exactly what the Israelis and Western scholars and Western media in general do: they define words and people. They are winning not only through money and the military, but also through defining words and who we are. It becomes a problem for me. I always have to defend myself; I am always either invisible or accused. If it is impossible to make such distortions in a subtle way or an unconscious way, then it is done bluntly, rudely, and consciously. I wish only to cite two very basic examples. Webster's dictionary defines Palestine as follows: "1. a territory on E. coast of Mediterranean, the country of the Jews in Biblical times, 2. part of this territory under a British mandate after World War I; divided into Israel and Jordan by action of UN in 1947."

The invisibility of the Palestinian people is not the issue I want to raise; it is common practice in Western scholarship. It is the lack of precision and the lies embedded in the statement. The United Nations resolution did not divide parts of Palestine into Israel and Jordan but into independent Arab and Jewish states. Jordan already existed on the East Bank of the Jordan River. The United Nations action is not a secret; it did not happen in distant times or distant lands; and it was not stated in controversial or vague terms or documents. It was stated clearly; it took place in 1947 in New York—where the dictionary was published—and is described in United Nations documents that are open for everyone to read.

The other example of "objectivity" in Western scholarship was at a conference on Islam that took place at Harvard University in the summer of 1985. The conference was organized by a well-known Zionist, financed by the CIA, and only Jews and Christians spoke about Islam: the ultimate objectivity! Just as in the case of Webster's definition, it is assumed that Harvard University cannot but be objective. Taking place at Harvard, the conference by definition was objective. I don't think that Khomeini even in his wildest dreams thought of having a conference in Teheran on Christianity at which only Buddhists and Muslims would speak. But at Harvard University it is not only dreamt of but it is also done. It is done without being noticed, or without an issue being made of it.

When we talk about fanaticism, this is the fanaticism that we have to worry about, not the fanaticism that is obvious, like Khomeini's. When Salman Rushdie wrote his book, everybody in the world heard about the threat that Khomeini made against Salman Rushdie. In contrast to the outcry by the "civilized Christian" world concerning Khomeini's threats against Salman Rushdie, this same world remains silent or comes out with a very faint voice when it comes to Palestinians. Writers and publishers of books supporting Palestinian rights are usually pressured and threatened. Noam Chomsky's books are one example.

To cite a very recent example, pressure against publishing Anne Nixon's report on the status of Palestinian children in the West Bank and Gaza Strip led the United States Save the Children Federation (which first supported it), the British Save the Children Fund, the Norwegian Save the Children, and the Ford Foundation to withdraw their support for funding and publishing the report. The reason for their withdrawal, they claimed, is that the report (which is on the status of children) is not within the mandate of the Save the Children Federation! The Swedish Save the Children, however, decided not to yield to the pressures and did support its publication.

Also virtually unnoticed by the "civilized Christian" Western world were the threats by Israel and the actual blowing-up of one ship that was supposed to sail from Athens to Haifa (in the summer of 1988) carrying Palestinians who were deported by Israel from the West Bank and Gaza since 1967. What is at stake here is fairness. And fairness has been a main value in the Christianity I internalized as a child through my parents. In contrast, winning (including winning converts), self-interest, and exploiting non-European peoples and lands seem to be the guiding values of Western Christianity, as I saw it being practiced on us.

This distortion of the world has been accomplished through an elaborate ideological structure and through European hegemony, of which Western Christianity has been an integral part. Hegemony and ideology are characterized not only by what they include but also by what they exclude—by what they render marginal, deem inferior, and make invisible. They substitute one kind of knowledge, education, and religion for another, in the context of a power relationship. Power, in this sense, is almost defined by what is excluded. Hegemony is successful when the ideology of the more powerful is taken or even assumed to be universal and superior.

This is exactly what has happened to my Christianity, my Arab Christianity, since Napoleon's invasion of Egypt and Palestine in 1798. Gradually, Arab Christianity was made marginal, inferior, or invisible. That woman who occupies our home in Jerusalem and who told me "you cannot be Christian and an Arab" is one example. Another example is the question, "When did you become Christian?" that I was constantly asked when I was studying in the United States, as if Christianity started somewhere near

Kansas City or Chicago. To consider being both from Jerusalem and Christian as a strange combination is an extreme example of how ideology works. My typical answer to such a question was, "I became Christian in the first century. When did you become Christian?" I was always tempted to add, "And when and why did you suppress and distort my Christianity?"

This brings us to the second topic: the basis for reclaiming our Christianity (which, by the way, is the only indigenous Christianity in the world), and the basis for redefining ourselves, as Arabs, as Christians, and as humans.

In searching for such a basis, I rely mainly on people who still carry the tradition and spirit of this indigenous Christianity, such as my parents, friends, and fellow Palestinians. My mother, for example, who never left Palestine and who never read a word in her life, embodied a Christianity that was completely different from the one that I was bombarded with from Westerners as a child, or from what I saw later in the United States. She did not, for example, mention the name of Christ a hundred times a day, but she always did things that I think were pleasing to God and to Christ; she did not try to win converts to her denomination; she did not hate communists, Muslims, or Jews. I strongly believe that if the devil took her to the Mount of Temptation in Jericho, she would have behaved just like Jesus. Satan would not have been able to twist her arm or make her kneel.

This is how the people in Beit Sahour, near Bethlehem, behaved when Israeli taxation officers tried to force or tempt people to pay. One woman from that town, after the army had taken everything from her house and had come to the kitchen, said to the officer, "Why don't you leave the refrigerator. I have small children and the milk will rot outside." Trying to tempt her, the officer said, "OK, pay 50 shekels as taxes [about $25] and I will return everything." She said, "I am not bargaining with you. I am appealing to you as a human being who probably has children." He said, "All right, pay ten shekels." She said, "You don't seem to understand." He said, "One shekel." She said, "Take the refrigerator!"

This is Christ in action. The "devil" could not tempt her. For half a dollar, she could have saved herself and her family lots of agony and lots of problems. That was very tempting. Like Jesus, however, she resisted the temptation. During the same week I heard that ex-president Reagan was not able to resist the temptation of an offer of two million dollars from the Japanese to go to Japan and say what they wanted him to say. He does not need money or fame, but he had his price. That woman from Beit Sahour did not. This is the type of woman, like my mother, like many others, that has been the target of Western Christian groups trying to convert them from their wonderful Christianity to some form which looks like Reagan's Christianity, from a Christianity of inner strength to a Christianity of outward power.

The behavior and the words of that woman from Beit Sahour manifested yet another aspect of Christianity: love your enemy. That woman tried to appeal to the officer's humanity. She tried to remind him of his humanity, of the similarity between her and him, of moving beyond military orders, greed, and power. She seems to have failed. But maybe she did not. Maybe that officer thought of her words later, of her appeal, of her concern and care, and of her attempt to communicate with him at a level different from that dictated by the structural relationship imposed on both of them. Moreover, through her behavior, that woman reminds us of what Christ said on that Mount of Temptation: one does not live by bread alone.

Distortion, hypocrisy, narrowness, and self-interest, which seem to have accompanied Western Christianity, are what I have been exposed to as a Palestinian, as an Arab, as a Christian, as a Muslim, and as a Jew. I say "as all of these" because this is the way my mother saw herself. This is how many Palestinian women saw themselves. One tradition among Christian women from Jerusalem was that any woman who could not conceive, went to Hebron (an Islamic town) to kneel under the tree of Abraham (a Jewish symbol) and pray to Christ in order to have children. For my mother, who believed in the practice, being a Christian, a Muslim, and a Jew at the same time was not a contradiction; rather, it was part of being human. What was alien to her thinking was to be purely a Christian, or purely a Muslim, or purely a Jew. Unlike the behavior of Western Christians (whose main concern seemed to be smaller and more divisions, and more precise and narrow definitions of who is what), her Christianity was an expansive one that included all others.

I would like to cite two more examples concerning the thinking and behavior of Palestinian Christians, this time about my father. One day in 1977 he came home from the center of the town of Ramallah [on the West Bank] feeling completely disturbed. He had just seen two Israeli soldiers holding the hair of an 8- or 9-year-old boy and smashing his face against the wall. After telling us what he had seen, he said, "These cannot be Jews." Obviously he was experiencing a dilemma: either God is wrong in considering Jews as a people of his or else these soldiers were not Jews. It was easier for him, it seems, to deny the Jewishness of the soldiers than to think that God was wrong. In this sense he was reasserting the original meaning of a "chosen people": people who do not willingly and consciously harm others. He was defending Judaism from the behavior of these soldiers.

Much earlier, in the late 1930s, when my father and my uncle were planning to open a shop in Jerusalem, my father put one condition: that they not sell liquor and cigarettes in the shop because they are harmful to people, and that is unchristian. My uncle tried to persuade him that not selling such things would not stop people from consuming them. Finally, however, my uncle yielded.

The most crucial issue the above discussion raises is that of the relation of Christianity to the world it inhabits, the relation of Christian Arabs to their own communities and environment, the political, economic, social, historical, cultural, and spiritual environment.

This brings us to the third and final part of this discussion: the task ahead of us. What are some of the guidelines that will help our thinking, strategy, and actions for the future?

To summarize the problem and the basis of solving it, we can say that Arab Christianity has been confiscated through Western hegemony. We have been denied the value of our experience and robbed of our voice and sense of self-worth. Value, language, and visibility are at stake here because they have been taken away from a people's fundamental activities. To me, therefore, liberation is to reclaim people's lives, their sense of self-worth, and their ways of thinking from hegemonic structures, and to facilitate their ability to articulate what they do and think about in order to provide a foundation for autonomous action. Liberation theology requires us to use our senses again, to make things visible, and to allow people to speak. It is reclaiming a people's voice. The crucial measure of any system, any social formation, is how much that system or social formation—whether political, social, educational, or religious—is built around the voice of the people.

The problem, then, lies not so much in the fact that we have been defined by others as in our acceptance of that outside definition. And, as I mentioned earlier, it was during the 1967 Israeli-Arab war and its aftermath that I began rediscovering Christianity, as I felt it conceived and practiced by my parents, and saw this as the basis of redefining ourselves as Christian Arabs. This awareness of the need to redefine ourselves and to restructure our thinking and social reality has been made more acute and urgent since the Intifada started in December of 1987.

To start with, we have to declare, as Christian Arabs, that we are not a part of the Christianity that helped plunder five continents, enslave people in many regions, and wipe out people and civilizations in North America and Australia, and is now threatening the Palestinians with a similar fate. As Palestinian Christians we have to declare with a loud voice that it has been Christianity, which accompanied capitalism, more than Zionism, that is at the root of many problems in the world today. Otherwise, it will be very difficult to explain why this "capitalist Christianity" has succeeded to a large extent in destroying the beautiful Christianity that flourished in Nicaragua and other Central and South American countries.

All the above has helped me realize that the Christian faith is not about pitying the poor, needy, and oppressed, but is rather about helping them change their conditions. It is about helping change the structures so that all people become partners in enjoying life and in acquiring the means to life. What the Palestinians in the Gaza Strip need is not some dollars, food, and clothes from American and European charitable "Christian" organizations and groups. Rather, what they need is to be free to use what belongs to them: land, water, and the sea. More than one-third of the land in the Gaza Strip has been confiscated by the Israelis, the use of water is restricted, and the Gazans are gradually being squeezed out of fishing.

The purpose of Christianity is not to stand in front of an altar, but, like

Christ, to be out in the street, in the field, and in the work place joining others in their efforts to make this world more just, more happy, and more humane. The New Testament is not so much about Christians, or about Christ and God, as it is about life, people, their conditions, as well as the personal involvement of God in life to help transform evil and inhuman conditions. God, according to the Christian faith, sacrificed his son for the sake of the world, and not vice versa.

Thus, the fact that Christ was born in a cave, in a manger, is not a call to idolize or glorify the cave or the manger but a reminder to us of the absurd and evil conditions in the world. It is a call to action so that babies will not have to be born in cold and unhealthy caves. Christ being born in a cave might be exotic to Western tourists, but for us, Palestinians, it is a reminder that the inhuman conditions under which Christ was born, including his flight with his parents to avoid being killed by soldiers, still exist in the world and, in particular, in the very place where Christ was born.

In other words, the gospel is about the poor and the oppressed and how to end poverty, greed, oppression, and exploitation. It is about making a people's voice clear and loud. The basic strategy or principle in accomplishing this is to love one another (in today's terminology, solidarity) and to discuss and to act in order to change the inhuman conditions. According to Luke's gospel, if we remain silent, the very stones will speak out. Foreign churches and clergy in the land of Palestine have three options: to be indifferent, to accept Israel's distortions of history and reality, or to play a positive role toward peace and justice.

Palestinian Christians are forced into a situation where we find ourselves also facing three options: leave, accept living in ghettos, or continue to assert our belonging to this land and to this culture, the Arab-Islamic culture. Christian Arabs are an integral part of this culture, not as a minority but more like an embroidery on a dress. No one calls the embroidery on a dress a minority, although it may occupy a small area on the dress. Without the dress, the embroidery cannot hold itself; without the embroidery, the dress loses much of its richness, value, and beauty. The locus of our identity as Palestinian Christians is, thus, not the Palestine-Israel conflict but rather, the Arab-Islamic context.

To bring a Christian from Australia to burn the Aqsa Mosque in Jerusalem in 1968; to approach Christians in the Bethlehem area, encouraging them to form militias in 1988; and many other such actions by Israel to put a wedge between Palestinian Christians and Palestinian Muslims will not succeed. Trying to convince Christians that Islamic fundamentalism is their main enemy ignores the fact that fundamentalism is a twentieth-century phenomenon and not an Islamic one. It is similar to the Crusaders' claim, almost a thousand years ago, that *jihad* in Islam meant a holy war. The Crusades were holy wars. The *jihad*, according to Islam, is a struggle against oppression and injustice in support of the poor, the weak, and the downtrodden.

According to Islam, the best form of *jihad* is to say a word of truth in the face of an unjust ruler. In this sense the actions of the Christian population of Beit Sahour exemplified *jihad* at its best. On the other hand, the way young Muslim Palestinians, the *shabab*, dealt with collaborators, especially during the first year of the Intifada, was a beautiful manifestation of "saving souls" in the Christian faith. Collaborators, in many places, were approached by the *shabab* and were told that they were members of the community, that they had probably followed the path they did because of need or coercion, that they should turn in the guns that were given to them by the Israeli military, and that they should declare over the mosque loudspeakers that they would not harm their people in the future. This reminds us of how Christ saved the soul of Zacchaeus. What was also significant was that the guns that were turned in by the collaborators were sent by the *shabab* through the *muktars* (traditional community chiefs) to the military governors with a note that the Israeli army might need them; the *shabab* have no use for them.

Islam, just like Christianity and Judaism, has been distorted to suit Western capitalist interests and ideology. Part of the challenge we face is to deal with this distortion of Islam. One extremely relevant fact to our discussion here is related to *al-Jame'* (the assembly or gathering place). There are two words in Arabic for mosque: *Masjed* and *Jame'*. *Masjed* refers mainly to a place where people can pray. *Jame'* is a place where people meet in order to discuss community affairs. The purpose of *al-Jame'* is the collective management of life, of community affairs: political, social, and educational. This original concept and practice of *al-Jame'* preceded the base Christian communities of liberation theology by fourteen centuries. It is both interesting and revealing to note that this meaning and function of the mosque was not translated into English or other European languages.

This function of *al-Jame'* was revitalized and was very obvious, in action, during the first year of the Intifada. This function of *al-Jame'* together with the flourishing of the neighborhood popular committees throughout the West Bank and Gaza Strip, form, in my opinion, the basic strategy we should follow. Unfortunately, Mu'aweya, the first Umayyad Caliph, wiped out this function of *al-Jame'*. The challenge we face, then, is how to revitalize this form of the collective management of affairs—whether we call it *al-Jame'*, or base communities, or popular committees—where people meet, discuss, and act in order to transform their reality. This form avoids, among other things, the main methods currently used in religious and educational institutions, that is, preaching and lecturing, whose principal function, in actual terms, is to suppress or silence people's voices.

This form of collective management of affairs at the grassroots level, of identifying and responding to problems and needs in one's community, is, however, very threatening to oppressive structures and to the people in power. The Israeli order of August 18, 1988, criminalizing the popular committees in the West Bank and Gaza, is one extreme example of crushing attempts to organize at the grassroots level. This order made it a crime for anyone to be involved in popular committees, including those concerned with gardening and teaching children in homes. The penalty for engaging in such activities was imprisonment for up to ten years. That's also why the concept of *al-Jame'* was suppressed by Mu'aweya, that's why Christ was crucified by the Romans, and that's why the children of Palestine today are tortured and killed by the Israelis. These children are the ones who exemplify today the true spirit of Christ, of *al-Jame'*, of the sacredness of life.

9

The Palestinian Christian Identity

GERIES KHOURY

It is not an easy task to discuss the Christian identity in the Holy Land. Speaking for myself, I cannot distinguish between the Christian-Palestinian identity and the Israeli-Palestinian conflict. There is a relationship between both. Before we can speak about such a conflict or its reasons, we in the Holy Land have the problem of speaking about the church or the local church. We do not yet have a real ecclesiological theology in which we can define locally what we mean by a local church in the Holy Land. Historically speaking, two thousand years of history have showed us a certain diversity.

Yet, if we are looking today at the church in the Holy Land or in Jerusalem alone, there are at least thirty different denominations. Each church would say that it is the local church. Every day we have new churches, and they try to take in people from other denominations. Then they too say that they are the local church.

For many years we have been in such difficulties because we do not really have an ecclesiological position about what we mean by a local church. This in itself is a major problem.

If we look back into our history we see that cultural challenges and political challenges both have contributed to diverting our Palestinian church.

The cultural challenge was the first challenge the local church faced. In the past the church was often able to provide solutions to those challenges. This is because the church cannot be restricted to time or to place. Yet this does not mean that it wanted or tried to remove the social and cultural values of its believers. Through God's unlimited love, the plurality of cultures could be accepted, even as Christ became incarnated, accepting the culture into which he came. This incarnation of the Word of God enables the church to interact with these cultures from within and to give the characteristics of faith through baptism.

Although Christ was brought up in a certain culture and civilization, we never see him in the New Testament restricting himself to the Jewish culture; he interacted with the Roman culture as well. This is clear in his message, teaching, and parables, which cannot really be understood unless we relate them to the culture in which they took place.

If we look into the history of Palestine and the Middle East we see that culture and politics were the main reasons for its division. I do not want to go back to the Alexandrian school or to the Antiochian school. I do not want to go back to the time of the Byzantines or to the Islamic period. But, if we go back into our history, we realize that culture and politics were the main two causes of such a division in the Oriental churches, the Jerusalem churches included.

The first question I would like to raise here is this: If cultures (Greek, Syrian, Coptic, and Arabic) led to the division of the church in the past, can the local culture in the Holy Land today be considered as a unifying factor for the local church? My second question is this: If the social-political factors in the past led to the division of the church, can the social and political situation in which the church lives here in Palestine become a unifying factor? My third question is: How should we work for the unity of the local church, and what is our Christian identity?

My answer to the first question is that of course I believe the cultural aspect today is a means to unify the local church. The cultural multiplicity in which the Oriental church lived and which led to its division does not exist anymore. Arabic language and culture have replaced the previous cultures and languages in the Orient, leaving the ancient languages only for liturgical celebrations and prayers. The Arabic language now is even gradually replacing the ancient languages in liturgical celebrations and prayers, so the members of those various communities may begin to understand the prayers, having been alienated from their own ancient languages, which are not spoken today.

The Arabic language is not a new language, for we note its development since the seventh century alongside the Arab culture. Many Christians participated in the making of the Arab culture through their translations, commentaries, and theological and philosophical writings in Arabic.

This Arabic-Christian heritage has been ignored in the East and in the West. I say this because there are thousands of thousands of theological manuscripts that remain neglected and unstudied; only a handful have been published in the last decade. Arabic was an important factor in the medieval period for the unity of the Oriental church because all the various groups wrote their theologies in Arabic, instead of their own church language. They also wrote ecumenical theology in which they expressed their desire for unity. In addition to this they confessed that the division in the church was not due so much to theology as to linguistic separations.

After the coming of Islam, the Christians wanted to write a local theology in order to explain their creed and to try to answer the questions of the

Islamic community. This led to dialogue on a very high level between the church and the Muslim caliphate, and stronger relations with the Muslims than with the Byzantine Christians. It was more important for those in the Oriental church to speak with a Muslim than with a Christian Byzantine. The Oriental church was able to survive in the Arab Muslim culture and civilization more than in the Byzantine culture and under its rules. The writings of the Syrian Patriarch Michael the Eighth testifies to that fact. He thanked God for the coming of the Muslims, who had set them free from the Byzantine persecution. In his book he explains with clear loyalty to his own church and people how Muslims liberated them from the Byzantines, who persecuted them, burned their churches, and destroyed their monasteries.

Today, the culture and language of the local Arab Palestinian is considered the main unifying factor for the local church, as well as an important factor in bringing the people of this land together. A united people call for being the people of God, the church. We Palestinians are a united people, Palestinian Christians and Muslims.

In response to the second question, we have noted how the social and political factors aided in dividing the church from its foundations until today, causing establishment of different denominations and churches. This led to weakness in the mother church and sometimes caused paralysis. Today, the problems before Palestinian Christians at all levels are the same for the various denominations because they are together in the same way in relation to the Palestinian cause.

Under occupation there is no difference between Orthodox and Catholic, Armenian or Syrian, Coptic and Maronite, Lutheran and Anglican, for we are all one nation, Palestinian, despite our different denominations. Our destiny is one, our pain is one, and our hope is one. This hope is in Jesus Christ, on one side, and in the liberation of our land, on the other side.

So, if the Lord is one, baptism is one, and our social political circumstances are one, then what could possibly prevent us, as Christians in Palestine, from unifying the local church? Although our Muslim brothers and sisters share with us the challenge of these political circumstances, as members of the same people, we have to be honest with ourselves and others and remember that, as Christians, we have kept our religious identity, but have been denied full participation in civil life under Islamic rule.

The third question is what do we have to do for the unity of the local church? The most important thing for the development of the church in Palestine is the writing of a local theology—Palestinian theology. Personally I am not very keen to call it liberation theology. I am not against such a nomination. Yet personally, I prefer to call it Palestinian theology.

Now, let us first remind ourselves that Palestinian theology is not a new work in Palestine. Palestinian theology is really as old as Christianity, because I consider that Jesus Christ was the first theologian in Palestine to teach liberation theology or Palestinian theology. If we read the Bible, we see the message very clearly there. After Jesus, the fathers of the church were able for several centuries, thanks to their flexibility in writing theology, to survive. A good example of that is Sophronius, the Patriarch of Jerusalem, who, in 636, in one of his sermons a few months before the coming of Islam, describes the Muslims as barbarians, as animals, as unmerciful and inhuman. Yet he was the one who gave the keys of the city to Caliph Omar and, on the following Christmas in his sermon, he addressed him in a very different speech than that before the coming of Islam. Sophronius was capable of writing in any way that could enable the faithful in Jerusalem to understand such new realities, to live with them, accept them, to have a dialogue with them, and in a certain way, to commune together and share one life and one future.

When we speak about a local theology or a Palestinian theology, what do we mean by it? Although general Christian theology assists us to understand Christian doctrine properly, it cannot answer all queries that occupy the heart of believers in every time or space. This is due to the diversity of the circumstances and conditions under which the communities of believers live. Hence, theology must contextualize the general theological thought under the present conditions in which the believers live, to find in this tradition something to assist them in understanding, formulating, and living their faith at a particular historical period, with all its appeals, challenges, questions, hopes, difficulties, and aspirations.

This theology is not intended only to be a repetition of past theologies by considering the present conditions, yet, on the other hand, it is not a completely new theology that develops in complete isolation and in contradiction with the general trend of Christian thought through the ages. Palestinian theology is but an extension of the general Christian thought within specific periods of time in which certain Christian communities live under particular conditions, so this thought can enable this community to live its faith in accordance with the present requirements.

The local church in Palestine lives under the particular circumstances of space and time from which it derives its own requirements. Theology in this cultural context picks up these characteristics, with all their diversities and realities, analyzes them, absorbs their depth, and sheds the light of God's Word on them to discover, among their faults, the call of God to this church here and now. In the long run it helps the church to discover its identity and real mission at this stage in its earthly course of life.

In relation to the historical turning point before which our Palestinian church stands, we can say that to contextualize theology is a call to read the events, challenges, aspirations, and hopes that occupy the conscience of the community of believers in the light of faith. The believers, in the light of faith and the everlasting Word of God, seek to find in these events signs of God's call and the motivation for the church's work and commitment in history. This will never be accomplished unless contextualized theory remains in a state of listening to what takes place around it, coexists and interacts in the events without any false compromise, and tries to interpret them in the light of faith. It must do so in a lively manner that promotes conscience, and explicit and intelligent commitment, without letting the believer lose his or her Christian identity.

This contextualized theology is able to give many special characteristics to the local church. It also raises many questions. The main question we face is what are the special characteristics of our church? What does our Christian faith say about those characteristics? How can the local Christian thought contribute to the linking of those characteristics with our Christian faith and our daily practices? The following characteristics cannot be complete and sufficient coverage, but serve as examples.

We are Arab Palestinian Christians. How did these elements come together to form our identity? What is the meaning of our presence here and now? What is the nature of our witness? What is the originality of our belonging to this geographical and cultural body which defines us? What has to be done to bring about this identity in the church? We are Christians distinguished by our ecclesiastical diversity, in addition to rifts in our vision and practice. What is our common vocation? What is our joint mission? What are the common factors that bring us together? What is the call that God directs to us in this respect? How can we turn the diverse traditions into a rich tradition common to all of us? How can we live and work for unity within diversity? How can we move away from introversion, separation, and isolation into open communication and cooperation?

We are Christians belonging to a nation—the Palestinian people—with a special characteristic and diverse historical experiences, old and new, including all our sufferings and hopes. What is our contribution, alongside that of our other brothers and sisters, to the progress of this community and the building of its future? What is the genius of this contribution? Does our Christian faith assist us in understanding the tragedy of our people and in committing ourselves to their issues and aspirations? I have many more questions about the other religions and about the Holy Land, about the pilgrims and about the theological quest which we have to ask ourselves.

Today, the local church cannot exist if it does not consider itself a part of the Palestinian people in the Holy Land. The local church is a Palestinian one and has all the Palestinian characteristics. It should be an integral part of the Palestinian community. Of course, it may have a different role from that of the Islamic community or other communities. The question we should ask ourselves is what is our position?

Our position is to be faithful to our Christian message. In the situation in which we live today as Palestinian Christians and a local church, we have to stand up and tell our occupiers, the Israelis, that occupation is a real sin and that they have to leave. As Palestinians, our theology should present God in a different way than many Jewish theologies present God to us and to others. We have to tell our people who the God is in whom we believe.

This God, of course, is not the one who is dividing the land between people and tribes. This God in whom we believe is not the god who gives orders to shoot innocent people, young or old. This God in whom we believe is not the God who demands other nations to oppress the Palestinian community.

We believe in a God from whom Jesus himself claimed his message when he was in Nazareth, when the book was given to him and he read the message from Isaiah. We believe in a God who is with the oppressed, the poor, and the sick. This is the only way in which Christians can put forward our identity clearly. As a local church we have to say to the Israeli Jews who misuse the Bible that they are misusing the Holy Bible in their political interpretations and that, through their theology, they oppress others. We have to be clear about it. As Christian Palestinians we have to tell Western Christians that their role is not just to have a dialogue with us but, what is more important, to work together for the future.

We also have to tell Western theologians that we are not responsible for what they are writing or doing, especially the fundamentalist groups. You cannot, in the name of God, write such terrible and horrible theologies. We have to tell the Christian people of the West that they cannot, because they feel guilty for what happened to the Jewish people, support what Israel is doing to the Palestinian people.

I would like to describe an incident that happened when I, as a Palestinian Christian, decided to speak with Israeli soldiers. I was in Bethlehem, and hundreds of Israeli soldiers were marching toward Beit Sahour. I wanted to know where they were headed. I said, "Where are you going? Don't you read your Holy Bible? Did you not pause at the sayings of Isaiah? How strange it is to do what you are doing in the name of God, as if you had never meditated on his words. Read your Bible and reread it. Read what God and the prophets have said to you and to us. Not to you only, but to you and to us. Read Isaiah, Amos, and Jeremiah, whose words are stronger than the bullets of the guns you carry while running in the lanes of the refugee camps. Read loudly the books of the prophets. Then perhaps your superiors would be willing to hear about your reading."

I said to them, "Where are you going? Has not prophet Isaiah said to you, 'But your iniquities had caused a separation between you and God?' Are you going to fire your arms at children or to steal their land?"

In my opinion we should not write a theology to please Shamir or to please the pope or the patriarchs in the West, or theologians, or the queen, or anyone else. In Palestine we must write theology in order to reflect the message of Jesus Christ and to say the truth to all, or else our theology cannot be called theology but hypocrisy.

10

The Identity of the Palestinian Christian in Israel

RIAH ABU EL-ASSAL

I will try briefly to address an issue that has addressed itself to many of us. This is the subject of our identity and loyalties as Arab Christians in general, and more specifically, as Arab Palestinian Christian citizens of the state of Israel. I would like to discuss this both in terms of the factors that have strengthened and those that have weakened our sense of identity.

In Israel, for the first time since the year 70 C.E., a Christian minority is living within a Jewish majority. Relations between the two communities are burdened by the history of anti-Semitism in the Western churches, by discrimination of the Jews in Europe, and complicated by the modern movement of Christian Zionism, but the confrontation between Judaism and Christianity in Israel is shrouded behind the tensions between the Jews and the larger Arab community to which the Christians belong. Thus our discussion will focus on the identity of Arab Christians within a largely Muslim Arab community, which itself is still coming to terms with its relegation to the role of minority within the new Jewish society in what was once its homeland. How has this development affected our perception of who we are, the continuity of our existence? How has it contributed to our alienation and confusion? How do we fit into the history of our Arab East? What are the factors that attempt to repudiate our Arabness and, more recently, our identity as Palestinians? How do our enemies exploit our confusion, and what are our dreams for the future? Do we have a common or special vision for our future and what contribution can we make to the national and regional causes that will determine our fate?

Christians make up 10 percent of the Arab nation, 2 percent of the population of the Holy Land, and 3 percent of the population of Israel. It would be easier to discuss our subject in terms of the "crisis of identity" this section of the Arab nation is experiencing, rather than in terms of its loyalties and sense of belonging. This crisis is neither artificial nor is it the result of an error made by our people. Our dilemma represents the net result of policies and objectives I shall be discussing. The mere fact that the issue is the subject of discussion indicates how the self-confidence of some of us has been shaken, how a subtle fear has found its way into the depth of the soul of Arab Palestinian Christians, as all around us whirls a bewildering kaleidoscope of political, religious, national, nationalistic, regional, partisan, and sectarian matters, all contributing to the present crisis.

It is important to point out that this situation is not new. It is not the result of a historical accident, nor is it the result of the experiences of the Arab nation over the last forty or even one hundred years. It began with the rise of Islam as the dominant power in what has become the Arab East and North Africa (the Arab Maghreb). However, very few written sources deal with this phenomenon, and even fewer scholars have studied it except to emphasize deliberately the role of Arab Christians in cultural and scientific fields, or their role in pioneering the Arab Awakening in the last one hundred or so years. It should be noted that what has been written has not been sufficient to fill Arab Christians with a sense of belonging or to persuade Christians in most Arab countries of the need to stay and to preserve their presence and heritage in their own societies. On the contrary, it has contributed to their wish to escape the present reality and turn toward exile and the West.

ARAB CHRISTIANS: WHO ARE WE AND WHERE DID WE COME FROM?

Arab Christians were and continue to be an inseparable part of the Arab nation, which extends from the Arabian Gulf to the Atlantic Ocean. Seven hundred years before Islam, we were. Let it suffice to point out that we were present, perhaps among the Arab converts to Judaism, in Jerusalem on the day of the Pentecost, as recorded in the Acts of the Apostles, chapter 2, verse 11. We can specifically go back to the days of the early apostles to find the early seeds of Arab Christianity. Just as the Christian faith spread in Asia Minor and other areas of the Roman Empire until it reached Rome through the early apostles, so it spread throughout the Arabian Peninsula and North Africa through the apostle Thomas, who found his way in 50 C.E. to the Indian subcontinent by way of the Arabian Peninsula.

The early historians tell us how diligently Thomas carried the good news of salvation, the Christian message, to the Arab tribes. Many of them believed, including the Ghassanids, the Manathris, and the Taghlib tribes, and some of the Lakhmid tribe, among others. Many became priests and bishops, and some are named among the saints of the church. In his works, Arfan Qa'war tells us how hundreds of them were martyred in the cause of the Christian faith. History is full of evidence of the contribution to and participation of Arab Christians in the development of life in the Arabian Peninsula in various fields of endeavor and of the effect of Christian thought upon religious life before and after Islam in the Arab countries. But these need no emphasizing, since we belong by virtue of all the circumstances of our lives, both historically and geographically, to the Arab nation.

As the Arabs are Semites, so are we. Just as they are descendants of Qahtan, so are we also. We are bound by the single language that we speak, with its many dialects. We have no civilization, no history, no culture, no heritage other than the Arab civilization, culture, history, and heritage. Despite all external influences, we do not live the culture, civilization, traditions, and customs of the French, the English, the Russians, the Greeks, the Italians, or lately, the Americans.

Yet this evident historical reality does not mean that there is no problem of disharmony between who we feel ourselves to be, where we come from, and our present reality. However, I see the contradictions as a merely transitional phase, affecting only certain aspects of our identity. I believe it is a passing phenomenon, which is not part of the essence of the reality either of the majority of the Arab nation or of the majority of the Arab Christian minority.

It is essential to mention here that the first era after the appearance of the Arab prophet Mohammed and the rise of Islam as the dominant and decisive force in the Arab East and North Africa did create a new uniform reality, which led in many cases to a confusion between the two religious understandings, to the point where it resulted in a large percentage of Arab Christians being torn away from their Christian faith. This happened for two important reasons:

1. The theological question pertaining to the doctrine of the Holy Trinity. What reached the Arabian Peninsula of this doctrine was not the Trinity of Father, Son, and Holy Ghost, but a belief in the Triad of Father, Mother, and Son, as we see it reflected in the text of the Qur'an (see Sura 5, verse 116; Sura 5, verse 77; Sura 4, verse 169). In the contrast, Islam preached a clear monotheism. And in an age characterized by many heresies, it was easy for many Arab Christians to accept Islam's call to monotheism.

2. The political question, or the matter of spiritual and ecclesiastical imperialism. Local Christians, most of them Arabs, had protested the injustice of the Byzantines and Ethiopians. Therefore, it was no wonder that the Arab Christians supported the Islamic conquests which were, in essence, Arab conquests. Such conquests reflected and expressed the Arab Christian desire for freedom and liberation from foreign spiritual leadership, which had dominated them and dictated not only their religious but also their national fate, relieving them of what had, in fact, constituted government by remote control. Is it any wonder, then, that the father of Saint John of Damascus was the first to open one of the gates of Damascus

to allow its conquest by the Arab and Islamic army under the leadership of Khalid Ibn Al-Walid? This is not surprising. Was not there also a tremendous joy among the Jews of Spain when they welcomed the army of Tariq Ibn Zayyad, the Arab and Muslim who liberated them from the Inquisition and other evils?

I believe that the relations of the "outside" to the "inside" have always been characterized by some form of "Christian over Christian" caste behavior. In this connection it is important to study the Catholic and Protestant missionary societies which, in my view, deepened the gap between Arab Christians and their true identity, roots, and loyalties.

THE IDENTITY OF THE ARAB PALESTINIAN CHRISTIAN IN ISRAEL

The Arab Palestinian Christian of Israel is Arab by birth in the flesh and Christian by spiritual birth. It is essential that we raise our present and future generations (if we wish to preserve for ourselves a future in our homeland) to understand that while we are baptized in the name of Christ to become Christians, we are born Arabs, and we are born Palestinians.

This applies equally to those whom destiny has permitted to remain in their homeland in what in 1948 became the state of Israel. We only became Israeli citizens some time after 1948. At first we were defined as Palestinian nationals, and this is what was entered in our identity cards in the early days after the creation of Israel. Also, that part of our lands which fell under Israeli rule was considered "occupied territory" at the time, until the failure of the Arab states to act and the failure of the Palestinian struggle to remove Israeli military rule from these areas led to their being incorporated into the territory of the state of Israel. When military rule was later abandoned, this was not an oversight but part of a devious policy that brought our lands under the sovereignty of Israel and made any call for their liberation not only illegal but also dangerous, since it was viewed as extremism and jingoism.

The Arab leader Gamal Abdel Nasser had previously made us aware of a great truth when he declared: "We are living today in a new age which is radically different from all previous epochs. A new awareness has been awakened in the peoples of the world, an awareness which makes it impossible to stop the current of nationalism and of progress." This is precisely what we are experiencing today. Thus we come to the factors and policies that were marshalled to undermine our identity.

FACTORS AND POLICIES THAT UNDERMINE THE IDENTITIES OF ARAB PALESTINIAN CHRISTIANS

In examining the factors and policies which serve to undermine the identity and sense of belonging of Arab Palestinian Christians, we must emphasize that these are not all part of the strategy of some enemy, although there are indeed devious and premeditated plans to deny our identity and our roots and to encourage us to abandon them, despite the fact that the Arabic language and Arab culture have enriched even those not originally Arab. All were affected by the spread of Islam which, under the leadership of the Prophet Mohammed and the Holy Qur'an, arrived in Arabic and could be read only in Arabic. But Aramaic thinking, Hellenistic thinking, and Roman thinking, as well as the Jewish religion, necessarily influenced those Arabs who had been converted to Christianity. It was natural for the Arab Christian to drink from the springs of those who were sitting on the thrones of the church. This influence came through reading the scriptures and repeating the liturgies, and led to Arab Christians giving their sons and daughters Christian names and following Christian customs and habits. I may point out here that colonialism does not occupy land only, but also infiltrates the spirit and the mind. I think this has had the greater effect, deliberately or otherwise, in shaking the confidence of Arab Christians in their own Arab identity. The division of the church into different denominations as the result of various heresies, each with its own spiritual if not temporal army, and each with its own customs, most of them far removed from the Arab heritage, has had a similar effect. I would like to point out that what occurred in the sixth and seventh centuries, the spread of heresies, was repeated during and after the Crusades, and again with the coming of the missionary movements, so that the Catholics among us became more Catholic than the pope, the Orthodox more Greek than Alexander the Great, the Anglicans more English than the Archbishop of Canterbury, the Lutherans more German than Luther, and the Southern Baptists more American than George Washington.

Anglicans among us, for example, despite the suffering we underwent at the hands of the British during the Mandate, continued meticulously to maintain the Anglican form in our churches: the prayer books, lifestyle, and even the cathedral talk, which was always in the King's English, even when no Englishman was anywhere to be seen. With some of us it reached the point where Anglicans insisted on taking high tea at four o'clock Greenwich Mean Time. Some continue to this day to believe that the Englishman, and after him the American, is naturally more competent than the Arab and should be given key positions in the Anglican hierarchy of the Holy Land.

I could give many other examples for each of our denominations and communities. Even the language used ecclesiastically plays an influential role. All of us know that language is part of the culture, the civilization, the history, and the aspirations of a people and a nation. The power and influence of those from "outside," including their financial power, have been used as part of a policy of divide and rule, and have had direct influence on our identity, even though a minority of us here and there have attempted to resist. Some of the methods that have been and continue to be used by our spiritual hierarchies to dampen the national spirit of the more active among us are devious and unchristian. They treat our attention to our identity, without abandoning our doctrines, as an excuse to brand us the black sheep of our churches.

I do not exaggerate when I state that the majority of us now appear closer to our patriarch or missionary supervisors than to our Lord Jesus Christ, and this mirroring of our foreign hierarchies has not only led to our being emptied of our Arab identity, but will eventually lead to the Arab countries being emptied of their Christian citizens.

Arab Christians as a Minority among the Majority of Muslim Arabs

Religious fundamentalism has contributed tremendously to making the national identity and affiliation of individuals a secondary matter, not only for Christians, but even for Arab Muslims. Arab countries have witnessed attempts to repudiate anything which is not Muslim, at all levels and in all spheres. This has forced some Arab Christian minorities to live a life of alienation in the homelands of their ancestors, or caused them to experience periods of intense worry and psychological and physical instability with respect to their fate and the future of their children and properties. Some have felt compelled to abandon their homeland, identity, and roots. However, they escape from one reality of alienation to another of exile in the West.

We could speak at length about the experience of some of these minorities in Syria, Lebanon, Iraq, and Egypt. A bitter reality is experienced by Arab Christians in the land of the "black gold," Saudi Arabia, where it has been impossible for most, if not all, to establish any harmony between their Arab and their Christian identities. Some have felt compelled to abandon outwardly their faith, simply in order to protect their financial interests. As soon as they have achieved this they escape to the West, seeking to compensate for what they have lost with excessive spiritual and doctrinal zeal.

We Arab Christians must value highly such people as the late leader Gamal Abdel Nasser, who was aware of the dangers of religious discrimination and fundamentalism and called for a unified pan-Arab movement. He resisted the Muslim Brotherhood, which was calling for a pan-Islamic movement. He was convinced that not every Arab is a Muslim and not every Muslim is an Arab. We, too, Arab Palestinian residents of the Holy Land, must monitor carefully suspicious religious movements. I do not say every religious movement is suspicious, but some movements do need to be monitored carefully, and we must attempt to reduce their influence on their adherents and on those who fall into their nets.

Palestinian Christians as a Minority among Palestinian Muslims

As Palestinian Christians we must also be alert to anti-nationalist slogans based on religious extremism, chauvinism, or sectarianism, especially in the difficult circumstances that the Palestinian cause is facing these days. We have heard many questions from non-Arabs about whether Christians are afraid that the Palestinian state, for example, will be an Islamic state, as some parties are advocating. They also ask about certain slogans that were heard during election time in Israel, such as "Islam is the answer" or "Islam is the alternative." Other inquirers remind us of the old slogan "When we are finished with Saturday, we will come to Sunday" (that is, when we have finished killing the Jews, we will turn to the Christians).

Yet none of these deviations justifies Arab Palestinian Christians abandoning their Arab and Palestinian identities. Being Arab and Palestinian is not limited to one religious group, and ultimately the religious current will not prevail.

Let me share with you my experiences and the reactions of some of my Muslim brothers in the Triangle and the Galilee districts of Israel at election time, when I ran for parliament. The Arab Democratic Party tried to take advantage of Muslims and Islam and called on the electorate to vote for "those who believe 'La illah ilallah' " ("There is no God but God," part of the Muslim creed). The general reaction was, "With Muslim votes we will send the first Christian clergyman to the Knesset." This was put into action by those such as the Muslim leader Sheikh Abdallah Nimer Darwish, who campaigned in the village of Kufur Qasem on behalf of the party I represented. We won there more than double the number of votes which went to all the other Arab parties combined.

Israeli Policy

The aim of official Israeli policy has been and continues to be not merely to deny and erase the identity of Arab Palestinians, but also to threaten their continued existence in their own country. The central authorities have therefore repeatedly used such definitions as to rob Palestinians of their true or full identity. Israeli citizens are classified either as "Jews and non-Jews" or as "Muslims, Christians, and Jews." The terms "Bedouins and Circassians" may be used, or even "Arabs and Christians," in a way reminiscent of Muslim fundamentalists, who insist that if an Arab is not a Muslim, he is not an Arab.

CONCLUSION

This atmosphere of religious chauvinism, and the definitions I have mentioned, have combined with fear and weakness to lead some Christians to respond positively to this policy. Some have tried to justify and confirm these ideas, and others have even gone as far as to support Lebanese Christian claims to being "Phoenicians," and to declare they are not Arabs. Some have called for setting up a Christian party or association, and others have even talked about setting up a Christian Zionist organization.

Yet all these attempts have met with utter failure, if compared with the reality experienced by Arab Palestinians. Arab Palestinians, including Arab

Palestinian Christians, have not only succeeded in maintaining their identity, but have led a movement which has solidified, deepened, rooted, and developed this identity. Many Arab Christians have contributed in different ways in enriching this identity through the spoken and written word, and through their daily activities in culture, education, social, and political life. Palestinian awareness continues to flow forth and increase in full harmony with the needs of our cause, side by side with the crystallization of clear responses to Israeli policies, both subtle and overt.

As a result, the followers of the "Christian Embassy" and of the idea of Israel as the fulfillment of prophecy, and the supporters of the Lebanonization of Arab Palestinians have all become totally marginalized, while Beit Sahour has become the symbol of the Arab Palestinian Christians. The people of Beit Sahour were not alone on this road, for the history of our nation and of the people to which we belong is full of such examples. This is in line with the major role that was played by Christian Arabs throughout the ages to deepen and solidify Arab identity, up to and including the pioneers of the Arab Awakening in the early twentieth century, whether Lebanese, Palestinians, Syrians, Iraqis, or Egyptians. They include Butrus Al-Bustani (1819-1883); Nasir Al-Yazeji (1800-1871); Bishara Al-Khoury (1895-1968); Jameel Al-Bahri (d. 1930); Gibran Khalil Gibran (1883-1931); Mikhael Na'emeh (1889-?); Khalil Mutran (1872-1949); Fares Shidyaq (1805-1887); Ibrahim Al-Yazeji (1842-1871); Suleiman Al-Bustani (1856-1925); Adeeb Ishaw (1856-1885); Georgi Zeidan (1861-1914); Khalil Bedas (1875-1945); Salim Qub'ain (1887-1951); Ya'goub Sarrouf (1852-1927); Fr. Louis Sheikho (1859-1927); Khalil Al-Sakakini (1878-1953); Mrs. Asma Rizk Toubi (?); and other giants of national and revolutionary thinking, such as Antoun Sa'adeh (d. 1973); Michel Aflak (d. 1990); George Habash; Kamal Nasser (d. 1973); Youssef, Anis, and Fayez Sayegh, sons of the late Rev. Abdullah Sayegh, pastor of the Church of Scotland in Tiberias; and Hilarion Kappuchi.

As we reach the recent years of the struggle of our people, we see that one generation has followed another with people of politics, and of ideas, authors and literary figures being engaged in deepening the awareness and solidifying the identity of the nation, sacrificing themselves for its soil and its olives. I will name only a few of these luminaries, such as Iskander Khoury, the poet (1888-1973); Jameel Al-Bahri (d. 1930); Hanna Naqara (1912-1985); and my contemporaries Hanna Abu Hanna; Emile Touma; George Qanazeh; Emile Habiby; Tawfiq Moammar; Jamal Qawar; Tawfiq Tobi; George Zreik; Mansour Kardoush; Anees Kardoush (d. 1975); Muneib Makhaul; Shafik Habib; Hanna Ibrahim; Michael Haddad; Fowzy Al Asmar.

Finally, I would like to mention the poet Fawzi Abdullah (1942-1988), whose famous poem "Palestine" held a revelation for me. Through it I was inspired to see the similarity between the Arabic word *hawiyeh* ("identity") and the Arabic *hawa* ("love"), when Abdullah wrote: "Blame me not if my Gods are more than One. My Faith is Love [*hawa*], and the Love of my Faith is Palestinian."

11

A Palestinian Christian Challenge to the West

ELIAS CHACOUR

My land is the land of Galilee—the land of inspiration, the cradle of three monotheistic religions. Yes, that same Galilee of the nations, for us Christians the Galilee of the resurrection, of hope, and of the restoration of humanity, the Galilee of our real identity as children of God. It is the Galilee of the incarnation of God, but also that of the divinization of man and woman. Every human being needs a Galilee and is entitled to have and to live in his or her own Galilee. The encounter between human beings and between human beings and God needs a place, a particular Galilee.

I grew up in a Palestinian Christian family from Galilee, not far from the Mount of Beatitudes, or rather the Mount of the Blessings, the Mount of urging children of God to dirty their hands if they are hungry and thirsty for justice. I grew up with the mentality of gratitude and joy—gratitude because God revealed to us his economy of salvation. It is there in Galilee that my Lord, my compatriot Jesus Christ proclaimed:

> The spirit of the Lord is on me,
> for he has anointed me
> to bring the good news to the afflicted.
> He has sent me to proclaim liberty to captives,
> sight to the blind,
> to let the oppressed go free,
> to proclaim a year of favor from the Lord (Lk 4:18-19).

I grew up with an attitude of joy because the Galilee of the nations, of the Gentiles,

> The people that lived in darkness
> have seen a great light;
> on those who lived in a country of shadow dark as death
> a light has dawned (Mt 4:16).

All my ministry has been with my Palestinian brothers and sisters—Muslims and Christians. It is from them, one who was my father, another my mother, another a relative or a friend, a child or an adult, I learned that we have persecuted brothers and sisters, the Jews. From them I learned to welcome the co-persecuted brothers and sisters. From them I learned that hatred is corruption and can solve no problem; it can only blind people.

It is from those simple Palestinian Christians that I learned the true meaning of the Sermon on the Mount. I was told that my compatriot Jesus never said that happy, or even blessed, are those who hunger and thirst or are persecuted. He could never have given a sermon about spiritual and emotional health care; the "be happy attitudes" cannot be the sermon describing the Man from Galilee. I was told that he spoke in Aramaic, saying *"ashrei"* (from the verb *yashar–yash-shar*, "get up," "move," "go ahead," "do something"). Get up, do something, move, you poor in spirit, you gentle, and you who mourn. Get up, move, go ahead, do something, you who hunger and thirst for justice. You merciful and pure in heart, get up, move, go ahead, do something, you peacemakers, you then shall, all of you, be called children of God.

We were told, "You are the salt of the earth." I grew up in Galilee aware that to be the salt of the earth means to humble oneself to serve, to give, but never to convert the earth into a pile of salt.

How often I was told by my simple father and mother to remember and remind other Christians to be the "light of the world"—a clear light that shows the way in the darkness, not a light to blind those who strive to see the way ahead. How often the Third World wants to shout at the Western world: Turn down your lights, you are blinding us. Yes, get up, go ahead, do something, get your hands dirty, don't be an admirer of peace or a contemplative of justice, but do it yourself, take the risk even of your life to make peace possible, to render justice a reality.

While I carry the sufferings of my people the Palestinians, I ache also for the sufferings of my brothers and sisters the Jews. Yes, we are deeply saddened by the tragedy of our two lights. We Palestinians became the victims of the empowerment of the children of the martyrs of the concentration camps. This is my daily bread.

Often the conflict between Jews and Palestinians has been interpreted with distorted biblical arguments and inspiration, and this abuse of religion is costing both a high price.

Israel is often compared with a modern David fighting and defeating the Arab Goliath. Now, since the Intifada, with the Palestinians using the very same weapons of David, the Jewish army is compared to Goliath and the children of oblivion from Gaza, the children of humiliation in the West Bank and in East Jerusalem, compared to David. Both comparisons are inaccurate. God does not kill. He never kills. David killed Goliath. The children of the Intifada did not kill. There have been some very rare, sad, and regrettable exceptions. Nevertheless, the Palestinian children want to change the situation, not reverse the roles.

I am a convinced Christian. My origins as a Christian go back into a distant past. Am I a descendant of Abraham the Iraqi, who became the father of the believers or, as the Muslims would call him, the friend of God? Or am I rather the one who received the errant Abraham in Palestine? Or am I rather the offspring of both the Iraqi newcomer and the old resident of Palestine? Whoever I might be, I am deeply rooted in the soil of Palestine. The 2,000-year-old olive trees tell the story of my ancestors, who planted them with the sweat of their brow.

They, my ancestors, were the first to hear the Sermon on the Mount and to accompany the Lord from one peak to another during his life, till they were promised to be elevated with him not only to glory but also and first to the cross, to death. Since then, we are crucified with him. You know the price we paid to share the Good News with the nations. We were, humanly speaking, powerless, but we had a faith that moved mountains. Today the results of that work of preaching to all nations cover the globe.

Did we take anything from the Lord, or have we given him his blood from Galilee, that he spilled for the salvation of humanity, to restore the real dignity to man and woman created in his image, gaining back, at least, the likeness with God? He did not create anything new but did renew everything created. I would call on all Christians to convert from the belief in Christian philosophy or theology or civilization to the belief in and to the following of Jesus Christ, the Man from Galilee, as his disciples.

The Christianity of the Holy Land is Palestinian. We share totally the plight of our people. We have begun to convert the world to Jesus Christ, but often Western Christianity cornered us, and this suggested to many that they should convert from Christianity to Islam. Presently, and during the past half-century, many Western Christians, overburdened with guilt feelings toward the Jews, have acted unilaterally in supporting the political national entity of Israel. Or else they rush to visit the shrines and antique stones, ignoring the "Living Stones" who struggle to survive and strive to protect their faith. Could the day come when Christians visiting the historical places in Palestine include a time of prayer and of fellowship with the Palestinian Christians, the ancestors of all Christians and the compatriots of Jesus Christ?

I am also an Arab, just as a Canadian might be an Anglophone or a Francophone. We Palestinians share a lot with the Arab world. Many among us are champions of Arab culture and civilization. At the same time we are not Lebanese, Syrian, Jordanian, Egyptian, or anything else among Arab nationalities. *We are Palestinians,* and, as such, we are the other side of the Israeli-Palestinian conflict. Should I enumerate, with tears and sadness, the successive holocausts of the Palestinians in several Arab countries and in Israel? I would rather spare the reader all these details of horror.

As Palestinians we have always loved Palestine. Is there any wonder, since even when God decided to become man, he chose Palestine as home and homeland? Palestinians never contemplated emigration as an alternative to living in Galilee. In Palestine the only alternative accepted, and not willingly, was and is still to be translated into glory. This is why, when needed, we did not have a lobby in Washington or in the West. We don't wish to have a lobby. We don't want to have weapons and military might. We succeeded in convincing our people—children and adults, boys and girls—that we have a message to the world.

Gandhi had his message of *Satyagraha*; Martin Luther King, his dream; Gorbachev, his *perestroika.* Palestinians give to the human family the resourceful reality of the Intifada. We don't wish the Intifada to finish or to stop. We want it to spread all over the world. We want everyone to ridicule the blind might of weapons and of militarism. We want everyone to shake off slavery and oppression, occupational, racial, economic, and social segregation.

We pray and act, we risk and get our hands dirty, we risk our valuable lives to stop the hostilities between the two persecuted brothers: the Jew and the Palestinian. We know who the Jews were before and during the Second World War. We see and know. We wonder if they know who they have become in Israel? The empowerment of the Jews in Israel brought much corruption, many oppressive attitudes and actions.

May I share a hidden fear in my heart? The Intifada, with the hundreds of Palestinian martyrs, is pregnant with the unavoidable birth of the Palestinian state. The Israeli army is presently fighting the newborn baby, Palestine. If the empowerment of the Palestinians in the near future, even in a Palestine neighboring Israel, would mean to forget the Intifada mentality and achievements and to follow the path of militarism and national or religious exclusivism, abandoning our beautiful dream of a pluralistic society, then a state is not worth it. Our martyrs, like the martyrs of others, would have died in vain. We learn the sad lesson from the past half-century of Jewish history and empowerment.

I am a Palestinian Arab Christian, but also, as intensively and dramatically, a citizen of Israel. I have Jewish friends, whom I respect and appreciate. They are both Israeli and foreign Jews. I was not born in Israel but in Palestine, before a part of it became the new state of Israel. I have learned from my life experience in Israel that whenever you meet with two Jews or two Palestinians, you have to face at least three opinions, each one's and their common opinion. I have learned that Jews and Palestinians are both right. None is absolutely right. Both survive under the heavy burden of the past. Aware of but not responsible for or accountable for the horrors of anti-Semitism in the Western world, the Palestinians are attempting to launch publicly the needed dynamism of solidarity and the vital embrace of reconciliation. Both Jews and Palestinians need to become emissaries of a solution to stop the vicious cycle of mutual corruption and self-destruction.

The Israeli Jews have done a lot in Palestine/Israel. The ingathering of the Jews is a challenge to the twentieth century. The devastating dispersal of the Palestinians is something tragic and horrible that they have also caused. The situation of neither war nor peace is a paralysis engulfing both sides. The injustice done to the Palestinians can and must be repaired, without causing a bigger injustice, whether to Jews or to others. It is imperative to declare no more inquisitions, no more concentration camps, no more labels "dirty Jews." It is as important and for the same reasons to declare no more Palestinian refugees, no more massacres of Palestinians, no more breaking of bones, no more *"Aravi miluchlach"* (dirty Arabs). Jews and Palestinians have to live together or die together. It is a common destiny, but it is also incumbent upon our friends, from both sides, to help us choose life and positive coexistence.

For twenty-five years of active presence in Galilee among the Palestinian minority in Israel, I have been building community centers, organizing kindergartens and youth activities involving sometimes over five thousand children. With the creation of Israel there was a destruction of every kind of infrastructure in the Palestinian society. I had the privilege to create and organize the first public library in our villages. I take pride in the 160,000 volumes I bought to equip the eight public libraries. The last of our activities are the institutions for higher education in such remote localities as northern Galilee, or the very successful Prophet Elias High School at Ibillin, which we began six years ago with ninety-two students; presently we have 585. For next September we have already registered 750 students: Muslims, Christians, and Druze adolescents between 14 and 19 years of age, 56 percent girls. Provided we succeed in raising funds for laboratories and equipment, we hope to introduce, in addition to the present six technological sections, ten others during the five coming years.

Our vision is for a school that would have over two thousand students, a school that will become a community college, the first of its kind ever to exist in Galilee for the Palestinians. In spite of, or rather, because of the alarming tensions between Jews and Palestinians, the Jews are not excluded from our vision. I did appoint two Jewish teachers on our staff. Our Peace Research Center promotes the school as a school of and for peace. Seminars, symposiums, conferences, and encounters are organized in that annex to Prophet Elias High School. The Fellowship of Reconciliation was born there. The Clergy for Peace, which includes Christian, Muslim, Jewish, and Druze "clergy" was also born in Ibillin's Prophet Elias High School.

I have many Jewish Israeli and non-Israeli friends whom I respect and love dearly. Very often we agree to disagree amiably; at other times we agree to agree, even painfully. Our interreligious dialogue is not, and cannot be, burdened with a guilt complex. We want them to convert, but to convert to God, as much as we wish for our people to convert to God. We stick to our own identity. We are followers of Jesus Christ; he is our champion in life.

Some would ask how I, a Palestinian, can believe in a Jewish Christ. It is easy for us to believe in the Iraqi/Mesopotamian Gentile father Abraham. We are not fanatics of Christ; we are his followers who love him and share that love with others. We still are able to love with our minds and to reflect and to think with our hearts. That's why our hands are always extended opened; they are never raised, waving a threatening fist.

This leads me to conclude with an appeal to all those concerned about the future of the Jews in Israel and of the Palestinians in Palestine. Your friendship with one side should not mean enmity or hostility to the other side. Often this is a sad result of ignorance or misinformation. This conflict has two sides; the one is the Israeli Jews, the other the Palestinians. Is it enough to know about these last from their opponents? Don't you think it important to know them directly?

I call Americans to support your friends, but not with weapons. Help stop the shipping of weapons to the Middle East. We want you to ship us thousands of copies of your Constitution. We need to live in a pluralistic kind of society. Theocracies, whether Christian, Muslim, or Jewish, cannot be other than discriminatory and oppressive. The three monotheistic religions have failed to reconcile or to unite and unify humanity.

My major ministerial function has been so far to proclaim the word of truth in the face of mighty people and never to flatter the poor to win their applause. I urge all Western people to try to risk, to build bridges among conflicting persons and groups. Yes, get your hands dirty with the leaven of justice; dirty your hands to build a human society that reflects God's presence and provides hope to hopeless people, homes to homeless people, and security to threatened people. Get your hands dirty as did Gandhi. Have a dream and risk for it, like Martin Luther King.

Liberate your own people and yourself; shake off the corruption of hatred. Yes, like my compatriot, the Man from Galilee, do not give charity, do not condescend to the poor and to the needy broken ones, but, like him, give of yourself. He wants a church, not for the service of the poor, but a church from and for the poor.

PART 3

POWER, JUSTICE, AND THE BIBLE

12

Biblical Justice, Law, and the Occupation

JONATHAN KUTTAB

The political systems prevailing in biblical times, both in the Old and New Testaments, were radically different from those prevailing today. The dominant system was an Oriental despotism where the ruler, whether monarch, emperor, or tribal chieftain, viewed his authority as absolute, and his wishes as law. Those who ran afoul of him—whether his defeated enemies or his own subjects—had no rights whatsoever. Their properties were forfeited, their liberty denied, and their lives subject to his whim. Even by surrendering and admitting defeat, enemies could only throw themselves at the mercy of the victor and hope to be spared to live as slaves. Harsh conditions of humiliation, and even the amputation of fingers, were not seen as unnatural. Samuel the prophet described vividly what the people of Israel could expect when they asked for a king "like all the other nations," and they got precisely what they asked for.

Yet in that world the divine commandments introduced restrictions on the authority of the ruler. They began with an assertion of the sovereignty of God as the ultimate ruler of the universe, and with the teaching that God was Lord over the kingdoms of humankind (Nebuchadnezzar). This meant that, while the king (Jew or Gentile) appeared to have absolute power, his power was only derivative. Jesus expressed this Old Testament principle when he replied to Pilate's arrogant assertion that he had authority to take or spare his life by telling him that he can only exercise that authority given to him from above.

Law was a second qualification imposed on the exercise of raw power. The commandments of the law were binding even on the king. His sins and the sins of his people would be punished. Physical penalties, as well as an absence of divine approval, were the expected sanctions against erring rulers.

One of the central roles of the Old Testament prophets was to call the attention of the rulers to the divine commands of justice and to "speak truth to power." Whether the king was giving vent to his own greed, or pride, or lust, or otherwise, the prophet was there to point the finger, and to tell the king to his face: "Thou art the man."

Few in the world today would be willing to assert that the authority of a ruler or a regime is absolute, or that it can find legitimacy in naked power. The international community has devised for itself elaborate rules and conventions governing the behavior of states, under the titles "rule of law," "human rights," and "international law." Before this century, when they were codified, the principles of justice often were referred to under the Eurocentric term of the norms of "civilized nations." By whatever name, these principles continue to be violated today, and the need continues to exist for a prophetic witness that will "speak truth to power" and that is willing to bear the consequences.

In our present context, the Palestinian people have found themselves living under the rule of another group, who exercises, by virtue of sheer power and brute force, total domination over their land, resources, and persons. The state of Israel, in its creation, asserted for itself and for the Jewish people worldwide, sovereign and total control in Palestine at the expense of and to the exclusion of its indigenous inhabitants. The majority of the Palestinians were forcibly evicted from their homes, driven into exile, and their homes and possessions turned over to new Jewish immigrants. The laws and structures of the new state openly discriminated against the non-Jewish inhabitants and in favor of Jews from all over the world.

In 1967, again by sheer force of military might and by right of conquest (covered up by the myth that Israel's Six Day War was a "preemptive defensive war"), Israel occupied the rest of the Palestinian homeland. It proceeded to rule the Occupied Territories in line with its discriminatory vision of serving the Jews and providing them with a state.

Such discrimination is inherent in the Zionist ideology and its professed goal of creating a Jewish state. Such a state was not brought about by the consent of the Palestinians, but by exercise of sheer power.

Law has always played an ambiguous role in the state of Israel, in the Occupied Territories, and indeed for the Zionist movement since its inception. Rather than serving as a control and restraint on the exercise of brute power, and in the interests of justice, law was conceived of as a useful tool in accomplishing the unjust deeds considered necessary for the success of the Zionist enterprise, clothing them with an aura of respectability and legitimacy. As such, great emphasis was placed on positive law being the expression of the will of the powerful and the rulers, rather than on the principles of justice.

For this reason the Zionist movement arduously courted the colonial powers in authority in Palestine for charters, promises, and permits to settle

Jews in Palestine, while spending little time or effort in obtaining the consent of the Palestinian population.

Once the state was formed, no constitution was drafted, in large part to avoid affirming broad principles of justice, which might assist the Arabs, on the one hand; or to declare unambiguously their second-class status, on the other. Their lands were expropriated, either by the Custodian of Absentee Property or as "public land." The latter was a most useful deception, since the world had already accepted that Israel was a "Jewish" country; therefore "public" land easily becomes "Jewish" land—for the exclusive use and benefit of Jews.

After driving out most of the indigenous Palestinians and bringing in from all over the world enough Jews to change the demographic balance in their favor, a new definition of democracy emerged whereby the individual, or the minority, can be suppressed with impunity as long as the majority (51 percent) in the Israeli Parliament pass a law permitting it. Under this "democratic" system, virtually unbridled exercise of state power against Palestinians, their property, institutions, and liberties was exercised. The rule of law was transformed in a subtle way into rule *by* law.

A further erosion of the principles of biblical and natural justice was facilitated by a new ideology: the idolatry of national security. Under the cover of security, which typically covers a multitude of sins, an entire system of laws is enforced that severely violates Palestinian human rights in a large variety of areas: administrative detention; deportations; house demolitions; travel restrictions; closure of schools, universities, and other institutions; uprooting of trees; prolonged curfews; shutoffs of electricity, water, telephone service, transportation, and other facilities; not to mention shootings, beatings, torture, denials of due process, and other deprivations.

In addition, the normal functionings of a government are subverted to permit a rigid system of controls and oppression by "legal" means. Every aspect of life is controlled by the requirement of licenses and permits, which are denied, or else they are regulated on the basis of the interests of those in power. The power to grant or withhold those licenses is so broad as to be totally discretionary, and it is often wielded in a thoroughly arbitrary fashion.

The world and the Israeli public are told that this discretion is subject to judicial review by the Israeli High Court. The Palestinians know otherwise. Those who have been naive or idealistic enough to try the High Court soon discovered its in-built self-imposed limitations and that the word *security* whispered into a judge's ear ends all matters. If further proof is needed, a "secret file" can always be relied upon to quiet the conscience of any skeptical judge. But, in most cases, this is unnecessary, for matters can be defined to be outside the scope of judicial scrutiny—which becomes limited to ensuring that the military follows its own rules, until it finds it easier to change them.

The High Court has itself participated in this diabolical scheme by providing and accepting convoluted legal arguments, of brilliant sophistication, to avoid the application of international law, particularly the Geneva Conventions, and to sanction the wholesale theft of land and the systematic denials of human rights through use of Emergency Regulations. Practices like deportation, which is prohibited as a war crime under international law, were permitted, and the demolition of houses sanctioned. Collective punishment, that cries out to the high heavens in its unfairness, is condoned as a "preventive, not punitive" measure.

If the law in the state of Israel is to be restored to its proper biblical function as a restraint to the arbitrariness of power, and if justice is to prevail, there must be a revival of the prophetic tradition. There must be men and women who are willing to risk the wrath of the authorities, the frustrating agony of being misunderstood, and the false accusations of "anti-Semitism" or "self-hating Jew." This can also mean the loss of favor of publishers, and funders, and the dreaded isolation imposed on those who take unpopular positions, as well as the physical sanctions available to the state. We must be willing to risk these dangers as we endeavor to "speak truth to power."

13

Law, Power, Justice, and the Bible

MITRI RAHEB

The topic of law, power, justice, and the Bible is very interesting, fundamental, and important. It is a topic that is strongly related to our present world and the current issues and problems. In particular, it is related to us, the Palestinians, who have experienced the fact that might is right and that the oppressed is accused of disorder and disregard for the law, although it is well known that we seek justice and only justice.

I am not going to present a detailed theological essay concerning each of the biblical terms—law, power, and justice—but I would like to elucidate some biblical aspects of the crucial relationship among these three basic concepts and the effect of such relationship on our Palestinian reality.

The Bible shows that there is a definite interrelation among law, power, and justice. These three factors are not independent of each other, but are related in a very definite and precise functional equation. Law lays the framework by which we deal with others in such a way that injustice does not prevail (Ex 20:1-17). For that reason God has given us kings, rulers, and governors, authority and power (Rom 13:1-5). Furthermore, law and power are connected. Law is protected by power so that it will not go out of control to become an instrument of injustice, oppression, and dictatorship. Therefore law and power are the tools of justice. This is the correct equation for this triad.

The Bible reminds us that, through the fall into sin, this equation has been thrown out of balance. Law has become a tool in the hands of the powerful and the domineering. They write it, interpret it according to their own personal whims, and they execute it accordingly. So the powerful determine what is right and wrong, and what is just and unjust. The equation, therefore, has been upset and the law has become subservient to the mighty.

Justice has become the plaything of those who are in positions of power.

This is the reality of our world as it is presented in the Holy Bible. And this is the real world experienced by our Palestinian people. Our people have witnessed the loss of their homeland and their bounty. They have suffered under oppression and injustice. When our people started crying for their rights, they found that the cries of the oppressed are faint and barely can be heard by the deaf ears of the world. The world hears and listens to the voice of the powerful.

This experience has led our people to the undisputed conclusion that might is seen as right. Confronted with such bitter experience and as a counteraction our people resorted to violence to make themselves heard. This angry, tumultuous cry echoed throughout the world, proving that our world is a strange one, indifferent to the moans of the meek but shaking at the thunder of guns. Such a reaction on the part of a small group has gained us the name of terrorists. Again, the world has shown its one-sided bias to power. The meek, who resorted to violence in a moment of desperation, becomes the terrorist, and the oppressor, who stockpiles weapons and subjugates other people, is seen as a democratic and law-abiding nation. Thus the world has shown that the coined phrases it creates are prejudiced and biased.

Now we wonder if the world can or will hear and respond to the peaceful outcry of the Intifada. Or will it turn a deaf ear to the sighs of countless mothers and keep upholding the powerful?

If the biblical equation of law, power, and justice is reversed, then the concept of justice will be altered. Based upon this, justice in the Bible does not mean neutrality, nor does it imply charity.

Many simple Christians think that justice is being neutral and playing the role of mediator between the two contestants. So many Western Christians try to bring Palestinians and Israelis together in an effort to create some form of reconciliation. The basic problem is that these people of goodwill do not pay enough attention to the fundamental equation mentioned above. It is not enough to bring individuals together, it is necessary that the disturbed equation be restored to its true form.

The Palestinian problem is not a matter of individual hate; it is a problem of power imbalance. It is a problem of a system based upon oppression, of law used to protect the strong, and power utilized to deprive other people of their land and basic human rights. It is a problem of two conflicting interests: one wants to perpetuate the status quo, and the other wants to change the prevailing system, as is pointed out in the *Kairos Document.*

Justice, according to the Bible, is the redistribution of power, the placement of law in its proper place and perspective, and the toppling of the current system. It is the restoration of the three components of the equation to their proper relation, so that law and power become the true instruments of justice.

The song of Hannah confirms this:

The bow of the mighty has been broken
but those who were tottering
  are now braced with strength.
The full fed
  are hiring themselves out for bread
but the hungry need labor no more. . . .
Yahweh gives death and life. . . .
He raises the poor from the dust
he lifts the needy from the dunghill
to give them a place with princes,
to assign them a seat of honor;
for to Yahweh belong the pillars
  of the earth
on these he has poised the world (1 Sm 2:4-8).

The same fact is echoed in Mary's magnificat (see Lk 1:46-55).

Justice does not mean neutrality, neither does it mean charity. Justice is not a gift from the powerful to the weak, nor is it an act of welfare from the rich to the poor. It is the undisputed right of the oppressed. It is their own dignity. When the Palestinian people started calling for justice, many thought they were begging for a charity. So too many have come to their aid, not to uphold them, but to silence them, thus pacifying their own tortured consciences. They rose up and rushed in, not to restore the Palestinians' lost land, but to give some drops of oil, a few handfuls of flour, forgetting that the Palestinians are not asking for charity but for justice. They do not want to be overwhelmed with refugee aid, but they did expect to have "justice flow like water, and uprightness like a never-failing stream" (Am 5:24).

Today, after the Intifada has gained momentum, alerting the world to a people whose basic rights have been forgotten in the maze of international diplomacy, let it be known that we are not seeking the charity of autonomy, or municipal elections, but our irrefutable right to have our own identity and the right of self-determination.

One of the most beautiful and illustrative tales of the relationship between law, power, and justice is the story of Exodus in the Old Testament. This narrative tells the story of a group of people that belonged to a poor working class without any rights and who were used as cheap labor. They were deprived of a dignified living and were excluded from positions of power, authority, and the protection of the law (see Ex 1–2). The justice they sought was not mere pennies thrown at them, but the toppling of the system that had enslaved and humiliated them, bringing them salvation and liberty.

In his first action, God wrecked the political power of Pharaoh and his economical system. The second thing God did was to give the liberated people the Torah, the Law, to strike the right balance between power and justice. This liberated people should have remembered that once they were weak, without power or influence, and that they were persecuted and subjected to an oppressive, unjust law, so that they can handle power properly and not be overwhelmed by the arrogance of power. History repeats itself, and the Jewish people found themselves oppressed and persecuted by the Nazis. It is ironic that the one oppressed has become the oppressor, and the one that was persecuted has become the persecutor. Those who were deprived of all their rights have become drunk in their own power, robbing the basic rights of other people. We Palestinians face this same challenge once we gain our rights and come into a position of power. The pains of the past should not be forgotten, and the law should dictate our behavior.

The life of Christ is another example of the relationship between law, power, and justice. By the incarnation God "emptied himself, taking the form of a slave, becoming as human beings are" (Phil 2:7). In his life Jesus refused to be neutral. Instead he chose the persecuted, the outcast, standing by them, defending them, giving them their sense of dignity. Jesus chose his disciples from poor simple fishermen so that, through them, he could catch the hearts and minds of all humankind through service. Jesus in effect told his disciples: "In this world the kings and great men order their slaves around, and the slaves have no choice but to like it! But among you, the one who serves you best will be your leader. Out in the world the master sits at the table and is served by his servants. But not here! For I am your servant."

He taught them to use the law to serve humanity, and power for the interest of the poor. Jesus taught us the same thing through his death, proving by his resurrection that God does not forsake the meek and the weak but will uplift them from their graves, giving them power as a tool for justice (see Rom 6:13). Accordingly, Jesus transforms the love of power into the power of love (see 1 Jn 3:10).

In Jesus, humankind is king and master over all; therefore, humanity is strong and has its rights; simultaneously humanity is a loyal servant to all. Where humankind is only king and master, it becomes a dictator and arrogant; where a mere servant, oppressed and humiliated. Humanity is powerful, but uses its power to uphold justice and to spread love. So it is not only maintaining the law but is fulfilling the will of the heavenly Father.

Let us hope that this will be the role of the Christians in the Israeli-Palestinian conflict.

14

Faith, Nonviolence, and the Palestinian Struggle

ZOUGHBI ELIAS ZOUGHBI

Bernard Shaw once said, "If you break a nation's nationality, it will think of nothing else but getting it set again. It will listen to no reformer, to no philosopher, to no preacher, until the demands of the nationalist are granted. It will attend to no business, however vital, except the business of unification and liberation."[1] Herein lies the message of the Uprising, its causes and its consequences, its techniques and goals, its effects and impacts. The Intifada is the culmination of long-simmering frustration over the past forty years of Israeli injustice. Indeed, the Palestinian Uprising against the Israeli occupation, born of anger, frustration, and despair, proves to be the most effective expression and the most authentic picture of Palestinian nationalist ambitions.

The Intifada, as a relatively nonviolent struggle, is not a new development in Palestinian history. Palestinians have used nonviolence alongside armed struggle since the beginning of this century in an attempt to achieve their national aspirations. It is worth mentioning here that most nonviolent activities, such as peaceful demonstrations, tax resistance, distributing leaflets, and so on, are considered illegal according to Israeli laws and military orders. In spite of this fact, many Palestinians have conducted a nonviolent campaign against the Israeli occupation. Not long ago the leadership of the Uprising printed some leaflets in Hebrew and distributed them to the Israeli soldiers, explaining that "the Intifada was not directed against them personally, but simply working for the rights of Palestinians."[2]

According to Gene Sharp, the director of the program on nonviolent sanctions at Harvard University's Center for International Affairs, there are three classes of methods in conducting nonviolence. They include 1) symbolic forms of nonviolent protest, 2) noncooperation, 3) nonviolent intervention.[3] The Intifada draws on the first two methods and on the third through international diplomacy.

Before exploring the reasons that nonviolence has been effective, I would like to emphasize two important points. The first is that indulging in the debate over whether national liberation movements should use violence or not is not as important as actively working to speed up the end of occupation, colonialism, imperialism, and racism. And, secondly, whether or not resorting to violence by the oppressed is considered evil, the greater evil will always be occupation. The Palestinians have the full right to struggle against occupation by the most effective means available. Therefore, I believe the ultimate goal is to support objectives and ambitions that will end occupation, achieve justice with dignity, and liberate Palestine from Israeli occupation.

There are two major aspects of nonviolence in the Palestinian struggle. First, there is the nonviolence of the Palestinians in Occupied Palestine, and second, there is the political route of the PLO, which uses diplomacy and proposes peace initiatives. Nonviolence is a commonly misunderstood term. By nonviolence, I do not mean passiveness, weakness, or surrender. Rather, it is an empowerment and an ongoing struggle that requires inner strength and perseverance.

I would like to highlight some of the reasons nonviolence can be effective and valid in the Palestinian Uprising. First, as a Palestinian Christian, I believe violence dehumanizes human beings. Therefore, through nonviolent struggle, we find the common ground among Judaism, Christianity, and Islam in their belief that human beings are created in the image of God.

Second, through nonviolence we not only seek the liberation of our nation, but also seek the liberation of our enemy by alleviating Israeli fears of an inevitable Palestinian state. As the educator Paulo Freire says, "Only power that springs from the oppressed will be sufficiently strong to free both."[4] When we consider the dehumanizing acts the Israeli government has asked its citizens to perform,—beating, maiming, killing, terrorizing, and torturing—we must think of the repercussions these sanctioned acts will have on the future of Israeli society. What kind of citizens will this generation's soldiers make? And, if this policy continues, how many generations following them will learn to be racist and to deal with fear and anger with violence? Because of the Palestinians' unique position, they are able to liberate Israeli society from learning to dehumanize, abuse, and degrade itself.

Third, given Israel's nuclear arsenal and defense strategy, there is little hope of defeating Israel by war. But, with the Palestinian commitment to struggle, there is no way that Israel can maintain the status quo and obliterate the Palestinian national identity. Israelis must eventually accept the inevitability of change. The Intifada has brought us to this point, and because of the relative nonviolence of the Uprising, the Israelis should have received the message that we want peace, security, and justice for all. It is worth mentioning here that the PLO leaders have issued orders restricting and prohibiting the use of firearms in the Uprising. Nonviolence should address these facts in order to pave the way of coexistence by laying the solid foundation of a two-state solution.

Fourth, through the Uprising we have so far achieved what violence has not been able to achieve. Palestinians have gained world sympathy for their cause, recognition that occupation is no longer viable, and affirmation from more than one hundred nation-states recognizing the right of Palestinians to have their own state. Some might argue that the armed struggle of the first decade (1964-1974) of the Palestinian revolution has put the Palestinians on the world map. I cannot deny that historical background. But being on the world political map is not enough. We need to foster our existence on the geographical map.

Fifth, based on the experience of previous and present popular struggles, I believe nonviolence will foster our relations with peace-loving people who would be mobilized to support the unarmed oppressed in the light of the atrocities and brutalities of the oppressor. This simply illustrates our vision of a new world order based on peace, economic well-being, social justice, and ecological balance.

A sixth point is that a nonviolent strategy can help us address Israeli society by working with those who cannot tolerate the unjust acts of their government. Palestinians can educate Israelis and break down stereotypes, but only Israelis themselves can change the policy of the government. The Jaffe Center for Strategic Studies at Tel Aviv University, headed by Aharon Yariv, a former chief in army intelligence, issued a report on "Israel's Option for Peace" which stated, "As long as the PLO maintains the moderate course it developed in late 1988, and an Israeli policy that rejects unconditionally any dialogue with it does not appear to be sustainable over time, it would generate increasing unrest within Israel, a sharp conflict with world Jewry, and Israel's own growing isolation."[5]

A seventh point is that as we see ourselves as members of the world community and are aware of the international impact of the Israel-Palestine conflict, we also realize the need for international support. Opting for nonviolence requires the support of others across the world to exert pressure to fulfill our aims. This would complement the local strategies.

The eighth point is that we should not be dragged into the swamp of violence into which Israel is trying to pull us. Palestinians should heed the words of Napoleon, who said, "Never do what your enemy wants you to do, if only because he wants you to do it."[6] Through its daily provocations Israel tries to push us to use greater violence, precisely because the Israelis are well equipped to deal with violence. It seems that they are threatened more by thoughts of peace and nonviolence than by war. Their whole system is trained for war, but they are not well equipped to face peace.

Therefore, it seems clear that Israel does not want peace; and neither does it wish to recognize the rights of the Palestinians to self-determination and statehood. Instead, it attempts to buy time and deceive the world by directing the world's attention away from the plight of the Palestinians to the issue of Soviet Jewish immigration. There is a faint ray of hope in some of the small changes taking place within Israeli society, but the government still adheres to its policy of creating facts on the ground, such as expanding settlements and deporting Palestinians, blocking any possibility for resolving the conflict through peaceful means.

However, the Intifada has created a new *real politik* in the region. It is a new phase in the history of Palestine in which the people, their society, and leaders have shaken the Israeli system as well as being shaken up themselves. The Intifada has conveyed a very clear message; it rejects past myths and proposals aimed to prevent the PLO from participating in negotiations which would determine their fate. Occupation can no longer be seen as benevolent, enlightened, and humane. There is no such thing as humane occupation.

And Israel's claim that there is a silent majority content with the occupation now falls on deaf ears. The Intifada, as a mass popular campaign of civil disobedience cutting across barriers of class, sex, religion, and political and factional affiliations, has shown to Israel and to the world that the Palestinian people are tired of occupation. Benvenisti describes the Intifada as "an entire community which refuses to obey the law."[7]

Any Israeli peace plans which do not take these realities into consideration are worthless. The Labor Party's so-called Jordanian option was therefore born dead. Its lack of a future was confirmed in 1974 when the United Nations recognized the representative nature of the PLO and then again in August 1988 when King Hussein renounced any claim by the Hashemite Kingdom of Jordan to the West Bank.

Similarly, the Likud Party's plans for limited autonomy and Prime Minister Shamir's election plan are farcical, in spite of Shamir's attempts to make them sound plausible. Even Israel's Chief of Military Intelligence, Brg. Amnon Shahak, in a secret report to senior cabinet ministers, linked peace talks with the PLO, saying, "Israel must reverse its long-standing attitude and talk to the PLO if it wants to end the Arab uprising in the Occupied Territories."[8]

The Intifada tells Israel, as it tells the world, that this is "the age of national rebirth and not the age of the demise of nations."[9] Already the establishment of alternative Palestinian institutions and committees is preparing the infrastructure for the Palestinian state. Thus the time of autonomy has passed and the liberation has been born.

In spite of this, the Israeli government has tried several times to create an alternative leadership for the Palestinians, usually composed of collaborators and agents, such as the "Village Leagues" in 1982. Even now it tries to undermine the PLO through its support of fundamentalist groups. But it is not succeeding. Israeli journalist Joel Greenberg says, "Slowly, inexorably and despite government opposition, the PLO is gaining legitimacy as a negotiating partner in Israeli eyes."[10]

The Palestinians are becoming more and more realistic and pragmatic. This is the sobering truth, the kind of realism that the Uprising has produced. Gone are the days of romanticism and wishful thinking. As George Mottell says, "The Intifada has boosted Palestinians' self-image, but also made them more willing to compromise with Israel."[11] Indeed, the PLO, whose original charter denied the Israeli state the right to exist, has now recognized Israel's right to security in exchange for Israel's recognition of parallel rights for Palestinians!

The PLO's policy has lately been centered on diplomacy and political solutions. Since 1974 the PLO has opted for political routes, thereby minimizing the role of armed struggle as the only means of liberating Palestine. As Dr. Muhammad Hallaj, the editor of *Palestine Perspectives*, says, "The Palestinian struggle seeks to redress rather than avenge an injustice. For that reason it has been accommodationist rather than rejectionist."[12]

The PLO's commitment to resolve the Palestinian-Israeli conflict pushed it to adopt a political strategy where it could break the wall of distrust and fear among the Israeli and Palestinian people. All the indicators related to this conflict point out that the political solution is the most viable solution. For Afif Safieh, an advisor in the PLO and head of the PLO office in The Netherlands, "the future Palestinian state is only possible through a joining of struggles; on one hand, the struggle of those who want 'to liberate the territories occupied by Israel in 1967,' and on the other, the struggle undertaken by those who want 'to liberate Israel from its occupied territories.' "[13]

The Palestinians have done their homework. Perhaps it is time the Israelis did their homework also. Safieh elaborates, "The political approach requires a radical change from within Israeli society, more specifically, an Israeli awakening."[14] Promoting such ideas means encouraging the peace movements in Israel by increasing contacts and engaging in talks and dialogue based on mutually acceptable peace.

Recognizing these realities, the PLO has followed a constructive strategy by pursuing diplomatic channels that favor "arms of dialogue rather than dialogue of arms." This positive policy has been crowned by the PLO political program, which was announced on the fourth day of the nineteenth PNC in 1988. It includes the following principal points:

1. The PLO is committed to pursuing a peaceful solution to the conflict with Israel on the basis of Resolutions 242 and 338.

2. The PLO will negotiate with Israel in the context of an international peace conference that will be held on the basis of Israel's acceptance of the Palestinian's political rights as a nation.

3. The PLO retains the right to resist Israeli occupation inside the Occupied Territories, but it rejects all forms of terrorism. It will do so in accordance with the United Nations Resolutions.[15]

The Intifada has captured the world's attention and gained global sympathy because it is an unbalanced war between the relatively unarmed captive Palestinians and the strongest military power in the Middle East. Whenever I become frustrated and think that the Uprising is not gaining any ground, I remind myself that nothing in Israel's forty-year history has stopped it for two years as the Intifada has done. Had we Palestinians used real violence against the Israelis, the Intifada would have been over in a short time. It is easy to justify the use of violence when one is confronted with violence, but it is very difficult to justify violence when confronted with nonviolence, as Israel has learned. The ultimate conclusion is that the PLO is ready for peace. It has clung to any initiative which might lead to dialogue with Israel. The question is whether the Israeli government is ready for peace or not.

"Today I have come bearing an olive branch and a freedom fighter's gun. . . . Do not let the olive branch fall from my hand!"[16] With these words, the PLO Chairman Yasser Arafat addressed the world community before the United Nations General Assembly in 1974. They are as valid now as they were at that time. "Do not make me drop the olive branch" is the message as well as the appeal to the world community who work and assume responsibility for peace. Can the world community afford to let the opportunity for a peaceful settlement in the Middle East slip away? This is the question and the ultimate challenge.

NOTES

1. Bernard Shaw, cited in *Palestine Perspective* (May/June 1988), p. 3.
2. Vicki Kemper, "The Road to Palestine," *Sojourners* (April 1989), p. 14.
3. Gene Sharp, "The Intifada and Nonviolent Struggle," *Journal of Palestine Studies* 73 (Autumn 1989), p. 4.
4. Paulo Freire, "Pedagogy of the Oppressed," *Towards a Just World Order*, vol. 1 (Boulder, Col.: Westview Press, 1982), p. 49.
5. Joel Greenberg, "Shamir Says No, But Israelis Edge Close to PLO Talks," *The Christian Science Monitor* (March 15, 1989), p. 3.
6. Sharp, p. 13.
7. Benvenisti, cited in Joseph Bernard, "Benvenisti Sees Non-violent Campaign as Serious Challenge," *The Jerusalem Post*, 8 January 1988.
8. Amnon Shahak, quoted in Glen Frankel, "Israeli Intelligence Agency Links Peace to Talks with the PLO," *Washington Post*, 21 March 1989, pp. A1, A15.
9. Muhammad Hallaj, "Revolt in Occupied Palestine," *American Arab Affairs* (Spring 1988), p. 41.
10. Greenberg, p. 3.
11. George Mottel, "Arab Uprising Brings Gain and Pain," *The Christian Science Monitor*, 7 December 1988, p. 1.
12. Muhammad Hallaj, "The Palestinian Contribution to the Middle East Peace Process," *Arab Perspective*, p. 12.
13. Afif Safieh, "Dead Ends," *Middle East* (July 1986), p. 8.
14. Ibid. p. 9.

15. Yousef Ibrahim, "PLO Proclaims to Be an Independent State; Hints at Recognizing Israel," *New York Times*, 15 November 1988, p. 6.

16. Yehuda Luckas, ed., *Documents on the Israeli-Palestinian Conflict* (Cambridge: Cambridge University Press, 1967-1983), p. 181.

15

Biblical Perspectives on the Land

NAIM S. ATEEK

The 1967 war was a great turning point in the Israel-Palestine conflict. Religion in Israel caught up with the Zionist dream and appropriated it in a special way. The state of Israel gradually became the servant of religion, and religion became the servant of the state. The political had become inseparable from the religious claims to the land.

Anywhere else in the world a conflict like ours would be considered a political one. A people, living in their own country, are overrun by a group of people who come from outside. These outsiders are determined to take over the country. They are stronger and equipped to do so. Such an act is a violation of the political and human rights of the indigenous population; it has no special religious significance. Arbitration, therefore, should be based on international law.

But in Israel-Palestine today, the Bible is being quoted to give the primary claim over the land to Jews. In the mind of many religious Jews and fundamentalist Christians the solution to the conflict lies in Palestinian recognition that God has given the Jews the land of Palestine forever.[1] Palestinians are asked to accept this as a basic truth. Any settlement that is not based on such a foundation is seen as contrary to the promises and covenant of God with the Jewish people.

Today this kind of abuse of the Bible and of religion is precisely the religious argument presented by most religious Jews and fundamentalist Christians. Therefore, Palestinian Christians must tackle the issue of land from a biblical perspective, not because I believe that the religious argument over the land is of the *bene esse* of the conflict, but because we are driven to it as a result of the religious-political abuse of biblical interpretation.

I would like to begin by calling attention to some of the abuses of the Bible which we frequently encounter. Recently a document came my way, prepared by some Anglican fundamentalist, on the issue of the land. This person wrote:

> a) I counted that on 109 occasions the Old Testament refers to the land as given or promised to the Jewish people. b) In addition, on a further 36 occasions, it states that God swore a solemn oath to give them the land. c) And on a further 15 occasions, the land is promised "forever." d) So strong is the emphasis on this in the Old Testament that it is clear that the people and the land are very deeply and closely associated. If the two are separated something is seriously wrong.

Later in the document this person concludes that since God swore an oath that the land is an eternal possession of Israel, though they did not deserve it, "Would it not be strange if God decided against fulfilling his strong and numerous promises to Israel about the land? If God breaks such promises, how reliable is he in other promises?"

This is only one sample of the way some of these fundamentalists argue. Any look at the Old Testament shows how often the issue of the land is mentioned. A mere count of the word *land* in the Old Testament (without any study of context) shows that the three Hebrew words most often translated land, *adamah*, *erez*, and *sadeh*, appear in the text of the Old Testament more than fifteen hundred times. By comparison, in the New Testament the two Greek words that are most often translated as land are *agros* and *ge*, and they appear forty-one times.

One cannot deny at all that there is a great difference between the outlook of the Old Testament and that of the New Testament on the issue of the land. The issue of the land is very much bound up in the life of the people of the Old Testament. The same is not true for the New Testament. I would, therefore, like to submit the following points:

1. The Old Testament makes it very clear that the land belongs to God.[2] There are a number of references in the Old Testament that God is the owner of the land. In one place in the Torah the divine claim to the land is so emphasized that the Israelites are regarded as strangers and foreigners themselves: "Land will not be sold absolutely, for the land belongs to me, and you are only strangers and guests of mine" (Lv 25:23; see Jer 16:18).

Another emphasis is that the Israelites were not supposed to defile the land. In Jeremiah it becomes clear that the defilement of the land had actually taken place, "But when you entered you defiled my country and made my heritage loathsome" (Jer 2:7). Those who live in the land must, therefore, obey the owner. Disobedience of God defiles the land. When the land is defiled, it would thrust its inhabitants out (see Lv 20:22; Deut 4:25–26, 28:63; Jos 23:15–16).

Furthermore, we know from the Old Testament that the God who was thought to be one among many gods (Ps 95:3) and then the greatest God above other gods, was eventually perceived as the only one God, creator of the world (Ps 96:5; 97). God was no more the owner of the land of Palestine, but the owner of the whole world. The whole world becomes sanctified because it is God's world and because God dwells in it. "To Yahweh belong the earth and all it contains, the world and all who live there" (Ps 24:1).

I believe that the lesson God has tried to teach the ancient Hebrews all along is the importance of understanding God's promises. The Bible witnesses to the misunderstood promises of God. Chosenness, which was intended to be a responsibility for service, was understood as a privilege to hoard. From one point of view the first exile from the land was meant to shatter the people's narrow concept of God and the land. They had to learn that God existed without the land and outside of it. They needed to learn that God is concerned about other people besides themselves.[3] The exile was meant to help them mature in their understanding of God. One observes that some post-exile prophets put the emphasis on the people who are returning rather than on the land itself. Second Isaiah made the remarkable discovery that the promise of God to the people after the exile was not about land and nationhood, but about the outpouring of God's Spirit on the people.

> For I shall pour out water
>   on the thirsty soil
> and streams on the dry ground.
> I shall pour out my spirit
>   on your descendants,
> my blessing on your offspring,
> and they will spring up among the grass,
> like willows on the banks of a stream (Is 44:3-4).

If the people are going to be a light to the nations, then they have to be the carriers of that blessing, rather than hoarding it. Unfortunately, the lesson of the exile was never fully learned; the people were easily swayed by fanatics to adopt a narrow view of the land, which led to the destruction of the nation in 70 C.E. Again, the people were given another chance to learn the lessons of history and of the period extended to eighteen hundred years. We observe, sadly, that many Jews have not been willing to learn the lesson that it is wrong to put one's heart on the land. To do so is to invite disaster and another exile.

In other words, within the pages of the Old Testament itself there is a developing understanding of God and the land. There is a movement, mostly in a zigzag way, from a narrow concept of God and the land to a broader, deeper, and more inclusive concept.

2. The second point that one observes in the Old Testament regarding this whole issue of the land has to do with the exodus. In fact, the Old Testament talks about two exoduses. The first is the one that took place

when the children of Israel came out of Egypt. The second happened when the exiles returned from Babylon in the sixth century B.C.E. Most of us are very familiar with the first exodus. Its dramatic stories are very well known to many people: the plagues against the Egyptians, the dramatic escape from Egypt into Sinai, the forty years in the wilderness, the invasion of Canaan, the battle of Jericho, the command of God to annihilate all the inhabitants, and many other exciting stories people enjoy and cherish about the wonderful acts of God for his people.

Very few people know about the second exodus. It is more quiet. It is significantly less dramatic than the first. Yet some of the prophets like Jeremiah thought that it would be a greater event than the first exodus.

> So, look, the days are coming, Yahweh declares, when people will no longer say, "As Yahweh lives who brought the Israelites out of Egypt," but, "As Yahweh lives who led back and brought home the offspring of the House of Israel from the land of the north and all the countries to which he had driven them, to live on their own soil" (Jer 23:7-8).

When one compares the two exoduses, it is amazing that the first had all the negative attitudes toward the indigenous peoples who were already living in the land. Every time they are mentioned, the language is very hostile. They are supposed to be displaced or destroyed. There is no room for them in the land among the chosen people of God to whom the land was promised. The second is totally different. One gets the feeling that the returning exiles reflected greater realism. They were much more accepting of the people around them. In fact, one of the greatest passages that comes to us after the exile is from the prophet Ezekiel, who was speaking the word of the Lord to the people:

> You must distribute this country among yourselves, among the tribes of Israel. You must distribute it as a heritage for yourselves and the aliens settled among you who have fathered children among you, since you must treat them as citizens of Israel. They must draw lots for their heritage with you, among the tribes of Israel. You will give the alien his heritage in the tribe where he has settled—declares the Lord Yahweh (Ezek 47:21-23).

This is an amazing change in the approach to the indigenous population. There is an amazing switch from the hostile language of Joshua. Here there is a clear indication that, after the exile, when the second exodus took place, there is a new understanding of the relationship to the land. There is an acceptance of the changes of history. Certain demographic changes had taken place, and the prophet pronouncing the word of God exhorts the people to accept these changes and to share the land with those who are living on it.

It is difficult to understand why Jews have not emphasized the pragmatic nature of the second exodus, and why so much emphasis has been placed on the first war-like exodus, with its violent and bloody treatment of the indigenous people. We also see that, in the twentieth century, instead of living up to the ideal and realism of the second exodus, many have tried to draw their inspiration from the first. This is, indeed, a tragedy. The "third exodus" has glossed over the second, which expresses a greater understanding of the world. It has clung to the first, which reflects a more primitive concept of God and the world.

Part of the problem, as I perceive it, has to do with the central position of the Torah in Judaism. Although the Torah has in it the seed of a broader concept of God, much of it is narrow and reflects an exclusivist understanding of God. The book of Deuteronomy, for example, has made it impossible for a good Jew to live outside the land. Yet, we know that Jews had to live outside the land during the first and second exiles. In the nineteenth century some Jews in the Reform Movement were ready to break away from the landbound faith and emphasize the prophetic and ethical demands of the Jewish faith. Unfortunately, these have been swamped by Zionism. The tragedy is that there is very little use of the great prophetic material and its insistence on God's demand for justice. The tragedy today is that both the Jewish and Christian fundamentalists have received their inspiration from the vocabulary of the first return to the land, rather than from the spirit of the second return. The first saw the indigenous inhabitants as wicked people who should be slaughtered and displaced. The second saw them realistically as people who should share the land. The returning exiles, in fact, were happy to accept a very small territory between Bethel and Hebron.

3. Any student of the New Testament is struck by the observation that the New Testament as a whole is not preoccupied with the issue of the land as was the Old Testament. Some scholars have suggested that in the process of writing the gospels there was a tendency to depoliticize them in order to decrease any tension between Christians and the Roman Empire. Others feel that the evangelists intentionally were de-Zionizing the tradition. There are other reasons scholars offer as they debate such phenomena. It seems to me, however, that the lack of interest in the land stems from the very nature of the gospel and its basic difference with an Orthodox Jewish outlook.

I believe that the gospels reflect genuinely and faithfully the message of Jesus. Some scholars have tried to suggest that Jesus was a revolutionary, that he was a Zealot. But I am convinced, as some scholars have argued, that Jesus who knew very well the position of the Zealots, rejected it, and consciously chose to go in another direction.[4] The third temptation in Matthew 4, which speaks about gaining authority over the kingdoms of this world by following the ways and strategy of the devil, is, I believe, the attractive message of the Zealots that Jesus considered and was confronted with but, early in his ministry, rejected. It faced him at other junctures, but he was able to resist it. It is clear, therefore, that the gospel writers, as well as other New Testament writers, have remained faithful to the basic message of Jesus. The land was of very little significance to them.

In this regard there is a difference between a New Testament view, and a later church's view of the land. In some places in the New Testament, the land, Jerusalem, and the Temple are viewed critically and negatively.[5] One way to illustrate this is by looking at the four places in Jewish life that had an ascendant order of significance: the land of Palestine, Jerusalem, the Temple, and the Holy of Holies. At Jesus' death the veil of the Temple was rent from top to bottom; that is, the way between the holy place and the Holy of Holies was now opened. The way between God and humans has been opened in Jesus Christ. Thus the Holy of Holies has lost its significance for the church. The Temple was destroyed in 70 C.E. and, in the minds of Christians, was no longer needed. Jesus himself had predicted its destruction. At one time he talked about his body as a temple, when he said, destroy this temple and in three days I will raise it up (Jn 2:19).

So, for Christians, Christ takes the place of the Temple. Paul talks of Christians as constituting the temple of God where the spirit of Christ dwells in them (1 Cor 3:16). Again, he is calling attention to the significance of people who carry the witness of God by the Spirit in their life, rather than the witness of a geographical place. Furthermore, the city of Jerusalem was also destroyed in 70 C.E. by the Romans. Jesus himself predicted its destruction and wept over it because it did not know "the things that make for peace" (Lk 19:42). The whole land of Palestine did not seem to be of great significance, because there is no more holiness in one area of the world than in another, but now there is the holiness and presence of Christ. So the New Testament message transcends the land, Jerusalem, and the Temple. The significance and holiness of place had been replaced by the significance and holiness of one person, Jesus Christ.

As one reflects further on this subject, it is important to emphasize two important points. First, the ministry of Jesus was very much preoccupied with the concept of the kingdom of God. In fact, the kingdom of God implies Jesus' radical understanding of God's relationship with the world. It is the true corrective for any misunderstanding of God's concern for one land. The kingdom of God stresses the reign of God in the hearts and minds of people, whoever and wherever they are. This is not dependent on one place or one region. It is dependent on faith. Where Christ is acknowledged as Lord, there God reigns. The concept of the kingdom of God, therefore, shatters any narrow concept of the land. I believe that Jesus' frequent use of the term, *kingdom of God*, was an intentional way to lift people's ideas and thoughts from a concentration on the land to the universality of God and of God's reign. This becomes an inclusive concept, and it fits the whole spirit and ethos of the New Testament.[6]

Second, the New Testament is concerned with the spreading of the gospel into the whole world. The narrow concept of the land has been replaced by a worldwide vision of God's concern for all people and in every country of the world. What started in the land in the birth, ministry, death, and resurrection of Christ must now be transported to every other place under the sun. The gospel must move from the vicinity of Jerusalem and reach the capital of the Roman Empire. The parameters have been expanded. The dimensions of the gospel have shattered the geographic focus on the land of Palestine. God's love for the world in Christ encompassed all people (see Jn 3:16, 1:12; Gal 3:26–29; Eph 3).

Later in the life of the church the land started again assuming greater significance. The church, after all, lives in the world. Geography is significant because of the incarnation. "The Word became flesh and dwelt among us" (Jn 1:14). Christ was born in Bethlehem. He grew up in Nazareth. He was baptized in the Jordan River. He ministered to people around the Sea of Galilee. He suffered, died, and was resurrected in Jerusalem. The church was born on Pentecost in Jerusalem. The land gradually started assuming greater significance for the church, because the church lives in history and because God in Christ had taken history very seriously. And Christians from early centuries made pilgrimage to the land, because the land hosted the Holy One. Recent studies have shown that this gradual shift in Christian attitudes to the land did not begin to take hold of Christians until after Constantine.[7]

What does all this have to do with the whole issue of the land today in the Israel-Palestine conflict?

1. Admittedly, Jews have come to understand their identity as being very much bound up with the land. Many of them today who emphasize this link from a religious understanding see no room for the Palestinians in the land. It is important to confront such groups with the challenge of a deeper investigation and study of their own Bible to discover that their own tradition has provided answers to such a dilemma by accepting sharing the land, or even the option of living away from the land and still maintaining faithfulness to God. We must encourage the more open understanding of God and the land as it is found in the Bible, rather than the more narrow and limited view.

One gets the impression today that the state of Israel denies history. It pretends that there was no history in Palestine between 135 C.E. and 1948 C.E. This is very clear when you visit the Israeli museum. Every period of Israelite history is well covered except the period between 135 and 1948, as if nothing happened in between. In Ezekiel 47 we hear the prophet say to the people, Do not deny history. There are now other people who are living on the land, and they have a right to it.

2. For Palestinian Christians the conflict over the land of Palestine is not a religiously motivated conflict. It is true that Palestinian Christians cherish and pride themselves on the fact that they live in the land where Jesus was born, died, and was resurrected. Such a historical fact has great

significance for many of them. At the same time, this is not the reason which is paramount when they defend their right to the land. For most of them the land is their *watan*, their homeland. This is the land of their birth. It is the land which God, in his wisdom, has chosen to give them as *watan*; in the same way as God has chosen to give you your own *watan*. They are fighting to maintain the God-given right to their own land. Any *watan* is a responsibility given by God to all the people of that land and country. It is not that they own their country, for in the final analysis God is really the owner as God is the owner of the whole world. But because they have been given the land, they have a responsibility before God. They would like to live in dignity as human beings on their land and as good stewards of it.

3. It seems to me that many Israeli Jews must come to accept the fact that, in order to live their religious faith, they do not have to have an exclusive political control of the whole of Palestine. In one sense, even at the height of Solomon's reign, there were certain parts of Palestine not under Israelite control.[8] Palestinians would like to assure Jews that, just as it is important to have a continued physical presence of Christian and Muslim communities in this land, it is equally important to have a continued presence of a Jewish community. But, in the same breath, we must emphasize that, in order to be living in the land and to fulfill our religious duties here, we do not need an exclusive political control over it all. The challenge before us is a challenge that would hammer out a new understanding of our relationship to the land. We can achieve a full expression of our religious life by sharing the land. Once this principle is affirmed, justice is not far off, and peace and reconciliation will become a welcomed reality.

NOTES

1. Much has been made of the words *for ever*, especially as pronounced by both fundamentalist Christians and Jews. But the Hebrew words *'ad 'olam* do not necessarily carry a literal meaning that deals with an unending duration of time. Sometimes it only applies to the length of a person's life (Deut 15:17). The words reflect a Semitic Eastern expression that contemporary Middle Eastern people still use to reflect a lengthy period of time but not an indefinite period. This is surely the meaning of the words in 1 Samuel 1:22. See Dewey M. Beegle, *Prophecy and Prediction* (Ann Arbor: Pryor Pettengill, 1978), p. 183; see also William W. Baker, *Theft of a Nation* (West Monrow, La.: Jireh Publications, 1982), pp. 84-86.

2. Naim S. Ateek, *Justice and Only Justice: A Palestinian Theology of Liberation* (Maryknoll, N.Y.: Orbis Books, 1989).

3. This point is eloquently expressed in the story of Jonah and God's concern for the people of Nineveh, that is, the Assyrians, who were one of the deadliest enemies of ancient Israel and Judah.

4. See John Yoder, *The Politics of Jesus* (Grand Rapids: Eerdmans, 1972).

5. I am heavily indebted to the excellent work of W. D. Davies, *Gospel and Land* (Berkeley: University of California Press, 1974).

6. Even the words of Jesus, "The kingdom of God is within you," reflect this

same view. People carry within them the seed of the kingdom in their faithfulness and obedience to God. It is no more the land as locus but the people.

7. See P.W.L. Walker, *Holy City Holy Places, Christian Attitudes to Jerusalem and the Holy Land in the Fourth Century* (Oxford: Clarendon Press, 1990).

8. Parts of the western coastal area were not part of Solomon's reign.

PART 4

WOMEN, FAITH, AND THE INTIFADA

16

Becoming Whole

The Challenge of the Palestinian Christian Woman

CEDAR DUAYBIS

In the Gospel According to St. Luke, chapter 2, verse 19, we read, "As for Mary, she treasured all these things and pondered them in her heart." How often have women kept their ponderings in their hearts? How often have they thought, "Well, I'm only a woman; who would want to listen to me?" As we continue in chapter 2 of Luke, we read how Mary was told that "a sword will pierce your soul." Again I stop to ponder. Faces pass before my eyes, faces of Palestinian mothers twisted with pain, pierced to their very souls.

Yes, Mary, we know very well how it feels. We know how it feels to watch your son tortured to death for refusing to give in to injustice. High indeed is the price of freedom, for while life is impossible without food and water and fresh air, it is completely undesirable without freedom and human dignity. All too often in situations of conflict, the dimension of human suffering tends to be overlooked and people talk only of procedures or statistics.

Whenever there is injustice, the heaviest burden almost inevitably falls on the shoulders of women. Palestinian women have had to bear the effects of the severest forms of repression under occupation and to make the greatest of sacrifices. They have had to keep the family together and to bear the burden of its survival, sometimes after the house has been demolished, a husband killed or injured, one or more sons imprisoned or disabled. They must carry on during extended curfews, often without water or electricity, with raids in the middle of the night, separations because of deportation, and searching from prison to prison for missing loved ones. The list goes on and on.

Perhaps the most agonizing of experiences Palestinian mothers face is to watch the dehumanizing effect of repression and prolonged deprivation on the children, to watch helplessly as they become hardened and radicalized or lose their faith. While other kids are spending their time in sports and hobbies, our children are withering away in prison.

Growing up has its problems in the best of circumstances. But, with the added intolerable practices of occupation, it becomes a desperate struggle for both children and parents. Added to all this, faith, instead of being a source of strength and consolidation, becomes a liability; rather than providing answers to our problems, it seems to be their cause. One of the main reasons for what has happened has been justified on religious grounds.

In our Palestinian Christian experience, the church did not provide answers to this problem, and church services became a time of estrangement rather than a homecoming. My children used to tell me: "We know that the nature of our problem is unlike any other, but surely Christianity must have answers for unique problems too. Or should we suspend our relationship with God until our problem is solved? Could God also consider us non-people whose very existence in our land seems to be the problem?"

As a Palestinian Christian woman, the conflict rages not only around me but also inside me, a frightening conflict between myself the Palestinian, myself the Christian, and myself the woman. How do I stand truly and actively as a Palestinian, without in any way compromising my faith? How do I bring up my children to resist the cruelest of occupations without sacrificing their humanity, for this is what qualifies them, in the first place, for a dignified life of freedom and statehood? How do I, as a woman, assert my personhood and my human right to participate fully and actively, alongside the "chosen sex," inside the church, his "promised land"?

I say "inside the church" for in public life the Palestinian woman has taken long strides and has left her mark since the beginning of the present century, although there is still a long way to go. Furthermore, the Intifada has brought about a stronger solidarity among Palestinian women. It has uncovered talents and abilities that had lain dormant. It has also emphasized the ability of women of different faiths to recognize common values and to get together in fruitful efforts to realize the rightful aspiration of their people.

There are special roadblocks in the way of our faith for Palestinians. The Old Testament has become out of bounds for us, for therein—we thought—lies the source of our misery. Many Christians have found a solution in liberation from theology, but fortunately others have discovered the liberating power of true theology. They discovered the liberating power of Christ who, by living in our midst, gave us a model for life. He revealed to us what it means to be truly alive. He came that we may have life in all its fullness, something we cannot achieve when others around us are denied life.

He showed us that being fully alive means being fully involved. It means struggling with the oppressed for justice and freedom. It means sharing the suffering and joy of our neighbor. It means serving, rather than being served. It means carrying the cross of the persecuted and, with them, anticipating resurrection. For the church to carry his mission faithfully, it has to be fully alive. For a Christian it becomes a duty, an obligation, and not just a matter of choice, to stand for justice.

But too often the church has put itself under "church arrest" and its faith under curfew. Many of its pastoral fields became closed military zones with signs that said "Beware—Politics." It lags behind and fails to take the initiative. It reacts rather than acts. However, women, who, until recently, were the Third World of the church—clergymen and laymen being the first two—today are also discovering the liberating power Jesus has for them.

The story of Jesus and the Samaritan woman has always fascinated me, especially after living for fourteen years in Nablus, a town in the heart of the West Bank, located on the site of Jacob's well where the gospel story took place. We were an Anglican pastor's family. Every time I entered our church, St. Philip's, I read above the altar that verse, imparted to the woman of Samaria during that brief, yet so rich encounter Jesus had with her: "God is spirit, and they that worship Him must worship Him in spirit and in truth." Nothing short of a complete change in attitude satisfied him. It was not so-called holy places he cared for. It was people and their attitude toward God and each other that concerned him, for when that is correct, everything else falls into place.

Our time in Nablus was a very challenging one. It was there that I learned what it was like to feel my knees turn to water at the sound of Israeli soldiers' boots on our doorstep, or my mouth go dry as they searched the house for I never knew what. It was there that the term *tongue-tied* became real, and I thought my 12-year-old daughter would never speak again. It was there that we saw our teen-age son completely broken, unable to take any more, and seeking release from life. It was there that I stood shivering alongside my neighbor, as she first laid eyes on the bullet-ridden body of her 17-year-old daughter, and I tried in vain to comfort her.

It was in Nablus that we, as a family, wrestled with our faith. We tried to pull ourselves through and help others along the way. All this and much, much more happened before the Intifada. I suppose some people would call it child's play compared to what they have been through since the Intifada began. I said at the onset that there was a conflict raging inside me between the Palestinian, the Christian, and the woman. But, through the mediation of the gospel, my peace process had begun. The tripartite meeting took place; peace and harmony won, and a Palestinian Christian woman became one whole person.

17

God Hears the Cry of My People

NORA KORT

How blessed are the poor in spirit:
the kingdom of Heaven is theirs.
Blessed are the gentle:
they shall have the earth as inheritance.
Blessed are those who mourn:
they shall be comforted.
Blessed are those who hunger and thirst for uprightness:
they shall have their fill (Mt 5:3-6).

Since December 9, 1987, the Occupied Territories have been gripped by an intense Palestinian uprising against twenty years of Israeli occupation, suppression, and subjugation. The Israeli attempt to crush the "Intifada" uprising has been savage and brutal. It has been carried out by means that are in blatant violation of basic human rights and of the Geneva Convention, to which Israel itself is a signatory.

The first two years of the Uprising, up until December 31, 1989, have claimed 823 lives. The deaths resulted from direct official responsibility, which included killings by occupation forces/army, bodyguards, police, prison guards, and interrogators, as well as settlers and collaborators using Israeli-licensed weapons. Shooting, beating, burning, stoning, and teargas were the primary causes of deaths. Eighty thousand Palestinians have been seriously injured. A large percentage of the injured were treated anonymously in emergency rooms, private clinics, and homes for fear of arrests by the Israeli Defense Forces.

Gaza statistics alone have indicated that the number of children (15 years and below) who were shot with live ammunition, marble and square rubber bullets, reached approximately sixteen thousand, thus constituting 38 percent of the forty-two thousand wounded there. Sixty-one children were reported to have lost their lives out of 273, thus comprising 22.2 percent of the total number of deaths. Twenty-eight children and thirty-two adults have lost one or both eyes due to bullets.

In the Occupied Territories as a whole, fifty thousand Palestinians have been arrested, over one thousand of them women. There are still fourteen thousand in prisons. Many are the breadwinners of their families. Eighty-five thousand have been put under administrative detention (six months to two years) without even a trial. Approximately eighteen hundred are still in detention, many for their second, third, or fourth order, subjected to all kinds of torture, harassment, and dehumanization.

More than twelve hundred houses have been demolished, allegedly for security reasons; 130 houses have been partially or totally sealed off. The number of the displaced and dispossessed has topped 10,500. Many families have become refugees for a second time, living in tents provided by the Red Cross. On October 29, 1988, twenty-five houses were bulldozed within fifteen minutes, in the village of Keisan, a Bedouin resettlement, about eight miles southwest of Bethlehem, and 320 people were made homeless on their own land, primarily for settlements, in particular the expansion of the military settlement of Maale Amos.

The suffering of the dispossessed families there has been intense, especially in the harsh wild winter days and nights. My heart was saddened as I heard them crying out,

> Why, Yahweh, do you keep so distant,
> stay hidden in times of trouble?
> In his pride the wicked hunts down the weak. . . .
>
> He watches intently for the downtrodden,
> lurking unseen like a lion in his lair,
> lurking to pounce on the poor;
> he pounces on him and drags him off in his net.
>
> He keeps watch, crouching down low,
> the poor wretch falls into his clutches (Ps 10:1-2, 8-10).

Every day the Uprising has witnessed curfews, closures, and sieges. The number of people affected has ranged from a few thousand to several hundred thousand. The Gaza Strip has been under night curfew for most of the Uprising, and some West Bank areas had similar curfews for prolonged periods, particularly in Nablus' Old City where the poor and impoverished live. In Kabaha village in the Jenin District, fifty-five Palestinian breadwinners have been expelled to south Lebanon and their families left behind. Women, babies, and elderly people in their seventies have been deported to Jordan for not possessing identity cards.

Arise, Yahweh, in your anger,
rise up against the arrogance of my foes.
  Awake, my God,
  you demand judgment.
Let the assembly of nations gather round you;
  return above it on high! . . .
Put an end to the malice of the wicked,
  make the upright stand firm (Ps 7:6-7, 9).

My people's economy has been shattered. Israel is attempting to crush it in order to keep the Palestinian economy in total dependence. Beit Sahour has been a good example of this economic war. This town maintained nonviolent resistance to taxation, despite all the Israeli military measures. These included the unprecedented closure of the whole area for six weeks, arbitrary confiscation of furniture and machines, the arrest of shop owners, craftsmen, pharmacists, and professionals; and intense persecution of the whole community.

Economic sanctions against Palestinian products, mainly agricultural, the backbone of the economy, have been harsh. Olive and fruit trees have been uprooted—77,688 trees over the past two years have been uprooted. Intentional damage to agricultural exports, mainly citrus from Gaza, has been carried out by Israeli officials. The European Community's ambassador to Israel has criticized and protested the security checks, calling them "unacceptable."

Palestinian laborers have been laid off work by their Israeli employers when they abide by the strike days observed by their community. According to the Bank of Israel Statistics of 1989, the number of laborers has dropped from 110,000 to 32,000. Released prisoners and young activists have been given plastic identity cards that restrict their movement. The Palestinian society is confronted with the increasing number of handicapped youth and children due to injuries. Over two thousand have become permanently handicapped in the West Bank and Gaza Strip. One hundred such children are from the Gaza Strip alone.

Land confiscation has continued, both for settlement and de facto annexation. Colleges and universities have been closed since December 1987. Primary and secondary schools were reopened following fifteen months of total closure due to international outcry, yet they are still faced with continual forced closures. Collective punishment, such as cutting off water and electricity supplies, continues; inadequate social and health services are major problems in the Occupied Territories.

But, despite all of these injustices, my people continue to struggle for their right and self-determination. St. James teaches us that faith without good deeds is useless. A living and true faith enables us to hear the voice of the crucified. In the words of Jesus:

> "For I was hungry and you gave me food, I was thirsty and you gave me drink, I was a stranger and you made me welcome, lacking clothes and you clothed me, sick and you visited me, in prison and you came to see me. . . . In truth I tell you, in so far as you did this to one of the least of these brothers of mine, you did it for me" (Mt 25:35-37, 40).

As a social worker at a humanitarian relief and development agency, whose mandate is to the poor and needy, I have been working with the oppressed of my country. We help the unprotected, the dispossessed, the injured, the sick, and the handicapped in cities, villages, and refugee camps, regardless of their sex, creed, or religion. I have heard the wails of the bereaved mothers, the cries of homeless children and hungry babies, the aches of the injured. I have witnessed the strength of the imprisoned, the wounded, and those in hiding. I have been in the most affected areas of the Occupied Territories. I have witnessed the struggle of women and men who seek righteousness and justice.

I believe that God is especially close to those who are oppressed. God hears their cry and resolves to set them free (Ex 3:7-8). God is father of all but in particular father and defender of those who are oppressed and treated unjustly. This is and has been my mission and commitment, despite all the risks and dangers involved. On February 26, 1990, I was subjected to a three-hour interrogation at the civil administration in Nablus.

> Yahweh is my shepherd, I lack nothing. . . .
> He guides me in paths of saving justice
> as befits his name.
> Even were I to walk in a ravine as dark as death
> I should fear no danger, for you are at my side.
> Your staff and your crook are there to soothe me
> (Ps 23:1, 3-4).

Yet I know we must continue our struggle, despite all these hardships. God hears the cry of the oppressed, even if the world turns a deaf ear.

18

The Intifada, Nonviolence, and the Bible

JEAN ZARU

As a Christian Palestinian woman, native of the Holy Land, I have been confronted all my life with social, economic, political, and religious structures of injustice that violated my dignity and self-esteem. The church, as well as my mother, taught me not to resist, for this is not Christian and is not in favor of peace, the way they understood it. Even now, I remember very vividly that the only time my mother ever hit me and was really angry with me (as a child of eight) was when I did not listen to her and climbed the fig tree in our backyard and picked figs. She claimed this made my grandmother angry, and that I should not make her angry. I thought I had a right to the tree, to my father's and grandfather's property, just as my grandmother had. I could not understand why I could not have some of our figs. Peace for my mother meant submission and relinquishment of rights. I have come to see that this results in doing violence to ourselves and others.

The rebel in me started searching, agonizing, and asking questions. I kept asking myself, if we say there is something of God in every person, why is it often so difficult to see that presence of God in others? Why is there so much evil and suffering in our world? For many years I struggled with this Christian truth, that we are made in the image and likeness of God. I was happy to learn that the belief in the divinity seems to be part of all religions. "The kingdom of God is within you," said Jesus. "You are the temple of God," wrote St. Paul. "He who knows himself knows God," said the Prophet Mohammed, and this is echoed by many Sufis.

This recognition of our shared brotherhood and sisterhood convinced me that it must lead to the disappearance of injustice, exploitation, oppression, and everything that comes from false beliefs that justify ourselves and degrade others. So, acknowledgment of our true selves is revolutionary. It must lead to great changes and to peace. Thus, the search for peace and for the recognition of true reality are identical.

All along, as Palestinians and as women, we were told to be peaceful. This was understood to mean being passive, being nice, allowing ourselves to be walked over. The Israelis talked to us about a "peace" that was achieved by pounding the opposition into submission, a "peace" maintained by crushing protest against injustice, a "peace" for the rulers at the expense of and through the misery of the ruled.

In December 1987 our Intifada started. With it we created an atmosphere of nonviolent action—notice I say "action"—by which we hoped to resolve our problems of occupation and oppression and to promote peace. We started by affirming one another. All of us felt empowered. We had a sense of our own inner power and worth, young and old, men and women, rich and poor. This affirmation and morale building helped us to think clearly and gave us the confidence to take creative action. We started sharing feelings, information, and experiences with others, and this helped to break down the sense of isolation we had been experiencing. This was done through Al-Kuds radio, demonstrations, worship services in mosques and churches, leaflets, funerals, strikes, films, fasts, sit-ins, and many other activities in the community. We helped reveal the violence of the Israeli army, and the world realized that the power of our Intifada is moral.

This is a true revolution that has united us as a people, while the violence of the Israeli authorities has divided them and isolated them. Our Intifada is based on respect, education, nonviolent struggle, and the faith and courage of the oppressed. We are all telling each other that we can do it, that we all count, and that everyone is part of the solution to the conflict. We have overcome fear. Our self-esteem is high, and we feel optimistic and more competent, in spite of the suffering and death. The Israeli government thinks that by using more oppressive measures against us, we will give up our struggle and submit. But the Intifada has taught us not to relinquish the power to make our own decisions about how we want our lives to be. The Intifada contradicts the idea that our situation is hopeless and that we are helpless in solving it. We are not helpless, and it is not hopeless. Isn't this also the message of the resurrection?

We live daily as persons and as communities in the midst of violence. We often find ourselves willingly or unwillingly participating in social organizations that practice and embody violence. We may deliberately act in violent or nonviolent ways to promote justice. Can we say to those who have opted for violence against injustice that we would rather see you die than defend yourselves? Who will throw the first stone to condemn them? Who is morally superior? There are many Palestinians who sacrificed their lives so we may have life with dignity and freedom. Isn't this Jesus' message?

As we opt for violence or nonviolence in our revolution, we know that the liberty to choose is not always there. I believe the division between the pacifist and the non-pacifist is not an absolute one. The pacifist and the non-pacifist, both committed to the struggle for a just future, should regard one another as allies on most issues. The conflict is not between them, but between those who support the oppressive structures of the status quo and those on the side of liberation. As Christians, the gospel compels us not to support the oppressive structures. Such an alternative is not possible for us today.

One peculiar strength of nonviolence comes from the dual nature of its approach—the offering of respect and concern, on the one hand, and of defiance and stubborn noncooperation with injustice, on the other. Put into a feminist perspective, nonviolence is the merging of our uncompromising rage at patriarchy's brutal destructiveness with a refusal to adopt its ways, a refusal to give in to despair or hate. To rage against, yet refuse to destroy, is a true revolution, not just a shuffle of death-wielding power.

No matter what our situation, life presents a succession of choices between life and death. Many of these choices may be subtle, and sometimes we scarcely take notice of them. But there is always, among the range of options available, one which is suitable to our present spiritual resources and practical circumstances, one which affirms truth. The Intifada is that right path for us today.

I once visited the Jalazone refugee camp after three weeks of curfew. The people there had been punished by having their electricity cut off and their supply of gas curtailed. Women told us how determined they were to find a way to bake their own bread. They collected wood and rubbish and made a communal fire, which was kept alight by burning old shoes and rags. When the soldiers came to put the fire out and throw away the dough, the women resisted, shouting, "Go tell your leaders that no matter what you do, we will not allow our children to starve. We will find a way to bake bread, and all your efforts to destroy our spirit are not going to succeed. What God has created, no one can destroy."

I visit the refugee camps often because the YWCA has many projects there. We ask women whose houses were demolished, who have no work or security, and whose husbands, fathers, or brothers are in jail, "How do you manage?" They say such things as, "God who created us will not forget us. Sometimes we wake up in the morning to find food supplies at our doorstep. On Easter, some young people tried to share eggs with their poorer neighbors. Every house they knocked at to offer a gift of eggs referred them to a more needy person, for they said, 'Thanks be to God, we are not starving.' " Their faith challenged me and reminded me of what Jesus told us: "Your God will feed you; see how God feeds the birds and clothes the flowers; therefore, be not anxious." Jesus taught us not to worry, but to seek first and find God's kingdom and to align ourselves to its righteousness (Mt 6:25-33).

We are seeking God's kingdom, God's will where peace will prevail. Searching for this peace is often a cause for strife. Jesus himself foresaw this. "Do not think that I have come to bring peace to earth. I have not come to bring peace, but a sword!" Where can we find peace? Many people, including women, think that they can find peace by running away from the world, by doing nothing about it. The churches have become a refuge for tired folk. But this is not the message of the gospels, for God loved the world, so we should be in the world that God loved and loves. The world is full of strife, and it is our duty as Christians to bring peace. We cannot bring peace only by proclaiming it. We should work. Wherever injustice and wrong exist, we should be there to say, this is not the will of God, this should be changed. But, we cannot fulfill this duty if we are not at peace with ourselves. The saddest thing in our time is that Christians have found it so difficult to live at peace with one another, locally and internationally.

There are many Christians whose theology brings to me, as a Palestinian and a woman, strife and confusion. These Christians are part of the structures of injustice we are facing. An example of this is the phenomenon of Christian fundamentalism in the West. Many of these Western Christians give blind support to Israel. They never question what Israel is doing, because they see the Jews as the "chosen people" and Israel as a "fulfillment of prophecy." Interpretations such as these affect us directly as Palestinians.

For the last two years, our people have been bleeding. Daily we are reminded of life and death, of the crucifixion. We feel the words of Jesus, who said, "Weep for yourselves and your children" (Lk 23:27-31). We often pray as Jesus did that the bitter cup of death may be taken away. We often shout with a loud voice, God, why have you forsaken us? But, until we surrender to God as Jesus did, and until we reach that stage where we can forgive those who have offended us, we will not have peace, and we will not have liberation.

19

Women in the Intifada and in the Churches

SUAD YOUNAN

The main object of this essay is to tackle the issue of oppression from the perspective of liberation theology, and also our interpretation of the latest developments on the Palestinian scene. Its subsidiary object is to tackle the position of the churches in relation to the Palestinian oppression and also in relation to their own interior matters.

In these days we seem to be seeing the realization of the belief that all men are created equal, that they are endowed by their creator with certain inalienable rights, that among these are life, liberty, and the pursuit of happiness. The real scandal is that, for millions of women and men in this world, this goal is still very far from being achieved.

Nowadays, there has developed in the world a theology of liberation, which seeks to meet the distress of the people on the basis of the biblical message. As a Palestinian, I regard liberation theology as an essential expression of faith in the message of Christ, to liberate woman and man without discrimination of gender and race. This stems from our faith, but this faith must be transformed into practice in our daily challenges and at the grassroots level. As a Christian, I see Jesus as a unique revelation of true humanism and personhood, for he helps us to understand our personhood. His life displays characteristics of love and compassion. In him, women and men, oppressed and oppressor, are set free to work together on behalf of the liberating purpose of God.

As I see it, liberation theology stems from faith. My only concern is that it might become exclusively male, clerical, and "very academic." It should rather be a praxis that involves all God's creatures in their search for new structures and for a better living that can overcome oppression, for both the oppressor and the oppressed. It ought to be the prophetic voice of the grassroots and should perpetually speak to difficult issues, in the fashion of the Hebrew prophets, who fearlessly conveyed God's message to both leaders and people. It is an act of incorporation and interaction and a call to the Christian community at all levels, in spite of all its mistakes, to be a sign of a new humanity where new lifestyles can emerge.

Our faith ought to guide and steer our involvement in the political and social process, and not the other way around. When politics manipulate faith, there is a tendency toward partiality. Nevertheless, we, as faithful women and men, need to work together to set our society and especially our churches free for their true calling to participate in God's mission in the world, a mission of impartial justice and liberation.

Our Intifada is a cry for justice and peace and a cry for the realization and actualization of human rights. It is directed to the world to hear the cry of an oppressed nation and to the Israeli conscience to abstain from acts of oppression inflicted on our people. What we have here is a vicious circle that dehumanizes both the oppressor and the oppressed.

Our Uprising and our revolution has to be an ongoing struggle. Our gaze must be constantly focused on ways of changing the status quo and the hierarchical structure of our society. The Uprising is also a cry directed to the inner Palestinian society. The Palestinian woman is forming a new identity. How can it be achieved?

To search for a Palestinian woman's identity is neither to copy the West nor to defend the "traditional" system, which had a restricted view of her role and status and cast certain prohibitions against her active participation in society. The Uprising is characterized by its geographical and human totality. It includes the whole occupied Palestine and all the Palestinian social classes. The women, as a part of this social system, were affected by and are effective in this new reality, not only socially as a mother, sister, or wife of a detainee, martyr, or owner of a demolished house, but also as an active partner in this society, at the political, the economic, and the social levels.

The Uprising has seen an increasing women's participation in all areas, for women are taking an active role in the struggle, at home and in the street. She is no longer the secondary partner to man in the national struggle. She is working now, and effectively at all levels, at demonstrations, peaceful sit-ins, and collection of food, supplies, and clothing for areas under siege. She takes part in the medical relief actions. She resists soldiers and stands as a human barricade to free detainees. This is a source of feminist pride. Women are trying to work for justice and peace on all levels. This role should continue to serve as a prototype for the post-Intifada epoch, both for men and for the church.

When we talk about justice and peace, we should always remember that charity begins at home. The question is: Does the local Palestinian church practice justice when it comes to women?

Although Lutheran and Anglican women have entered spheres which were stereotypically male, there is still a long way to go. Nevertheless, in light of the developments in the Palestinian streets, where women are involved in the struggle for a better and more dignified life, and the quest for genuine peace based on justice, I am positive that eventually this will have an effect on her active life and full participation in church and its decision-making.

The faith of the Palestinian Christian woman propels and motivates her to seek a new lifestyle. This is a continuing process of Koinonia, based on justice and equality. This is a challenge that is posed to male church members and to our leadership and clergy. As a church, we cannot claim to be catalytic agents without attempting to change our interior system. We, women and men, ought to walk side by side, fully aware of the important changes and developments of our society.

We, Palestinian Christian women, have a prophetic role that has been perhaps overlooked by men. This role is that we can, with the grace of God, transform injustice into justice, hatred to love, and selfishness into full participation. This must include the inevitable future ordination of women, although now the mere mention of it is considered blasphemous by most of the present church leaders and clergy. If Paul were living in the Intifada, he would have said, "Let the woman talk and work without ceasing in the church for justice and peace."

I have here briefly displayed a few crucial points in a feminist perspective and from a Palestinian Christian point of view. Women and men can learn to think their way into new actions and cooperative lifestyles, if they begin with agreement on the need for basic changes. This, in my opinion, is the foundation of any solution, because it has a great potential. Basic changes have taken place in our Palestinian society following the Intifada. It has been an intentional and contractual formation of a process.

This should also take place in our churches today. We should move in the dialectic of liberation toward a new awareness and ability to act, motivated by our faith in Jesus, the liberator, and in the justice of our cause. I ask you not to misinterpret my words, because this discussion is not a personal one, but it is about action.

The gospel of liberation clearly teaches that Christ died for the many, including all classes and groups and both men and women. The building of our community can only begin with dialogue, when we take seriously the understanding of salvation and liberation and begin to deal with various obstacles to communication. We need God's help and enlightenment in this process.

PART 5

INTERNATIONAL RESPONSES TO THE QUEST FOR PALESTINIAN THEOLOGY

20

Between Jerusalem and Bethlehem

Reflections on the Western Ecumenical Dialogue

MARC H. ELLIS

Over the last few years almost every person that I have met who is involved in the ecumenical dialogue between Western Christians and Jews shares a heartfelt despair as a well-kept secret. Simply put, the secret is that the ecumenical dialogue is at an impasse because the issue at its center—unrelenting abuse of the Palestinian people at the hands of Jewish Israelis—hovers over every meeting. Typically, the Israeli-Palestinian crisis is either passed over in silence (the issue not allowed to be raised), or discussed by way of defensive maneuvers or in terms of anguish. Thus the Jewish side either answers that the criticism of Israel is an anti-Jewish argument, or laments policies of the state of Israel which liberal diaspora Jews cannot control.

Among Jewish participants, a combination of strategic responses—silence, anti-Semitism, anguish—is most often employed, while the Christian participants nod knowingly, feeling their responsibility has been met merely in raising the question itself. Sometimes when the Christians feel particularly brave or angry, they import a dissenting Jew, by definition a person unaffiliated with any major Jewish organization, to speak at a meeting. Christians then feel good about the "truth" having been spoken and promptly retreat to safer ground. Thus the coziness of career ecumenical dialogue participants reasserts itself and the discussion returns to the relatively safe terrain of whether there is one covenant or two, whether Martin Luther was a vicious or nuanced anti-Semite, or—the most current—how to organize a Holocaust remembrance or an ecumenical protest over the painting of a swastika on a local synagogue.

The problem with all of this, of course, can be stated simply, though with endless details and ramifications. And it is starkly visible travelling with Palestinians and hearing them speak their stories. First, what we are witnessing in Israel and the Occupied Territories is the culmination of a 60-year communal and now state-sponsored program of limiting or, if possible, ending the presence of Palestinians and Palestinian culture in Israel and Palestine. That is, we are witnessing today the final stages of what we can only call ethnocide.

This has been done historically and is being done today through the combination of terror, for example, the slaying of seven Palestinians and wounding of ten others by a former Israeli soldier on May 20, 1990; and systematic "legal" extension of Jewish sovereignty into occupied Palestine, which is illustrated by the Knesset approval of new appropriations for roads and Jewish settlements in the West Bank and Gaza the day after the massacre, even as dozens more Palestinians were being killed and almost one thousand wounded.

Of course, a major theme of the conference was the reality of ethnocide and how it affects Palestinians in the choices before them: to be forcibly transferred out of the remaining and greatly diminished area of Palestine, to voluntarily join the ever-growing Palestinian diaspora, or to accept a subservient place in a completely Jewish-dominated reality. But as I listened to the Palestinians discuss their plight, I also realized how these policies affect Jewish Israelis and Jews around the world. On the one hand it threatens to make definitive what Palestinians have claimed all along: that Jews have come to Palestine as conquerors. At the same time it reinforces the Arab view that the expansion of Israeli power is relentless and unlikely to stop even at all of Palestine, thus renewing traditional Arab fears of a Western, colonial, expansionist power in their midst. Finally, and here the Western ecumenical dialogue again reappears, the end of indigenous Palestinian culture in Israel and Palestine means the end of any meaningful Jewish claims vis-à-vis Jewish suffering and the end of the Jewish tradition as communicated in these dialogues: as a small, suffering, ethically-oriented people in a hostile world.

Rest assured, however, that little or none of this analysis will be injected into this special sphere where the maintenance of "victim status" and innocence in history is the foundational element of the Jewish-Christian dialogue and virtually the only reason Jews participate in it. Jews will not inject these elements precisely because those who would speak of ethnocide and Jewish crimes would hardly be chosen to represent the Jewish interests of victimization and innocence. Western Christians will not speak in these terms, at least not consistently or forcefully, because for the most part they entered the dialogue out of a spirit of repentance for Christian sins vis-à-vis the Jewish people and a desire to include those who were too often placed outside religious and human discourse. Those Christians who realize, even dimly, that the relationship of Jews and Christians has changed dramatically rarely know how to speak of the present reality. They are literally without a framework, theological or otherwise, to analyze, let alone articulate the end of Jewish innocence. What does the ecumenical dialogue look like if Christians no longer oppress Jews and if Jews actually oppress Palestinians? Where does the ecumenical discussion move if Jews are not powerless but rather are powerful and too often use that power to subjugate another people?

The other reality, the physical and cultural destruction of the Palestinians, is hardly recognized as important in and of itself, independent of how Jews and Christians feel about one another. The dialogue is frozen in historic mirror images: both Jews and Christians are seen as emerging from the Holocaust, hence Christian complicity, Jewish innocence. In this framework the Palestinian people do not exist historically or in the present; they may be a side issue, perhaps, but are not accorded a central role in the dialogue.

There are, as it develops, unhealthy and unholy ties of dependence between Jews and Western Christians in these institutional dialogues. Too often the dialogue participants see their jobs as representing their respective community positions and doctrines, outlining and, if need be, defending the "integrity" of each faith community. Much time is spent ingratiating themselves to one another, reassuring each of their own personal integrity in the quest to move beyond a bloody history. And of course there is the prestige that comes from meeting with the higher-ups of each community, of being personally involved in fulfilling a demanding mandate and occasionally being treated to an expensive dinner. Thus the dissenter, Jewish or Christian, is seen as an interloper in a prearranged dialogue, as a person who threatens a mutually agreed upon status. The dissenter may even be perceived as one who threatens to move the dialogue to a ground where the major participants of today are peripheral tomorrow, hence the end of a career.

So while everyone knows that the ecumenical dialogue is over, few if any act on that knowledge. The price of their intransigence is high. We might say that the ecumenical dialogue as we know it today helps legitimate, by omission or commission, the end of indigenous Palestinian culture in Israel and Palestine, not to mention the torture and death which accompanies Palestinians in their demise. This, then, is the ecumenical dialogue—culpability in ethnocide—and it includes such august bodies as the National and World Councils of Churches, despite their protests to the contrary. With this knowledge the ecumenical dialogue takes on a criminal aspect and those who continue it become liable in criminal activity. If this sounds too strong, perhaps one can suggest a better term for those who help legitimate the displacement of a people and the destruction of its culture? Certainly Jews have had little hesitation in defining this activity when it relates to their own community.

But if we can be critical of Jewish participants in the ecumenical dialogue, what are the questions confronting their Christian partners? As I listened to Palestinian Christians, here are some questions they seemed to pose to their Western coreligionists. Are Christians—especially those within the ecumenical dialogue—serious? Are they willing to risk criticism, accusations, a breach in friendships, even the loss of a place at the ecumenical dialogue? Are they willing to risk their own prestige, comfort, and peace of mind for Jews and Palestinians? Or are they content with the conspiracy of silence?

Many of the Christians involved with Jewish-Christian dialogue whom I meet are careerists, with all the limitations and risks attendant to that status. Too many of them are ignorant of what is occurring in Israel and Occupied Palestine and prefer that ignorance to avoid conflict with Jews and with their own perception of themselves and their achievements over the years. Thus a conspiracy of silence is joined by a conscious ignorance. Too many of these Christians are what may be called "free floaters," travelling around the world to reconcile others but with few, if any, commitments at all. I am amazed how many Christian ecumenists I meet on the issue of Israel and Palestine who, when the surface is scratched, seem to have little affection or even regard for either Jews or Palestinians.

So upon reflection on my visit with Palestinians, I state without hesitation and without equivocation: the ecumenical dialogue as presently constituted joins the conspiracy of silence and ignorance with a conspiracy of lies, lies that lead to the torture and death of the Palestinian people. Like most Jewish theology, the dialogue is complicit in the dispersion and humiliation of the Palestinian people. Thus it follows: if you care about Jews, about Palestinians, about Christian complicity, *end the ecumenical dialogue before it is too late.*

We must end the ecumenical dialogue now and begin moving toward a Jewish-Christian solidarity that has a new and unexpected foundation: a mutual repentance, a confession of transgressions by both Christians and Jews toward each other and against others. We as Jews and Christians are not innocent. There must be a mutual repentance and confession for playing out our eschatological dreams of redemption on others. For what Christians and Jews thought was redemptive for themselves, the reign of Christ over all humanity or the greater land of Israel, is for others an unredeemable catastrophe. The point here is for Jews and Christians to move beyond innocence and redemption into a shared humility, which also gives rise to a new honesty and renewed possibility.

This is an immensely difficult task for Jews and Christians to own up to the fact—and publicly at that—that the traditions we cherish are beautiful *and* bloody, especially when our status and identity are bound up with the certainty of our innocence.

Yet those who are suffering, those who have lived on the other side of the gospel and those who live on the other side of Israeli power, call us to a way of life beyond victimization and oppression, beyond innocence and redemption, to a shared life on a shared land. This, perhaps, is the message that Judaism and Christianity began with and that contemporary ecumenical solidarity might once again approach. Could it be that Palestinian Christians, indeed the Palestinian people, hold out this possibility for a Jewish and Christian future beyond innocence and redemption if we will only listen?

21

People, Power, and Pages

Issues in Ethical Interpretation

MARY H. SCHERTZ

As a New Testament scholar and biblical theologian, I am also a feminist. The primary importance the consultation on "Theology and the Israel-Palestine Conflict" has for my work is a renewed sense of urgency for the tasks of ethical interpretation. Because of my travel in Israel and Palestine, I am newly aware how important it is that those who interpret sacred texts from a liberation perspective work diligently and cooperatively to understand the dynamics of how those texts are used to empower or undermine groups of people. One specific issue, the use of the Bible as a source for feminist and Palestinian theologies, seems a point of entry into the larger discussion of ethical reading. Thus I will first compare two interpreters—one feminist, one Palestinian—and explore the implications of that comparison for the issues of liberation hermeneutics (or ethical reading).[1]

A COMMON DILEMMA

I think that the dilemma of the Palestinian Christians and the dilemma of Western feminist Christians have at least one aspect in common. Both dilemmas raise the critical question of whether and how the text of the church is useful. Is the text life-giving or life-draining? Is the text so problematic in relation to women and those who are not "chosen" that it has lost not only its authority as sacred text but also its relevance for the theological and social problems that constitute the modern context of the faith?

For feminists, the negativity of the text (both the Hebrew Bible and the Second Testament) toward women leads to the conclusion that the text is thoroughly patriarchal. The question is: If patriarchy is death-dealing to women, can a patriarchal text be liberating for them?[2]

For Palestinians, the Hebrew Bible notion of the chosen people has become problematic since the Israeli invasion of Palestine. The question is: Can a text partial to ancient Israel be life-giving for Palestinians who are being oppressed by modern Israelis?

Two representatives of people working on these dilemmas from within them resolve the issue of the text along lines that have some similarities as well as some differences. Both Elisabeth Schüssler-Fiorenza, a North American feminist theologian, and Naim Stifan Ateek, a Palestinian liberation theologian, take highly critical attitudes toward the texts while essentially retaining them as a source for theology and, in some ways, authoritative for modern life and thought.

Schüssler-Fiorenza contends that both the Hebrew biblical texts and the early Christian sources are texts which are thoroughly androcentric. As such, these texts do not reflect historical reality but "theological interpretations, argumentations, projections, and selections rooted in a patriarchal culture."[3] Given that circumstance, however, Schüssler-Fiorenza chooses not to address the question of the "authority" of the text directly. Instead, she says, the question of "theological legitimacy" might be better bracketed until "women can come into focus as historical agents and victims and until biblical history can be restored to women."[4] She then proceeds to analyze the New Testament texts in order to uncover and disclose the reality of women's experience in the early Christian movement as it is reflected dimly and covertly in the patriarchal texts.

In the end, Schüssler-Fiorenza does not explicitly return to the question of theological legitimacy; she implies that the answer to her bracketed question is at least a tentative yes. Thus she argues "that only in and through a critical evaluative process of feminist hermeneutics can Scripture be used as a resource in the liberation struggle of women and other 'subordinated' people."[5] That conclusion implies that *if* a feminist hermeneutic such as she describes *is* applied, then the Testaments can provide a "resource" for liberation. It is true that the term *resource* does not give large quarter to the authority of the biblical text. It is also clear, as she continues to summarize her case, that the biblical theme of the *ekklesia* of women is not only a concept that Schüssler-Fiorenza finds personally compelling but one that she feels should be taken seriously by the entire church. She says that "the gospel is not a matter of the individual soul; it is the communal proclamation of the life-giving power of Spirit-Sophia and of God's vision of an alternative community and world."[6] In other words, this concept she has uncovered or disclosed in the text claimed as the church's scripture has power and authority for the church which claims the text.[7]

In his book, *Justice and Only Justice: A Palestinian Theology of Liberation*, Naim Ateek moves in directions somewhat similar to Schüssler-Fiorenza's, even though the issues are discrete. He contends that if the primary issue for Palestinian Christians is political, then a second issue for them is the issue of the Bible. He says that while for most liberation theologians the Bible has been seen as "a dynamic source for their understanding of liberation," for Palestinians the establishment of the state of Israel has changed dramatically the connotations and mental associations of some biblical words and images.[8] He notes that since the creation of the state of Israel "many previously hidden problems" have arisen. "The God of the Bible, hitherto the God who saves and liberates, has come to be viewed by Palestinians as partial and discriminating. Before the creation of the Israeli state, the Old Testament was considered to be an essential part of Christian Scripture, pointing and witnessing to Jesus. Since the creation of the State, some Jewish and Christian interpreters have read the Old Testament largely as a Zionist text to such an extent that it has become almost repugnant to Palestinian Christians."[9]

Yet, as with Schüssler-Fiorenza, acknowledging the difficulty the text presents to a certain segment of its readership does not lead Ateek to reject the text as a whole. In fact, he expends a great deal of energy trying to preserve the significance of the text. He asks: "How can the Bible, which has apparently become a part of the problem in the Arab-Israeli conflict, become a part of its solution? How can the Bible, which has been used to bring a curse to the national aspirations of a whole people, again offer them a blessing? How can the Bible, through which many have been led to salvation, be itself saved and redeemed?"[10]

It is clear from the nature of these questions that part of Ateek's agenda is salvaging the text not only out of a sense of reverence and respect for the sacred text of the church but because he wants it to be useful for the present conflict. He wants it not only to survive the challenge of the Israeli-Palestinian conflict but also to become a vital and practical contributor to the solution of the problem.

Ateek works toward this goal by positing Jesus as a hermeneutical key. The person of Jesus offers evidence that the biblical concept of God has "matured through the period of biblical history."[11] He says:

> To understand God, therefore, the Palestinian Christian, like every other Christian, begins with Christ and goes backward to the Old Testament and forward to the New Testament and beyond them. This becomes the major premise for the Christian.
>
> Due to the human predicament of evil, however, one discovers that the use of this hermeneutic does not mean that all of our theological problems are solved automatically; but one can discover that the new hermeneutic (which after all is not new at all in the Church) is really liberating. The Bible for Palestinian Christians, thence, can be retained in its entirety, while its contents would be judged by this hermeneutic and scrutinized by the mind of Christ.[12]

Thus it would appear that from very different experiences, North American Christian feminists and Palestinian Christians share a common dilemma in that the texts held as sacred by the church are not always salvific in a practical way. As the work of Schüssler-Fiorenza and Ateek indicates, sometimes parts of these texts have to be rejected or dealt with in a specific hermeneutical move in order for the people reading them to experience the grace of God revealed in them as a whole. Despite the fact that Schüssler-Fiorenza favors a historical reconstruction and Ateek a theological reconstruction, both in the end turn to the figure of Jesus as the key to an egalitarian morality that unlocks scripture and makes it available to an ethical reading in the present situation of the oppression of the text's readers. In so doing, Schüssler-Fiorenza and Ateek both participate in a larger effort to preserve the text hermeneutically in a way that maintains a relevancy for the oppressed and offers a critique for the oppressor.

A FURTHER QUESTION

While I find both these interpreters genuinely helpful, on one level of the issue of what constitutes an ethical reading of the Bible, there is a second level of the issue with which neither deals directly enough. Schüssler-Fiorenza and Ateek convince me that there are ways of reading the Bible that are not harmful and are also helpful to women and Palestinians. But they both stop short of asking the more critical question of why oppressed people do and even should continue to read and live by a text that can and has been used against them. This second level question is perhaps more clearly focused in an article entitled "Feminist Uses of Biblical Materials" by Katharine Doob Sakenfeld. After outlining the various ways that feminists are working redemptively with biblical materials, Sakenfeld concludes that "no feminist use of biblical material is finally immune to the risk of finding the Bible hurtful, unhelpful, not revealing of God, and not worth the effort to come to grips with it. Regardless of approach, feminists may find that the Bible seems to drive them away from itself (and sometimes from God), rather than drawing them closer."[13] As previously stated, while Schüssler-Fiorenza alludes to this question, she deliberately postpones it and returns to it only implicitly. Likewise, perhaps because he can remember a time when "the name 'Israel' did not signify . . . any existing state on the face of the globe,"[14] Ateek also does not deal directly with the question of the helpfulness or hurtfulness of the Bible for oppressed people. He seems to accept the validity of the Bible and a biblical approach to a Palestinian theology of liberation as a given without carefully articulating the rationale for those decisions.

As threatening as this second level of questioning may be to theologians and lay persons of faith alike, it is one that an ethical reading cannot avoid. We cannot claim to have seriously heard the stories of women whose battering has been justified in the name of Christian submission or the stories of Palestinians whose oppression has been justified in the name of Jewish conquest unless we are willing to face this question honestly. I would contend that a straightforward appraisal of this issue can neither be postponed nor ignored. It is one of the most crucial questions of the age—presenting a profound challenge to the vitality of our faith. It is a question apart from which we can neither answer the concerns of our time nor think theologically about the struggles and suffering present in our world nor read the Bible ethically.

WHAT THE QUESTION DEMANDS

What pursuing this question of ethical reading to the heart of the matter entails is pushing the practice of liberation hermeneutics one step further. I would suggest that the familiar consensus surrounding the prejudicial positing of liberation as the highest value is only half the truth. Liberation may indeed be the most treasured value of the liberation theologian but rarely is it held purely, without tension in relation to other values.[15]

Liberation theologians have pioneered in pointing out the underlying investments of the status quo theology as well as straightforwardly claiming their own prejudices on behalf of the oppressed. This work on the exploration of the relationship between the investments of the interpreter and the outcomes of interpretation has been good, but perhaps we have not been rigorous enough. While we have been careful to explicate our primary commitments, we have for the most part been more covert about our secondary and tertiary commitments. A more rigorous investigation must include not only the usual political considerations but also go beyond them to explore other religious and cultural investments as well. As liberation theologians we must begin to lay before our readers our own denominational affiliations, social and economic class situations, educational status, and so forth. An ethical reading may well demand that our self-disclosure go beyond a celebration of liberation and an opposition to oppression to include other issues of social and religious location. In fact, the hermeneutics of suspicion must be applied both self-critically and toward other theologies from the "underside" in addition to applying it to dominant theologies. As liberation theologians, we must ask ourselves and each other what it is that we are holding in tension with the freedom and well-being of the people we represent.

For instance, Schüssler-Fiorenza and Ateek are both concerned with the liberation of their people *and something else*. Perhaps for Schüssler-Fiorenza it is the preservation of the church—a church chastened by feminist understanding but the church nevertheless. Perhaps for Ateek it is the biblical faith as it has been lived, historically and geographically, in Palestine over the years. But whatever these additional values are, the point is that each holds the quality of liberation as a human value in tension with other human values and that tension colors the theological outcome.

There are, of course, some risks to this further process. The introduction of additional sets of variables contains the possibility of further factionalization. For example, in the arena of feminist interpretation, we would need to look more seriously at the differences between Catholic and Protestant women's experiences. We would also need to look more seriously at the differences between women's experiences in mainline Protestant, evangelical, and historic peace churches. These additional complexities can be threatening in movements where solidarity is all too often both fragile and politically essential. These complexities can also be threatening to coalition and cooperation among different groups who are all too often forced to compete with each other for attention from an impatient and frequently uncaring majority. So the risks are great.

As great as the risks are, however, moving forward with a second level of self-disclosure and a deeper level of grappling with the issues of ethical reading or liberation hermeneutics is crucial. After returning from Occupied Palestine and thinking about what the struggle there means for my work as a New Testament scholar and theologian, I am more convinced than ever that oppressed groups of people must struggle in solidarity with other oppressed groups of people. Those of us whose piece of that solidarity entails thinking through biblical issues are, I think, called to renewed effort to think more rigorously about the issues of people, power, and sacred books. There are two things at stake. The first is the ethical foundations of our interpretations. The second is the contributions those readings make toward solidarity in the larger task of bringing the suffering of oppression to an end.

NOTES

1. Obviously, I am making several sweeping assumptions that cannot be adequately explicated or defended in this setting. I am assuming, for instance, that: 1) reading the Bible is a political and social act; 2) reading the Bible in a way that justifies oppression is unethical and immoral; 3) reading the Bible is a complex activity which cannot finally be located absolutely in either the text or the reader but only in an interaction between the content of the text and what the reader brings to the text.

2. That patriarchy is "death-dealing" for women is a common feminist assumption. Often the charge is leveled somewhat metaphorically—since women do not receive the same advantages as men in a patriarchal society, they do not thrive as well as their more privileged brothers. But sometimes the charge is leveled literally. Sonia Johnson, for instance, makes the point that more women have been murdered by men in the past three years than persons have died of AIDS in the same time—although AIDS has gotten far more attention by the press and the public. Sonia Johnson, *Wildfire: Igniting the She/Volution* (Albuquerque, New Mexico: Wildfire Books, 1990), p. 189.

3. Elisabeth Schüssler-Fiorenza, *In Memory of Her: A Feminist Theological Reconstruction of Christian Origins* (New York: Crossroad, 1983), p. 60.

4. Ibid. p. 27.

5. Ibid. p. 343.

6. Ibid. p. 344.

7. In this essay I am addressing the issue of authority in more nearly a classical Gadamerian sense than an evangelical sense. The question for feminist liberation theologians as I understand it is not the question of extrinsic or intrinsic authority but the very question of relevancy itself. Is this text one to which women freeing themselves from patriarchy ought to attend?

8. Naim S. Ateek, *Justice and Only Justice: A Palestinian Theology of Liberation* (Maryknoll, N.Y.: Orbis Books, 1989), p. 75.

9. Ibid. p. 77.

10. Ibid.

11. Ibid. p. 81.

12. Ibid. p. 80.

13. Katharine Doob Sakenfeld, "Feminist Uses of Biblical Material," in *Feminist Interpretation of the Bible*, ed. by Letty M. Russell (Philadelphia: Westminster Press, 1985), p. 64.

14. Ateek, p. 76.

15. At this point, I am using the term *prejudicial* in the positive, Gadamerian sense.

22

Western Christianity and Zionism

ROSEMARY RADFORD RUETHER

One of the most shocking and puzzling phenomena for Middle Eastern Christians is the behavior of Western Christians toward them. Far from showing concern about the sufferings of Palestinian Christians, as part of the Palestinian people, Western Christians ignore them, as if they don't exist. They rush to Israel to see ancient sites of the Hebrew and Christian Bible, but seem oblivious to the "living stones" of those descendants of ancient Christians in the Holy Land. Even worse, they add their own biblical and theological arguments to support the Zionist takeover of the land of the Palestinians and the oppression or expulsion of the Palestinian people.

What is the basis of this behavior of Western Christians? In this essay I try to show the roots of this type of Christian Zionism, which reads the Israeli-Palestinian conflict from the context of a Western set of agendas that have little roots or meaning for Palestinian Christians or Arab people generally. Although, as Naim Ateek has said, a Palestinian liberation theology has arisen, and has been forced to arise, to answer these types of religious claims from Jews and Western Christians,[1] I believe that it is particularly the responsibility of Western Christians and Jews to speak critically to their own communities about this misuse of theology to justify injustice. In this essay I examine and deconstruct these patterns of Christian Zionism which have been used to ignore and disregard Palestinian human and political rights and to justify occupation.

Support for Zionism and for the state of Israel have deep roots in Western Christianity. Patristic and Medieval Christianity had adhered to a myth of divine punishment of the Jews that included their exile and wandering outside the ancient homeland.[2] But Reformation Christianity, particularly Reformed or Calvinist Christianity, developed theological beliefs in a restoration of the Jews to their homeland. These ties of Reformed Christianity to the idea of the restoration of the Jews to Palestine were based on three major premises.

First, evangelical Christians nationalized the Christian idea of itself as the New Israel. This developed a new affinity for the Jews as representatives of the Old Israel. The English and the Americans, particularly, thought of their people and land as the new Israel and the new Zion. They came to think of the Jews less as a superseded or negated people, and more as a parallel people, a sibling people, with whom they had a special relationship. Reformed Christians discarded the Catholic saints as their religious ancestors and identified instead with the ancient Hebrews as their religious forebears. The Jews were thought of as the contemporary descendants of those ancient Hebrews.

Secondly, the mandate for restoration of the Jews to Palestine was part of a revised Protestant eschatology. Protestant Christians believed that the promises to the Jews in the Hebrew Scripture must be fulfilled as a precondition for the return of Christ and the final redemption of the world. So, restoration of the Jews to Palestine became an integral part of a new Christian eschatology, particularly among pre-millennialist evangelical Christians.

Finally, restoration of the Jews rests on a literalistic belief in Palestine as a land promised exclusively to the Jews by God, whether or not they are present in it. This idea of the promised land had been spiritualized and universalized in Patristic and Catholic Christianity. It became a symbol of the whole cosmos or of heaven. But Protestant Christianity abandoned classical allegorical hermeneutics for literal, historical interpretation of the Bible. This reinforced a new particularism of peoplehood and land, both for Christian identity and also in relation to the Jews and the biblical idea of the promised land.[3]

These ideas of the Jews' restoration were revived in the evangelical and pre-millennialist revivals in England and America in the second half of the nineteenth century. Both British and American evangelicals promoted ideas of Jewish restoration to Palestine. Ironically enough, these ideas were very much resisted by the Jewish community in both countries in this period. They were particularly resisted by Reform Jews, who had put aside the Jewish laws that had tied Jews to a separate communal way of life and were seeking integration and equal citizenship in a secular pluralistic definition of nationalism. Reform Jews suspected that Christian enthusiasm for Jewish restoration in the 1890s was tied to a desire to divert the flow of Jews from Russia to Western Europe and America. In this period hundreds of thousands of poor Jews were fleeing from the pogroms in Eastern Europe to the West. Reform Jews suspected, not without reason, that Christian restorationism was a cover for deportation of the Jews.[4]

This history of Christian restorationism is an essential part of the background for understanding the affinity with Zionism among both British and American Christians that has tied first the British and then the Americans to support for Israel. By pointing to these religious ties of Christians to Zionism, I do not deny that the chief reason for British and American support for Israel is that of colonialist self-interest. Israel has been seen, first, as a British-identified and then an American-identified state that supports the interests of these nations in the Middle East and the world. But the religious ties have been used to cover up this colonialist self-interest and to build strong emotional and symbolic identification between the two Western nations and Israel.

In this paper I will address four key religious arguments that are still operative in linking Christians in America to Israel. Three of these arguments are versions of the arguments I have already mentioned. The fourth argument has arisen from more recent European history, namely, the Nazi Holocaust.

The first and most important of the arguments that appeal for Christian support of Israel is the literalistic belief that God promised this land to the Jews in an eternal and exclusive sense. This belief in divine donation was not as important for earlier Western secular Zionists who were themselves either atheists or non-observant Jews. They appealed to the special relationship of the Jews to this area primarily as a part of Jewish ethnic, historical identity. But the religious form of the claim grew much more important after the 1967 war, with the growth of fundamentalist Jewish religious Zionism. For example, in a 1988 publication of the Friends of Zion, *Hashivah* or *Return*, it is stated that criticism of Israel in the recent uprising of the Palestinians stems from a loss of faith in the biblical promises, specifically among Christians.

> It is hardly surprising in a world where the majority of people reject the biblical promises of Israel's restoration and return to all the land given by God to Abraham and his seed through Isaac and Jacob. It is a pity that so-called Christian nations, influenced by centuries of Replacement Theology, frequently deny Israel's right to the ancient lands.[5]

A second appeal of religious Zionists to Christians is the belief that Jewish restoration to Palestine is part of a messianic or redemptive scenario. The Christian millennialist form of this redemptive scenario is different from that of Jewish fundamentalism. For Christian millennialists, the Jews' restoration is a precondition for the predestined conversion of 144,000 Jews to Christianity and the outbreak of Armageddon, which will kill all unconverted Jews, as well as other enemies of God, such as Arabs and Communists. Obviously these ideas of Jewish conversion and destruction are unacceptable to all Jews.

Nevertheless, Zionism, both of the official governmental variety and some sectors of religious Zionism, has made a marriage of convenience in recent years with Christian millennialist evangelicals. They see such evangelicals as staunch supporters of Israel, including its claims to an expanded territory in "Judea and Samaria." They seek either to detach, or else to ignore, these ties of immediate support to the long-range eschatological scenario of Jewish conversion, destruction of the unconverted Jews, and the world reign of Christ.[6]

However, belief that the founding of the state of Israel is a fulfillment of biblical prophecy is not simply a tenet of a relatively small group of pre-millennialist evangelicals. In a more general way, and not particularly tied to this pre-millennialist scenario, this belief is widely held among American Christians. A 1987 study showed that 57 percent of American Protestants and 37 percent of American Catholics agreed with this proposition.[7]

A third religious argument used to tie Christians to Zionism is the claim that Zionism is an essential part of Judaism. It is said that Judaism, unlike Christianity, has always been a communal religion, a religion in which Jewish nationalism is integral to its religious self-understanding. Therefore, to deny the right of the Jews to be a nation is to reject an essential part of Judaism. Anti-Zionism is, by its very nature, anti-Judaism.

A fourth and particularly potent argument for Christian support of Israel has to do with evocation of Christian guilt for the Holocaust. Christian anti-Semitism is seen as providing the foundation and milieu in which the Nazi Holocaust was possible. Israel is claimed to be essential to protection of Jews today from "another Holocaust." It is implied that without not only Israel as a state but also a state that is absolutely secure against all enemies, Jews are vulnerable to a new Holocaust, which might break out at any time. It is implied that if Christians are truly repentant of their guilt for the Holocaust, the only way to show this is by total and unflagging support for the state of Israel, including everything which the present government of that state claims as necessary for its "national security."

Appeal to the Holocaust threads through all the other arguments for Christian support of Israel as well. In each case, any doubt or questioning of Israel's right to the promised land, that the founding of that state is a fulfillment of biblical prophecy and a redemptive event and that Jewish nationalism is an integral part of Judaism is immediately ascribed to Christian anti-Judaism or anti-Semitism. Thus it is suggested that if Christians doubt any of these propositions, they are still in the grip of an unreconstructed anti-Judaism. It is this very anti-Judaism which was the root of the Holocaust. To be critical of Israel is to be still unrepentantly guilty of the Holocaust.

In the second part of this essay, I wish to briefly examine each of these religious arguments. Each demands a much fuller critique, but the limits of this paper will allow only a brief outline of what questions need to be raised about each of these arguments.

GOD'S PROMISES TO ABRAHAM GIVE THE JEWS AN ETERNAL AND EXCLUSIVE RIGHT TO ALL OF PALESTINE

A Christian exclusivist nationalism, either toward their own nation or toward the Jews as a nation, is a fundamental denial of the foundational

Christian belief that God is a God of all nations, that no one nation is especially favored by God. A Christian reversion to a tribalistic, exclusivist concept of God is theologically and ethically unacceptable. Christians have often misconstrued their own notions of universalism to deny Jewish particularity and also to turn Christian universalism into a cultural imperialism of Christian peoples. Authentic universalism must avoid both a reversion of tribal ethnocentrism and also universalist imperialism. This means it must affirm a multi-particularist vision of the co-humanity of many peoples and cultures. One cannot use Jewish particularity to deny the rights of Palestinians, or the reverse. One must affirm a co-humanity of Jews and Palestinians that seeks, as far as possible, a just coexistence of both national communities.

Christians are often led to a one-sided assumption that Jews have an exclusive right to Palestine by an ignorance of the actual history of this area. This land has never been a land of one people, but a land of many peoples. Many peoples lived there before the rise of the brief moments of Hebrew political hegemony in antiquity. Many people continued to live side by side with those Hebrews, even during those brief moments of hegemony. Many peoples have come together, in continual migrations and amalgamations of peoples and cultures in this region, for the last two thousand years. These peoples became predominantly Muslim in the seventh century, with a significant Christian minority and a small Jewish minority. All three religious communities became Arabized in culture and language.

The descendants of those people are the Palestinians. Properly speaking, these were the people with primary rights to the land of Palestine in modern times. These were the people who were still the majority, representing 70 percent of the population, when the land was partitioned in 1947. Thus whatever rights are given to the present Israeli Jewish population, it can only be on the basis of a recent construction of a national community in this region, not on the basis of ancient religious land claims. These recent "facts" of history must be adjusted to make place for, at least, an *equal* claim to the land of those who were present as the majority population in the land until their forcible and unjust displacement by the Israeli military in 1948.[8]

THE FOUNDING OF ISRAEL IS THE FULFILLMENT OF PROPHECY AND THE BEGINNING OF REDEMPTION

For both Jews and Christians the idea of a messianic return to the land as part of redemption is premised on an ethical vision of what redemption means. In the Bible, and in the Jewish and Christian traditions of future historical fulfillment of redemptive hope, this means a healing of the enmity between nations. Swords are beaten into plowshares. The instruments of violence and death are transformed into the instruments of creation and cultivation of new life. Redemption is characterized by a flowering of justice and peace among nations. Both Christian and Jewish militant fundamentalisms ignore these ethical criteria for what is redemptive. This allows them to ignore the obvious fact that the foundation of Israel has not been a means of healing between nations, but of an enormous outbreak of new enmity between nations. Plowshares have been turned into swords on every side. The means of human livelihood have been starved to create the instruments of death.

The foundation of Israel has been for Palestinians what they call "the catastrophe," an unparalleled disaster which evicted 780,000 people from their homes and land in 1948. From this disaster have flowed continual disasters of more land confiscation, more evictions, repression of those still on the land, continual denials of justice, continual violence, injury, and death. Tens of thousands of Palestinians have died in this violence; also tens of thousands of Lebanese, Jordanians, Egyptians, Syrians, and other Arabs; fourteen thousand Israeli Jews have also died. The numbers of the wounded, the numbers of those whose lives have been shattered, are uncountable. In short, the founding of Israel is *not* a redemptive event. It is an event that has taken place very much within unredeemed history and as an expression of unredeemed modes of behavior between human peoples. To call an event with such results "redemptive" and the "beginning of messianic times" is a travesty of what is meant by those terms. This is false messianism, an attempt to clothe evil-producing events with the aura of divine sanctity. This is a false messianism to which Christians themselves have been all too prone in the past, clothing their own evil-producing political projects with the garb of messianic fulfillment.

This does not mean that the state of Israel is any worse than any number of other political projects of human groups today, or in the past, which have produced disastrous results for other people, and often for one's own people. It simply means that it cannot be clothed with a garb of special sanctity that obscures its actual ethical deficiencies. It is the nature of all false messianisms that the garb of redemptive hope is used to prevent truthful recognition of evil. Zionism, like many other disaster-producing revolutionary projects, is still operating with the ethics of competition and negation of others. It, and every other project of human hope, will begin to become redemptive only when it overcomes the ethics of competition and domination and begins to shape itself with the ethics of mutuality or love of neighbor as oneself.

ZIONISM OR JEWISH NATIONALISM IS INTEGRAL TO JUDAISM

The claim that Zionism, or Jewish nationalism, is integral to Judaism rests on a confusion between the communal nature of Judaism, in its classical form, and the modern concept of a nation-state. It is not accidental that when Zionism first arose, the vast majority of the leaders of all forms of Judaism rejected it as contrary to their understanding of Judaism. For Orthodox Jews, Zionism was an unholy project carried out by non-observant

Jews and thus fundamentally contradictory to their religious belief in a messianic restoration of political sovereignty over the ancient homeland. For the Orthodox, this restoration could only take place as an expression of a redemptive process. This meant both the redemption of the Jews and a complementary redemption of all nations. It meant a restoration that would heal the enmity between the nations and bring world peace. These Orthodox leaders recognized that the Zionist secular political project, in the context of modern nationalism and imperialism, did not qualify as a fulfillment of this redemptive process.[9]

Reform Jews also rejected Zionism because it denied their political universalism. They sought to detach Judaism as a religion from secular political identity and make the Jews a people who could become full and equal citizens of all nations.[10]

It is incorrect to say that Judaism is unique in having a communal dimension that seeks to shape the entire familial, social, and political life of Jews as a whole. In fact, all classical religions have sought this same comprehensive scope. Christianity, in its classical form as Christendom, also Islam and Buddhism, among others, have in their classical form sought to shape a total system that informs all public and private life as religious states. It is precisely this political side of classical religion that has made it problematic for modern states, which are ethnically and religiously pluralistic. Both liberal Christianity and Reform Judaism sought to overcome this conflict by separating religion and state.

Today Jewish, Muslim, Christian, and even Buddhist and Hindu fundamentalisms threaten the establishment of just relations among different ethnic and religious groups living in the same state by reverting to these classical claims to religio-political exclusivism. The unjust treatment of the Palestinians by the state of Israel is rooted precisely in the effort to create an ethnically and religiously exclusive state, namely, a "Jewish state." It is this concept of Israel as a Jewish state that construes the existence of a nearly 40 percent population of Palestinians in Israel and the Occupied Territories as a "demographic problem." This is a "demographic problem" only if one defines Israel as a Jewish state, rather than accepting the fact that there are two national communities and three religious communities in this region. For justice and peace to be possible in Israel/Palestine, any state or states that encompass this region must accommodate and give equal civil rights to all members within this ethnic and religious pluralism.

REPENTANCE OF GUILT FOR THE HOLOCAUST DEMANDS UNCRITICAL SUPPORT OF ISRAEL

There is no doubt that Christians of the West bear a burden of guilt for the Holocaust because of their historical traditions of anti-Semitism and the way these traditions were used by Nazism to gain both active and passive acquiescence of Christians. However, one must ask what is appropriate repentance for the Holocaust. It would seem that the primary expressions of this must be to purge anti-Semitism from Christian teachings and their effects on Christian societies. It is not appropriate to construe such repentance as collaboration with injustice to another people, who are the victims of the state of Israel. To use guilt for the Holocaust to silence criticism of injustice to the Palestinians is not repentance but toadyism, on the Christian side, and blackmail, on the Jewish side.

On both the Christian and the Jewish side, I believe there must be a separation of the question of the Holocaust, and its theological and ethical consequences for each religion, and the questions raised by the state of Israel, with its ethical deficiencies. One has to examine how these two phenomena are interrelated symbolically and psychologically. In my talks on this issue of Israel and the Palestinians, I frequently get the question from Christians, "How can Jews, with their experience of the Holocaust, turn around and become oppressors of Palestinians?" This implies that the Holocaust should have made Jews very concerned to avoid the oppression of other people.

However, some Jews have suggested a psychological link between the oppression of Palestinians and the Holocaust. One Jewish friend, who works with battered women, suggested that Israelis are like battered batterers. Like people who have been battered and abused as children, Israelis have a psychological need to batter others. Abuse of Palestinians becomes the way of "getting even" for past abuse, of turning the tables of power and powerlessness.

I think there is some truth in this psychological connection between past abuse and a special Israeli psychological need to batter Palestinians. There is a clear tendency to turn Palestinians into symbolic Nazis, but powerless ones upon whom revenge can be meted out. There is also no doubt that the Holocaust has been enormously exploited by Zionist leaders to create in all Jews, in Israel and throughout the world, a psychology of fear and insecurity. This has been used to tie Jews to Israel as the symbol of security.

Yet the promotion of Israel as the place of "security" for Jews becomes increasingly contradictory. In fact, nowhere in the last forty years have so many Jews been killed or injured as in Israel. This is not because of an incomprehensible "cosmic hate" against Jews in general, but because the state of Israel has been built in an antagonistic relationship to the Arab and Palestinian communities which generates a cycle of violence. Israel, in this sense, is not the place of Jewish security, but the source of a new stage of Jewish insecurity.

However, these psychological and symbolic connections with the Holocaust serve to confuse the real issues, for the political root of the antagonistic relation of Israel to the Palestinians does not lie in the Holocaust. It lies in the patterns of ethnic nationalism that shaped the ideology of Zionism in the 1890s-1920s, and in the pattern of British colonialism that shaped the Israeli military in the 1930s. Already in the first decades of Zionist settlement, sensitive humanist Zionists, such as Ahad Ha-Am, were making horrified criticisms of the patterns of ethnic antagonism, displacement of the Palestinian peasantry, and violence toward this displaced peasantry that characterized the Zionist settlers.[11]

In 1930, Rabbi Judah Magnes was spelling out the consequence of an ethnically exclusive idea of a Jewish state that reads like a prediction of all that has happened since.[12] It was the British in 1937 who first proposed the idea of a "transfer of population"; that is, expulsion of Palestinians, as part of a scheme of partition of the land into a Jewish state and an Arab state which was to be annexed to Jordan.[13] Already in 1937, British officer Orde Wingate was training what were to become the chief Arab-fighters of the Israeli Defense Force, such as Moshe Dayan, in the techniques of total warfare against Palestinian villagers. The Iron Fist, which Israel has used against the Palestinians, employs not only the same techniques, but rests on the same laws, constructed by the British in 1936-39 to put down the Palestinian revolt of that period.[14]

Thus Israel's violent and discriminatory behavior toward Palestinians is rooted in a history of the Jewish *Yishuv* between 1910 and 1948. Holocaust survivors may have flocked there from 1948 to 1950, but they entered a state whose historical roots in the area were largely unknown to them. They did not shape nor did they control the actual policies of that state. They, and all other Jews, have received a mythical construction of the state of Israel as the solution to the Holocaust. This has served well to cement powerful emotional bonds to Israel. But these Holocaust survivors often found themselves treated with contempt by Israelis, who called them such names as "soaps." For Israelis, these survivors were the unpleasant reminder of vulnerability and history of suffering that they sought to negate.[15]

These survivors should not be victimized once more by suggesting that it is they who originated the oppression of the Palestinians. This oppression and its racist culture have their roots in a Jewish version of a European racial nationalism and colonialism. It was Israelis shaped by this system of colonialist domination under the British Mandate who then laid hold of the symbol of the Holocaust as a tool of power. They exploited the emotions linked to symbols of past Jewish victimization to cover up and disguise the reality of colonialist patterns of racism, land confiscation, and expulsion of indigenous people.

Both Christians and Jews must recognize that power construed as domination over others creates violence, injustice, and hatred. Christians have been amply guilty of this in the past toward Jews, and also toward other peoples they have colonized, as well as toward each other. Such possibilities of power as domination are new to Jews. It is perhaps hard for them to switch rhetorical gears and recognize that they too can not only gain power, but use power unjustly. But the refusal to recognize this fact is creating increasing ethical self-delusion among Jews. Jewish religious and moral health demands a shift to a new rhetoric of self-understanding that accepts the problems of this new reality.

The dialogue and collaboration of Jews and Christians today cannot be based primarily on the innocent victim/guilty victimizer relation. It must become a collaboration and solidarity of two people who know both that they can abuse power and are seeking to help each other regain their prophetic voice toward injustice within their own and other societies. This means that both Jews and Western Christians must overcome their religious and ethnic hostility to Arabs and Muslim peoples. They must extend their embrace of solidarity to the Arab world as well, without in any way becoming sentimentally blind to parallel tendencies to violence and competitive domination in this culture as well.

In all these relations, one seeks a conversion that shifts from an ethic of competitive domination to an ethic of co-humanity that fosters a quest for mutual justice between neighbors who must live together in one land and on one earth. This quest will call forth the best of all three religious traditions, the traditions of compassion, forgiveness, and neighbor love, rather than those religious ideologies that tend to foster violence, hatred, and mutual negation.

NOTES

1. Naim Ateek, First International Symposium on Palestinian Liberation Theology, 10-17 March, 1990.
2. Rosemary Ruether, *Faith and Fratricide: The Theological Roots of Anti-Semitism* (New York: Seabury Press, 1974), pp. 144-49.
3. Regina Sharif, *Non-Jewish Zionism: Its Roots in Western History* (London: Zed Press, 1983), pp. 17-18.
4. David A. Rausch, *Zionism within Early American Fundamentalism, 1878-1918* (New York: Edwin Mellon Press, 1979), pp. 79-125.
5. *Hashivah: Friends of Zion*, vol. xi, no. 1 (Spring 1988), p. 1.
6. See Merrill Simon, *Jerry Falwell and the Jews* (Middle Village, N.Y.: Jonathan David Publishers, 1984).
7. Ronald R. Stockton, "Christian Zionism—Prophecy and Public Opinion," *Middle East Journal*, vol. 41, no. 2 (Spring 1987), p. 246.
8. See Michael Palumbo, *The Palestinian Catastrophe: The 1948 Expulsion of a People from Their Homeland* (London: Faber and Faber, 1987).
9. See Klaus Herrmann, "Politics and Divine Promise," in *Judaism or Zionism: What Difference for the Middle East?* (London: Zed Press, 1986), pp. 29-30.
10. *Reform Judaism: A Historical Perspective*, ed. Joseph Blau (New York: Ktav, 1973).
11. Ahad Ha-am, *Nationalism and the Jewish Ethic*, ed. Hans Kohn (New York: Herald Press, 1967), pp. 203-4.
12. Judah Leon Magnes, "Like all the Nations?" (1930), in *The Zionist Idea: A Historical Analysis and Reader* (Philadelphia: Jewish Publication Society of America, 1960), pp. 443-49.
13. See Palumbo, pp. 2-3.

14. See Nevill Barbour, "The Dark Path of Repression, 1937-8," and David Ben-Gurion, "Our Friend: What Wingate Did For Us," in Walid Khalidi, *From Heaven to Conquest: Readings in Zionism and the Palestine Problem Until 1948* (Washington, D.C.: Institute for Palestine Studies, 1987), pp. 335ff. and 382ff.

15. See the introduction to the book by Holocaust survivor Leon Wells, *Who Speaks for the Vanquished: American Judaism and the Holocaust* (New York: Peter Lang Press, 1987), pp. vi-vii.

23

On Chomsky, Language, and Liberation

The Need for a United States Christian Ideological Intifada

MARK CHMIEL

In May 1990 several theologians from around the world had the opportunity to meet with Palestinians from Nazareth. While having lunch with several middle-aged Palestinians, I was struck when one woman, while telling her story of travail, exclaimed, "Look at me! Do I look like a terrorist?"

No, I had to admit, she didn't look like any terrorist as characterized by a hack Hollywood scriptwriter; in fact, she appeared in bearing, dress, and articulation like many women with whom I had worked in the United States on Central American issues. But I realized that this woman knew enough about Western propaganda to believe it possible that a normal United States citizen might be unsure as to her ontological status. I supposed that this woman had friends or relatives in the Palestinian diaspora in the United States who reported back to her the stereotypes about her people that abound in the popular media of the liberal, democratic United States.

This woman's pain and incredulity, I came to see, are but the tip of an iceberg that characterizes the Palestinian people. They have gone from being human beings with human rights to convenient caricatures for paranoid American consumption.

It is in the context of this experience—of the jarring difference between label and reality—that I set down these reflections. It is my contention that the Palestinian Intifada has much to teach Christians in the United States, not only about the Palestinian struggle, but about our own. "Our own" is that of educated, relatively privileged Christians struggling against an *ide-*

ological occupation, made all the more difficult by its permeation throughout economic, political, and social segments of United States life. As the Intifada is the Palestinian "shaking off" of the Israeli occupation and recovering a dignity that has been systematically insulted and injured, so then an Intifada in the United States is required to throw off the flood of propaganda and indoctrination about the United States government's role in the Middle East, and throughout much of the world, that serves to keep our population inert, passive, and unquestioning before the powers that be.

The simple fact is that many Christians in the United States are hoodwinked and consistently have had the wool pulled over their eyes by the mutually reinforcing dictates of government and mainstream media. And the basic "truth" repeated ad nauseam is that the United States government is only motivated by the purest and most righteous of intentions and is primarily concerned with the achievement of a just international order.

In his reflections sixteen years ago on the importance of Noam Chomsky's work on the Middle East, Edward Said wrote, "One senses that Chomsky, perhaps without intending it, lifted a corner of the wall-to-wall carpet on which liberal Americans have pranced for three decades. Not only has he released Arab Palestinians from the sacrifice imposed on them by Israel: he asserts that the only solution is to take their grievances seriously. As a moral absolute above criticism, Israel is thereby nullified."[1] Indeed, Chomsky is one of the United States' leading dissident intellectuals who marshals argument and evidence in the service, not of the super-state, but of the victims of that state. Inasmuch as it has been important, as Said correctly notes, for Palestinians to see how an American Jewish intellectual articulates an argument that upholds justice for the Palestinian people, so it is equally instructive for United States Christians to attend to Chomsky's analysis of United States power and ideology, and to what it reveals about us and our moral and intellectual culture.

In this essay I introduce Chomsky's work on the ways language is used in the United States to distort the reality of the Middle East conflict; as such, Chomsky's work can be a resource for a North American ideological Intifada. Further, I suggest that the broader dimensions of Chomsky's work can provide Christians with frameworks to better understand the idolatry of the American state.

Chomsky is an internationally acclaimed and influential linguist. His numerous works on United States foreign policy have focused on the ways language is used in the American political culture. As his 1986 lectures in Managua indicate, Chomsky's primary interest and concern is United States "power and ideology."[2] Chomsky analyzes the documentary and public record and then delineates certain principles that animate United States policy. Unless one is aware of these largely invariant principles, one runs the risk of naivete, innocence, or prolonged confusion before the United States propaganda machine. Once these principles are understood, the layperson is in a much better position to ask critical questions about what is taking place in the national and international arenas.

Simply put, Chomsky argues that the main concern for the ruling elites in the United States is the promotion of and preservation of the "Fifth Freedom," namely "the freedom to rob and exploit."[3] The other freedoms once enunciated by Franklin Roosevelt as central to the American mission during the Second World War will be heralded so long as the Fifth and most important freedom is guaranteed.

A second principle, taken from the same work, is that this fundamental truth cannot be revealed to the United States population on the assumption that we would not accept such blatant immoral uses of power to serve the needs of the elite few. Chomsky's perspective on why elite groups take such pains to exercise "thought control" is worth quoting in full:

> There are two basic reasons. The first is that reality is unpleasant to face, and it is therefore more convenient, both for the planners and for the educated classes who are responsible for ideological control, to construct a world of fable and fantasy while they proceed with their necessary chores. The second is that elite groups are afraid of the population. They are afraid that people are not gangsters. They know that the people they address would not steal food from a starving child if they knew no one was looking and they could get away with it, and that they would not torture and murder in pursuit of personal gain merely on the grounds that they are too powerful to suffer retaliation for their crimes. If the people they address were to learn the truth about the actions they support or passively tolerate, they would not permit them to succeed. Therefore, we must live in a world of lies and fantasies, under the Orwellian principle that Ignorance is Strength.[4]

Chomsky has written two recent books that deal particularly with this striking principle. The first, co-authored with Edward Herman, is called *Manufacturing Consent: The Political Economy of the Mass Media.*[5] The other work is *Necessary Illusions: Thought Control in Democratic Societies.*[6] Throughout Chomsky's extensive body of work, from his essays on Vietnam to his present debunking of the New World Order, this aspect of "thought control" constitutes his most brilliant and provocative contribution to our understanding of United States political and intellectual culture.

In a social system that requires "necessary illusions" (the phrase is theologian Reinhold Niebuhr's) to pacify the people and keep them distracted from the reality of United States policy, there are often two levels of meaning to particular terms. Chomsky notes that political leaders ringingly use words like *democracy* and *freedom* on an official level for public consumption. Thus, whatever the United States does is in support of democracy because democracy is a great and moral enterprise, and we must promote such a great endeavor. But it is important to understand that these words have an operative meaning as well. Here, as above, Chomsky usually reminds his audience that we are living "in the post-Orwellian age." United States elite groups have among themselves a functional, Newspeak understanding of democracy—a system of government in other countries that we can control. That is why, on the official level, United States aid to the military government of El Salvador is said to be in promotion of the evolving democracy there, and the American citizenry can then feel justifiably proud of this noble support; on the operative level, however, the Salvadoran government *is* a budding democracy precisely and only because it does our bidding.

One of the principles that Chomsky elucidates is that the media function to limit the range of thinkable thought. This is accomplished by allowing only certain voices to be heard in the public debate on a given topic. Invariably these voices reflect a conservative-liberal tactical difference on some issues, though the underlying principles are agreed to by both parties. This, then, is known as "respectable and serious" thought or commentary. Dissident opinion on principled grounds is thus excluded a priori as unthinkable, for to gain access to the debate one must "play by the rules." Not only does this largely eliminate controversial views, it gives the illusion of a vigorous debate between the "hawks" and the "doves." To give an example from Central America: in the debate that raged on about Nicaragua in the 1980s, both liberals and conservatives in the United States agreed that Nicaragua had to be "contained" in some way, with one camp arguing for the military solution, and the other advocating a combination of diplomatic and economic pressures. Rare was the voice allowed into the mainstream press or television media that raised the issue of the illegitimacy of United States intervention in subverting the sovereignty of another country, thereby violating international law.

This United States pursuit of the freedom to rob and exploit won't be threatened as long as the system of necessary illusions to manufacture popular consent is maintained—and as long as the population asks no bothersome questions about the government's activities. Official rhetoric and the framework of thinkable thought help to ensure this.

These principles have a remarkable relevance to the conflict in the Middle East. Knowing that some words have both official and operative meanings can clarify United States aims and interests. I consider in turn three words that regularly crop up in discussions pertaining to the Arab-Israeli conflict: *rejectionist*, *terrorism*, and *the peace process.* Awareness of this manipulation of language can begin to free us from the Orwellian principle of Ignorance is Strength.

In *The Fateful Triangle* Chomsky spends the entire second chapter analyzing the options of "rejectionism" and "accommodation."[7] To begin the discussion, Chomsky adopts two principles:

> Israeli Jews and Palestinian Arabs are human beings with human rights, equal rights; more specifically, they have essentially equal rights within the territory of the former Palestine. Each group has a valid right to national self-determination in this territory. Furthermore, I will assume that the State of Israel within its pre-June 1967 borders had, and retains, whatever one regards as the valid rights of any state within the existing international system.[8]

Chomsky advises that the term *rejectionist* should refer to those who reject the legitimate claim of national self-determination of Jews or Palestinians. In United States government and mainstream media circles, however, only a selective use of *rejectionist* comes into play. That is, the meaning of *rejectionist* is anyone who denies the Jews a national right of self-determination. For Chomsky, this use is essentially racist because it excludes those who deny the Palestinians equal rights. The way the United States ideological system functions, then, is to put forth a selective definition of *rejectionism* and frame the debate in such a way that only the Palestinian Arabs can be seen as rejectionist, regardless of the facts.

Chomsky next analyzes the stands of the United States, the two major groups in Israel, Labor and Likud, and the Palestinians, in light of the international consensus for a peaceful settlement of the conflict. Those in consensus include Europe, the Soviet Union, and most non-aligned countries. The consensus was originally for a settlement "along approximately the pre-June 1967 borders, with security guarantees, recognized borders, and various devices to help assure peace and tranquility; it envisioned the gradual integration of Israel into the region while it would remain, in essence, a Western European society."[9] This is the essence of U.N. Resolution 242. Since the mid-seventies, Chomsky notes that the international consensus has been modified to include what was previously missing: that the Palestinians' right to national self-determination be recognized in the areas of the Gaza Strip and the West Bank.

Vis-à-vis the international consensus, the position of the United States is consistently rejectionist because the Palestinians' rights have always been viewed as inconsequential compared to the importance of supporting a "Greater Israel" in the region as a "strategic asset" to ensure order and stability to the benefit of United States economic and military interests. Chomsky stresses, however, that there has been an internal debate among United States elites since the early seventies, between the position associated with former Secretary of State William Rogers (accommodation along the lines of international settlement) and that of Henry Kissinger (supporting a "Greater Israel," that is, Israeli settlements in the Occupied Territories). Kissinger's position came to be accepted as the guarantor of United States interests in the region: control over the vast petroleum reserves of the Arabian peninsula. As a loyal Spartan client, Israel serves as the local policeman for United States interests against the great threat of "radical Arab nationalism" by asserting its military prowess to keep other nationalist movements in line. The message is clear: Israel is the top power in the region, and Israel represents the United States.[10]

The United States position is still further rejectionist because it rejects the right of the Palestinian people to select their own representatives in the negotiations for a peace settlement. Since the early seventies the Palestinians have made it definitively clear that the Palestine Liberation Organization (PLO) does and should represent the entire Palestinian people. Chomsky comments, "Had someone denied Jews the right to be represented in negotiations by the Zionists in 1947, we would have spoken of a resurgence of Nazism; the principles are no different in the present case. The issue is not what one thinks about the PLO or the Zionist movement, but rather basic human rights."[11] Once Israel resorted to a level of brutality to stop the Intifada that even pricked their consciences, liberals and progressives protested this policy. Chomsky considers one example of the narrowness of the political spectrum in the United States:

> In a January 26 [1988] letter to the *Times* considered so important as to merit notice in the news columns, Irving Howe, Arthur Hertzberg, Henry Rosovsky, and Michael Walzer write that Israel's "strong-arm methods . . . strengthen the hand" of the Arab and Jewish "extremists" who "reject negotiations" and refuse a political settlement, neglecting to mention that the Arab extremists include Qaddafi and the Rejection Front of the PLO, while the extremists on the other side include both major political groupings in Israel, both U.S. political parties, the major U.S. media—and, for many years, the writers of this letter.[12]

Such rejectionism plays a key role in shoring up thinkable thought in the United States.

For Chomsky, both Labor and Likud in Israel are consistently rejectionist, using various proposals to overtly or covertly deny the right of the Palestinians to govern their own life in their own land. The rationale given for Israeli rejectionism, stressed at all turns in the United States, is the need for Israel's security. Chomsky elaborates:

> This presupposed framework of discussion again reflects the profound racism of the American approach to the topic. Evidently, the indigenous population also has a "security problem"; in fact, the Palestinians have already suffered the catastrophe that Israelis justly fear. . . . It is argued that the Arabs already have 22 states, so the Palestinians have no valid claim to self-determination, no claim comparable to that of the European Jews who established the State of Israel in 1948; at a similar moral level, a fanatic anti-Semite could have argued in 1947 that there are, after all, many European states, and Palesti-

> nians of the Mosaic persuasion could settle there if they were not satisfied with minority status in an Arab region.[13]

As the debate rages on today, both the United States and Israel are thorough rejectionists. The PLO, on the other hand, has agreed to the international consensus (at least since January 1976) and has supported a two-state solution. Yet, in the mainstream press and scholarship, the Palestinians are seen as the intransigent "rejectionists" who want only to wipe out Israel.

One way this shift has been accomplished is the elaborate public relations campaign on international "terrorism." Chomsky's work on this issue begins as follows:

> St. Augustine tells the story of a pirate captured by Alexander the Great, who asked him "how he dares molest the sea." "How dare you molest the whole world?" the pirate replied: "Because I do it with a little ship only, I am called a thief; you, doing it with a great navy, are called an Emperor."[14]

In contemporary discourse *terrorism* is framed as the alleged or real hostile acts committed by the "pirates," for example, factions of the PLO, Libya, Cuba, and Nicaragua. The terrorism of the emperor, the United States, is systematically excluded from examination in the public record (for example, United States support for Salvadoran terrorism directed against its own people). And while the emperor and his clients (in this discussion, Israel) reserve the right to engage in "self-defense against future attack," no pirates are allowed a similar right. This framework cynically justifies violent United States attacks as "retaliation" (the bombing of Libya in April 1986) and elicits hysterical outrage from American pundits when a pirate, such as a rejectionist faction of the PLO, engages in small-scale terrorism. Thus the moral rectitude of the United States and Israel is safely guarded by this deception while the depravity of the Palestinians is duly noted and condemned. Israel, the world's fourth most powerful military, is portrayed as a hapless victim, while the Palestinians are seen as irrational aggressors.

Chomsky reveals the use of the "terrorism" framework in his analysis of the period before the Israeli invasion of Lebanon:

> While the PLO refrained from cross-border actions for a year prior to the Israeli invasion, the border was far from quiet, since Israeli terror continued, killing many civilians; the border was "quiet" only in the racist terms of U.S. discourse, once again. Furthermore, neither [*New York Times* correspondent David] Shipler nor his associates recall that while 29 people were killed in northern Israel from 1978,

thousands were killed by Israeli bombardments in Lebanon, barely noted here, and in no sense "retaliatory."[15]

Furthermore, Arafat has been demonized as the master terrorist, while no such denigration is laid at the feet of Menachem Begin and Yitzhak Shamir, who both perpetrated violence against innocent civilians in the 1940s, or Ariel Sharon, who presided over the "Peace for Galilee" invasion and devastation of southern Lebanon in 1982. The point here is neither to ignore nor to rationalize Palestinian violence against innocent civilians. Rather, it is to confront the ideological distortion that makes an exaggerated issue of the violence of the "pirate," certainly deplorable, while at the same time ignoring the far greater atrocities carried out by Israelis under the (U.S.) "emperor's" influence and assistance. This framework of "terrorism" throughout the 1970s and 1980s reinforced the rejectionist conviction in the United States by dehumanizing the Palestinians in toto as reckless mockers of innocent life and by obscuring the ongoing, large-scale violence Israel employs to scatter and eliminate the Palestinians.

A third example of United States disinformation about the Middle East conflict is the "peace process." Certainly everyone should support the peace process, in the official sense, supporting those policies that lead to peace. The operative definition, Chomsky asserts, is rather different:

> The term refers to whatever the U.S. government happens to be doing at the moment. It therefore follows that the U.S. government is pursuing peace, whatever the facts may be, and that its enemies stand in the way of the peace process. In respectable discourse, one will not find such a phrase as "the U.S. government is opposing the peace process." That is a logical contradiction. While it might appear unlikely that even the most sublime regime is always pursuing peace, it is true for the U.S. government—by definition. The conclusion requires no laborious inquiry into the annoying facts.[16]

As noted earlier, the United States and Israel have blocked the path to any peaceful settlement with their consistent rejectionist positions vis-à-vis the international consensus. With the Iraq war, both nations have preferred to continue the process of settlements in the West Bank which, in addition to being a flagrant violation of international law, is a chief impediment to any reasonable political settlement. Too often, both nations reject the prospect of an international conference to deal with the conflict. Both nations have resorted to violent aggression rather than diplomacy to work for peace.[17]

Chomsky refers on occasion to the United States as constituting the "Holy State." In so doing, he echoes the expression the "Holy Church," from a time in the church's history where it claimed absolute authority over the lives of believers. Obviously, in the late twentieth century the Roman

Catholic Church cannot command the unquestioning obedience that it may have previously held in past centuries. But Chomsky notes that since the dawn of the modern period, it has been the nation-state that effectively replaced the church as the supreme authority in people's lives.

In a cogent passage from *Necessary Illusions* Chomsky describes elite contempt for the popular masses by echoing Dostoyevsky's dramatic confrontation in *The Brothers Karamazov*:

> At its root, the logic is that of the Grand Inquisitor, who bitterly assailed Christ for offering people freedom and thus condemning them to misery. The Church must correct the evil work of Christ by offering the miserable mass of humanity the gift they most desire and need: absolute submission. It must "vanquish freedom" so as "to make men happy" and provide the total "community of worship" that they avidly seek. In the modern secular age, this means worship of the state religion, which in the Western democracies incorporates the doctrine of submission to the masters of public subsidy, private profit called free enterprise. The people must be kept in ignorance, reduced to jingoist incantations, for their own good. And like the Grand Inquisitor, who employs the forces of miracle, mystery, and authority "to conquer and hold captive forever the consciences of these impotent rebels for their happiness" and to deny them the freedom of choice they so fear and despise, so the "cool observers" must create the "necessary illusions" and "emotionally potent oversimplifications" that keep the ignorant and stupid masses disciplined and content.[18]

Chomsky's critique of the state brings to mind the work of psychoanalyst Erich Fromm, who argued that "idology," the systematic study of idols, is a more pressing task than theology in our contemporary world.[19] We moderns may laugh superciliously at the ancient superstitions of primitives who worshipped objects made of wood, stone, or metal. Yet Fromm cautions us against such pride when he identifies *our* idolatrous equivalents: "Honor, flag, state, mother, family, fame, production, consumption, . . . "[20] Christians can understand Chomsky's secular critique at a deeper level by utilizing it within the idological framework suggested by Fromm. The United States state *is* an idol that demands worship, obedience, and awe; it perpetuates violence around the world; and it requires massive human sacrifice in pursuit of its self-proclaimed sacred goals.

Chomsky contends that intellectuals do have a significant role to play in public life, namely, "to analyze the nature of power and oppression in our present societies."[21] One of his consistent themes is how rarely intellectuals fulfill this critical function. Many citizens and believers do not have an intellectual vocation; they are not prepared to engage in full-scale idological research. Since, as Chomsky has noted regarding the techniques the Holy State employs to keep people in line,

> Few are willing to undertake the tedious task of refuting the regular flood of lies; they have little access to the public in any event, and they can always be dismissed by the charge that they are apologists for the enemy and its actual crimes. This standard device is sometimes used consciously as a technique to preserve the crucial Right to Lie in the Service of the State; or, for the more deeply indoctrinated, it may simply be impossible to conceive of criticism of the Holy State as anything but support for its official enemies, principled criticism of the divine institution being unimaginable. In either case, the discussion shifts to the evil deeds of the official enemy and the critic can be dismissed as an apologist for these crimes, as having a "double standard," etc.: the Holy State and the Right to Lie in its service are secure.[22]

Subverting both the "Holy State" and the "secular priesthood" that support it by exposing their violence and hypocrisy, Chomsky's work illuminates the sources of much misery in El Salvador, Guatemala, Nicaragua, the West Bank and Gaza Strip, East Timor, Brazil, Vietnam, Laos, Panama, and other places in which the United States has intervened. His analysis leads us to ask: Who are we as Americans? What do we do in the world? In addition, Chomsky has given citizens tools to use in apprehending what is happening in the world, and with such knowledge, what *ought* to be our role. Christians can borrow these tools and frameworks of critical thinking in order to develop our own, home-grown idology. Such idology will be a necessary dimension of any "prophetic theology," to use the term South African Christians identified in their *Kairos Document.*

In sum, it is imperative for United States Christians to throw off naivete and indifference regarding the American state's role in the world. Serious idology, or decoding the discourse of the idolatrous Holy State, can be likened to the first steps of an Intifada to recover the precious practice of thinking for oneself and to participate in matters that affect our communal lives.

Furthermore, in confrontations with the idol, United States Christians must keep in mind the many victims of United States policies. These victims are often scapegoats, unjustly persecuted in order to provide a distraction or release from crises erupting at home. That the Palestinians have become a scapegoat, a victim that attracts unwarranted blame, is known all too well by the Palestinian women with whom we met in Nazareth. The language used in the United States to describe the Palestinians—"rejectionist," "terrorist," and "aggressor"—only underscores this scapegoat status.

As Christians whose tradition frequently engaged in the vicious scapegoating of Jews, we would do well not to repeat our sins of commission or complicity in the scapegoating of the Palestinians. To resist the idol of the Holy State is to take the side of the Palestinians in affirming their human and national rights. It is appropriate to recall literary critic Rene Girard's reflections on the Holy Spirit:

> *Parakleitos*, in Greek, is the exact equivalent of advocate or the Latin *ad-vocatus*. The Paraclete is called on behalf of the prisoner, the victim, to speak in his [sic] place and in his name, to act in his defense. Paraclete is the universal advocate, the chief defender of all innocent victims, *the destroyer of every representation of persecution*. He is truly the spirit of truth that dissipates the fog of mythology.[23]

The fog of mythology and indoctrination that surrounds America's role in the world and obscures the suffering of the Palestinians has remained thick for far too long. The work of, and in, the Spirit is before us.

NOTES

1. Edward Said, "Chomsky and the Question of Palestine," *Journal of Palestine Studies* 15 (Spring 1975), p. 94.
2. Noam Chomsky, *On Power and Ideology: The Managua Lectures* (Boston: South End Press, 1987).
3. Noam Chomsky, *Turning the Tide: U.S. Interventionism in Central America and the Struggle for Peace* (Boston: South End Press, 1985), p. 47.
4. Ibid. p. 170.
5. Edward S. Herman and Noam Chomsky, *Manufacturing Consent: The Political Economy of the Mass Media* (New York: Pantheon, 1989).
6. Noam Chomsky, *Necessary Illusions: Thought Control in Democratic Societies* (Boston: South End Press, 1990).
7. Noam Chomsky, *The Fateful Triangle: The United States, Israel and the Palestinians* (Boston: South End Press, 1983), pp. 39-88.
8. Chomsky, *The Fateful Triangle*, p. 39.
9. Ibid. p. 40.
10. For a succinct version of Chomsky's argument, see his essay, "Israel's Role in US Foreign Policy," in *Intifada: The Palestinian Uprising Against Israeli Occupation*, ed. Zachary Lockman and Joel Beinin (Boston: South End Press, 1989), pp. 253–73.
11. Noam Chomsky, "Scenes from the Uprising," *Zeta Magazine* (July-Aug. 1988), p. 18.
12. Ibid. p. 21.
13. Chomsky, *The Fateful Triangle*, p. 45.
14. Chomsky, *Pirates and Emperors*, p. 1.
15. Ibid. p. 73.
16. Noam Chomsky, "The Trollope Ploy and Middle East Diplomacy," *Zeta Magazine*, vol. 2, no. 3 (March 1989), p. 19. This essay critiques the media depiction of the PLO's alleged capitulation to U.S. demands in December 1988.
17. See particularly Chomsky's examination of the "Peace for Galilee" in *The Fateful Triangle*, chapter 5, "The Reasons for the Invasion of Lebanon."
18. Chomsky, *Necessary Illusions*, p. 18.

19. Erich Fromm, *You Shall Be As Gods: A Radical Reinterpretation of the Old Testament and Its Tradition* (New York: Fawcett Premier, 1966), p. 40.

20. Ibid.

21. Noam Chomsky, *Language and Responsibility* (New York: Pantheon, 1979), p. 80.

22. Chomsky, *Turning the Tide*, p. 78.

23. Rene Girard, *The Scapegoat* (Baltimore: Johns Hopkins University Press, 1986), p. 207.

24

Liberation Theology

Pastoral Care and the Spirituality of Violence

ARTHUR PRESSLEY

Prayer for the Children of the Intifada:

"Do not weep for me but for yourselves and your children."

Once again men and women of compassion are disturbed by the tragedy of soldiers shooting children for throwing stones. We feel the fear and frustration of these children who fight for their land in the only way they know how. We are aware of the insecurity of children who feel the future holds no promise for them and share their helpless rage at life. Tell us the meaning, dear God, of soldiers shooting children for throwing stones.

O God, we would ask for your deliverance, but we do not know how. We offer our predicament and that of our children to your love, with the hope that you will not turn your back on our pain. We wait for the peace that only you can give, O God, our mother, our father.

"How do I explain—to my wife, my children, my friends—that I loved war as much as anything before or since?"[1]

INTRODUCTION

There is much about the Israel-Palestinian conflict that is difficult for most outside this situation to understand. Since the beginning of the Intifada approximately one-third of the eighty thousand victims have been children. Initially, it seems unimaginable that so much violence would be directed toward children. What also feels strange is that after a time we are accustomed to the statistics and are less disturbed by the stories of shooting children. We would like to believe that during civil and international strife violence would be directed toward military personnel or adults, as much as possible. This would be more "civilized."

As the strife continues, we simply accept the shooting of children and innocent persons as a natural consequence of war and, to some degree, of life in general. If we can understand the way we are transformed by hearing the reports of violence we may understand the spirituality of violence. This is important, for without this perspective we will create theological and religious belief systems that support violent behavior. Although it may be difficult for those of us living outside the Middle East to completely understand the conflict there, we are able to have some insights by understanding our own culture of violence. Conversely, we can better understand the meaning of our violence as we struggle to understand the nature of violence in other places.

Thus I feel it important to explore the meaning, the spiritual quest of violence from the perspectives of liberation theology and pastoral care. One of the conclusions I have reached is that there are forms of spirituality that are only available through violence, and that much of our pastoral care and liberation theology supports this form of spirituality. History is replete with interpersonal and social acts of violence, but its connection with religious striving and meaning is seldom acknowledged.

Kenneth Clark once described black inner-city adolescents as seeking their salvation in defiant, aggressive and, in the end, self-destructive behavior.[2] Initially I thought Clark was merely being poetic, describing these youth as seeking "salvation" in aggressive behavior. After considering this statement in light of biblical injunctions to kill every living thing to possess the "promised land" for God, and the ritual reenactment of a brutal killing considered to signify ultimate meaning, I am forced to rethink the meaning of Clark's statement. More recently, I came across Robert Jay Lifton's book *The Broken Connection*, in which he agrees with Becker that violence may become a way of transcending one's finitude. Lifton argues that "violence cannot be understood without including its close relationship to symbolization of immediate or ultimate vitality."[3] The question of the meaning of violence is poignant, because most attempts to change or redirect violence of any type fail. Perhaps Ronald Goetz is correct in suggesting that we, too, quickly romanticize the soteriological necessity of the cross in the New Testament gospels.[4]

Violence has been a constant reality of black life in America. The history of African-Americans includes periods when a black man, woman, or child was lynched every three and one-half days. African-Americans have heard the story of children bombed in churches as they sat in Sunday School classes and of the shooting of a 66-year-old grandmother and children for their tennis shoes. The interchangeable nature of victims is characteristic of violence in the United States, in the Middle East, and elsewhere in the world.

Violence against African-Americans has not been limited to acts by whites, but includes blacks committing acts of violence against other blacks. Overt acts of violence, in combination with institutional and social policies that diminish the quality of life, have created a culture of violence that must be clearly understood if it is to be changed. We must ask questions about the nature of violence from a psychosocial and political perspective; for example, What are the structures and processes which encourage violent behavior? We must also inquire about the spiritual striving that gives substance and meaning to this sickness.

Violence must be understood from the perspective of liberation theology and pastoral care if the various levels of its meaning are to be uncovered. The question must be asked in this way: Is there a unity of meaning, a form of spirituality, and a way of coming before the face of God, sought through violence, that is different from other paths of spirituality? If so, does this form of spirituality have an appeal that is lacking in other pathways of spiritual direction?

The essence of violence is the destruction of human beings. This includes not only killing, but creating conditions that destroy or diminish human dignity, happiness, and the capacity to fulfill basic material needs.[5] An interesting characteristic of violence is that both the person who commits the act and the victims of such acts endeavor to find ways to avoid confronting its destructive effects. Loyd Delany reports that when the bodies of three civil rights workers—Chaney, Goodman, and Schwerner—were being sought, other bodies were found in the Mississippi and Pearl Rivers. After the bodies of the civil rights workers were found there was no investigation about the other deaths and the dragging of the rivers ceased.[6]

Delany appeared shocked at the lack of concern about the identities of the other dead persons or the circumstances surrounding their death. What was equally puzzling to him was the indifference, the sense that these murders were just a normal part of life, part of what whites do to blacks and blacks do to other blacks. The apparent indifference to the day-to-day violence of our culture must lead us to conclude that people feel powerless in the face of chronic problems. Yet, we also ask if violence has deep spiritual meaning to those directly affected, and even to those who only hear the stories. Perhaps both are true, given that most people feel a mild excitement as the death toll climbs during a tragedy, or as we watched television during the bombing of Iraq.

LIBERATION THEOLOGY

Liberation theology in the United States and elsewhere develops in situations where people are subjected to some form of socially legitimated violence. The violence is usually a combination of physical, emotional, and social aggression which dehumanizes the person victimized and the persons inflicting the injury. Liberation theology also flourishes in a context where people of faith feel their condition has not been responded to by the majority of the religious community. In addition, there are feelings that conventional interpretations of the gospel are unable to sustain meaning or advocate for significant change. A more significant problem is that traditional theological interpretations do not speak to the condition of oppressed people who feel separated and alienated from their culture. This is of paramount concern, since the gospel is communicated through culture as well as through religious experience and ritual.

A Negro spiritual concludes with the line, "True to our God, true to our native land." The relationship to the divine and the place where people are connected geographically and emotionally are central issues for those attempting to locate who they are. The identity of a people is related to its community, which is both physical and emotional space. The Palestinian asks a pastor, "How can I know myself in another land? How can I find myself if I am not in my village?" It is reminiscent of the question about being able to sing the Lord's song in a strange land. Thus the way in which people feel they control themselves, and how they feel they control physical space, is related to how they experience the divine.[7]

Vincent Harding describes the spirituality of African-American religious traditions as one of wrestling with angels. Wrestling with angels is the attempt to discover meaning and purpose in life, despite suffering that diminishes the quality of life. To wrestle with the meaning of life is to confront the creator of life. Liberating theology has attempted to understand the nature of divine activity in a context characterized by emotional and physical violence. This theological reflection by Africans in diaspora in America has had several different emphases during the past three centuries as they have sought to understand the violence inflicted upon them. An important part of this question is why God brought Africans to this land to experience these hardships.

Beginning in the 1700s black churches in America attempted to meet the spiritual and social needs of their members by organizing to support each other in sickness and for the benefit of widows and fatherless children. Immediately after slavery was ended the concern of the black church was to understand the consequences and effects of slavery and to encourage blacks not to give whites further reason to oppress them. There was a growing belief among blacks that self-reliance in economic, political, religious, and intellectual life was necessary if freedom and equality were to be secured.[8]

Liberation theology has also been formed in response to the corporate and cultural identity of African-Americans. It has given meaning to the community's suffering, and it has indicated direction for change. Within the United States this has meant understanding the identity of black Americans in terms of persistent African traits, in spite of the degradation of those traits by the larger society. This context becomes a source of stress as the community acknowledges itself as marginally African and marginally American. Acknowledging its African heritage also has served to bond this people with a larger community both as a source of ethical norms and as a way of avoiding a sense of isolation, which is an aspect of oppression.

The identification of social and political struggles with the spiritual quest is most evident in religious services of the oppressed. Robert Williams argued that within black religion, as expressed in its African and Afro-American forms, worship as ritual is almost always associated with moral conflict and social problems. Through black religion, worship, ritual, drama, and the power of the divinity are correlated.[9]

James Cone describes the theological process within the black church as seeking to define its existence in light of God's activity in the world.[10] Liberation theology is not only concerned with correcting social and political injustices, but also with viewing these in relationship to salvation. Cornell West defined salvation as a divine gift and the center of any acceptable social vision. The understanding of salvation requires an accountability of institutions and leaders to their peoples. This assumes that covenantal communities created to struggle for liberation must reflect the values that they seek to instill in the larger society.[11] Salvation as an internal experience must be expressed in social systems that reflect the ethical norms of justice. The questions that arise are whether liberation theology has focused too much on the external experience, and if so, what is the meaning of such a focus for sustaining corporate and individual forms of violence.

Liberation theology has sought to understand the activity of God on the assumption that the oppressed are a chosen people. The assumption is that if God is fundamentally oriented toward justice, and the oppressed have not received justice, it must follow that God has their condition as a primary concern. A concept of justice that implies a just God and a just universe might lead to the unconscious belief or assumption that the poor are wicked and unworthy, and that they are receiving what they deserve. Possibly the only other conclusion to be reached from the assumption that God is just and works in history would be that the people of God need to rise up and defeat their enemies and make the kingdom of God a reality. The latter view may be one of the few options available, if there is little recognition of redemption and renewal for one's self or one's enemies in the theological discourse about the nature of God.

In general, what attention has been given to describing the nature of God within liberation theology has focused on the power and authority of God and seldom on the wonder and mystery of God. The God of Exodus is committed to justice and to controlling everything from our going to sleep at night to our early morning rising. It follows that if the external environment reflects symbols of justice and love, the internal experience of individuals will eventually mirror this change. The problem with this approach is that it reinforces assumptions that the interior and exterior worlds of individuals are separate. This assumption can lead to the belief that only a strong external force can break down the wall that separates these two aspects of being, thereby making violence a necessity.

The experience of God cannot be totally transcendent or rest completely on objective criteria. This statement is not intended to deny the need for external validation of the internal experience of God. What is suggested is that the emphasis on the power and justice of God may reflect a strong dependence on finding physical evidence of the workings of the divine. There must be some confirmation of God in the internal experience of the individual, and the individual must be able to perceive the activity of God in social history.

The problem with depending too heavily on external validation of the working of God is that it reinforces a dichotomy between the internal and external environments. How an individual experiences the world depends as much on internal experiences as on the world perceived by the senses. The paradox is that the external experience of God must find validation in the individual's cultural context, although this is never a one-to-one correlation.

A major problem of oppression and racism is the dichotomy created between the internal experiences of the oppressed and the experience of the external environment. This universal problem keeps all human beings hidden from themselves and from others. This problem is exacerbated in situations of oppression. Ernest Becker states that by the time we grow up we are masters at dissimulation, at the cultivation of a self the world cannot probe. "As human beings we relate to people only with our exteriors, physically and externally. Individuals tend to interact with each other only in terms of their exterior selves, yet each has a rich interior life that needs and seeks expression in the external environment."[12] Becker claims that we become hopelessly lost trying to communicate our insides to others.

We are created as social beings who live very much alone within ourselves. The universal problem that we share is the desire and fear of being known. In *Jesus and the Disinherited* Howard Thurman argues that keeping what is inside hidden is one of the survival strategies that the oppressed have had to learn. He also points out that this keeps us hidden from ourselves, our families, and from knowing God. Religion must provide language that connects the interior and exterior of our being.[13]

Historically, pastoral care has focused on the care of individuals and the exploration of their inner world. It has sought to assist individuals to discover meaning in their life during suffering, situational or developmental crises, and to understand their relationship with God and with others. The assumption of pastoral care has been that as individuals understand their personal experiences, they will better understand the activity of the divine in the world. This process often begins with the questions of suffering and theodicy.

The weakness of pastoral care is that it has chosen to attend primarily to individual crises of faith and intimacy. For the most part, pastoral care as a discipline has maintained the assumption that, if the individuals were emotionally integrated, they could withstand and overcome external crisis. Thus it has consistently ignored significant social problems, such as institutional violence and racism, and in so doing has given insufficient attention to understanding social structures and process. One of the major issues unaddressed by both pastoral care and liberation theology is the meaning of violence for both individuals and communities. Frequently the consequence, effects, and strategies for confronting violence are addressed, but its meaning is not explored.

VIOLENCE AND TRANSFORMATION

In cross-cultural studies of the concept of the self, a universal theme is the need for transformation. There is the desire for individuals and their community to undergo radical change to become their ideal. This assumes that natural developmental processes are never enough by themselves to achieve their ultimate state of being. Thus strategies for change, such as rituals, sacrifice, extreme discipline, or meditation, are created to move them toward their divinely appointed goals.

This assumes that some aspect of human or social existence somehow hides or diminishes the true spiritual self. A special event or additional energy, often intense and communal, is necessary to complete the journey toward the ideal state of being. Violence is an age-old response to this human predicament. The act of violence is and can be transforming and give meaning and direction to both the persons who act this out as well as to their victims. Studies of soldiers from World War II and Vietnam demonstrate how these individuals went through predictable phases as their individual coping systems were altered during the process of the war. During this transformation many claimed to have felt more alive, to have experienced themselves as part of a community, and to have a purpose in life. They felt they had clarity about the nature of the world and how to resolve problems accordingly.[14]

Victims and bystanders are also transformed by acts of violence. Literature in the fields of domestic violence and of other forms of violence describes a process in which the perception of the self and the social world is altered. Violence is a transforming experience, intense and unique. It both makes persons aware of their own finitude and gives the fantasy of having defeated this threat to being. It gives assurance that the individual has confronted the ultimate threat to existence and has survived.

The victims deny the need for adequately defending themselves and their families against the violence, and survival takes on ultimate meaning. The victims begin to see themselves as part of a vast community of sufferers, with unbroken historical continuity, which will move into eternity. Those who act out the violence also see themselves as connected to the long tradition of the righteous warrior, willing to fight and suffer for the good. Both victims and aggressors see themselves involved in divine activity. They are doing the work of the God of the Old and New Testaments, defeating the evil that threatens to consume the good.[15]

Those who act out their aggression against others feel that they live in a violent and meaningless world and that their acts are a method of transcending this meaningless and chaotic situation and granting them some sense of identity. The process of killing denies the absurdity of life and at the same time takes the absurdity of the situation to its logical conclusion. This allows the person to transcend the situation. The violence gives the individual a reason for existence and renders the death and suffering of others meaningful. It gives a sense of providing moral order to the individual's universe. The violent person has little awareness of anything other than the harm that has been done to him or her by others and the harm he or she might inflict upon others, the hated adversary. The act of killing defines the evil of the enemy and evokes the necessity of one's actions and one's relationship to what is virtuous.[16]

The act of violence is reinforced by recalling earlier moments of being attacked by others. The actors must be able to see themselves as victims. Every act of violence is seen as anticipatory defense or an appropriate act of revenge.[17] The act of violence also makes sin and its effect a concrete reality that can be eliminated. The existing belief is that if the work of God is to stamp out evil, then we must do that work as God's chosen representatives on the earth.

The process of spiritual formation is difficult for most individuals. Many who begin this type of pilgrimage typically report several experiences which may cause them great emotional discomfort. These difficult experiences include passivity or waiting for the movement of the other toward them. The passivity of waiting on the divine frequently causes people to feel that nothing is happening. They may also feel out of control of their life. What becomes even more difficult for those seeking spiritual transformation are the feelings of emptiness and of being submerged in an oceanic void where they lose their identity. Another problem with traditional forms of spirituality is that persons cannot point to anything concrete which has happened or that they know that was not previously known. All they can claim is that they have met the divine.[18]

People who act out violence do not have these feelings of passivity. They own the initiation. Since they have done the work of God, they have earned their salvation. The intensity of their activity, the virtue of their cause, clearly define who they are in relationship to ultimate issues. Many individuals and communities define their identity by understanding themselves as over and against the enemy. Their acts of violence and killing not only define the enemy, but also evoke the necessity and ideology of their response. Therefore, the spirituality of violence may aid them to avoid the oceanic feeling of other forms of spirituality. The intensity of their activity, besides defining them against another, maintains their identity and separation from others. Individuals who are victims of violence are transformed by the constant state of terror, and they too have special claims before God.

SUMMARY

The violence of the Israeli-Palestinian conflict presents an enormous challenge for theologies of liberation. Liberation theology typically views situations of oppression in terms of victims and victimizers. This situation is one wherein both sides have suffered for centuries and presently fear annihilation. The Israelis have experienced years of persecution, the Holocaust in Europe during World War II, numerous wars with Middle Eastern neighbors, and acts of terrorism. There is ample evidence that the Jewish Israeli population has been transformed by this violence. It has been frequently noted that many of the acts of violence and terrorism directed toward the Palestinians parallel the Jewish experience in Nazi Germany.

The Palestinians have suffered the destruction of hundreds of villages, deportations, prolonged curfews, school closings, and the confiscation of land which had belonged to families for decades. About one-fourth of the population has been imprisoned since the beginning of the Intifada, and live with daily intimidation and harassment from Israeli soldiers. The physical, economic, and institutional violence suffered by the Palestinian population is staggering. There is evidence that this population is also being transformed by the enormity of the violence it has suffered and has begun to define its social and cultural identity in relationship to its enemies. It has been demonstrated in this chapter that this process not only gives meaning to their suffering but also becomes a form of spiritual striving.

The violence against Palestinian children and the interchangeable nature of victims in this conflict suggest a form of spirituality that must be understood if it is to be changed. Ed Wimberly argues that a major problem in contemporary society is that cultural symbols that once provided meaning and spiritual transformation collapse and are no longer able to communicate purpose. Therefore, individuals and communities withdraw from traditional symbols and seek new avenues of renewal and self-discovery. As more and more cultural symbols collapse, violence becomes a viable alternative to spiritual fulfillment. The attraction of violence is bolstered by theological and religious systems that support a dichotomy between internal and external existence. If religious communities are to be more effective in resolving situations such as the Palestinian-Israeli conflict, attention must be given to the spiritual striving and desire for transformation which always accompany conditions of political and economic oppression.

Religious experience must never devalue the work of God in this life or the need for individual growth and transformation. Gustavo Gutiérrez describes the interaction of the internal and external realms of existence as pointing to the qualitative nature of salvation. Salvation and personal integration are always tied to social freedom and justice. The black church has always understood itself as examining the relationship of liberation to salvation. The struggle of the black church in America has been to create external validation of the internal experience of God and a sense of dignity of worth for its members. In order for individuals to experience themselves as having meaning and purpose, there must be some validation of this in the external environment. This does not imply that the experience of the holy and the self must find complete validation in the surrounding environment, but individuals cannot withstand radical inconsistency between these two experiences.

Thus the capacity to experience oneself as loved or part of the community cannot be maintained if persons are lynched, deprived of basic human needs, or are forced to watch their loved ones and community abused. What is needed are ways of understanding social change and conflict that are consistent with a personal relationship with God. The gospel speaks about the unity of all human life—economic, political, and spiritual. It is my hope that the struggle of the African-American church to create a unity of experience may shed some insight for the Palestinian Christians as they struggle for liberation and meaning.

NOTES

1. William Broyles, "Why Men Love War," *Esquire* (November 1984), p. 55.

2. Kenneth Clark, *Dark Ghetto* (New York: Harper and Row, 1965), p. 13.

3. Robert Jay Lifton, *The Broken Connection* (New York: Basic Books, 1983), p. 161.

4. Ronald Goetz, "God's Plan to Kill Jesus," *The Christian Century* (11 April 1990), p. 363.

5. Ervin Staub, *The Roots of Evil* (New York: Cambridge University Press, 1989), p. 25.

6. Loyd Delany, "The Other Bodies in the River," in *Black Psychology* (San Francisco: Harper & Row, 1980), pp. 376-83.

7. David Augsburger, *Pastoral Counseling Across Cultures* (Philadelphia: Westminster Press, 1986), p. 82.

8. Sterling Stuckey, *The Ideological Origins of Black Nationalism* (Boston: Beacon Press, 1972), pp. 1-30.

9. Robert C. Williams, "Existence and Ritual in Howard Thurman's Vision of Spirituality." This essay was delivered at the second Howard Thurman Consultation at the Garrett-Evangelical Theological Seminary, 22-24 April 1985.

10. James Cone, *A Black Theology of Liberation* (Maryknoll, N.Y.: Orbis Books, 1986), pp. 1-20.

11. Cornell West, *Prophesy Deliverance* (Philadelphia: Westminster Press, 1982), pp. 15-19.

12. Ernest Becker, *The Birth and Death of Meaning* (Bellevue, Wash.: The Free Press, 1962), pp. 27-31.

13. Howard Thurman, *Jesus and the Disinherited* (Richmond, Ind.: Friends United Press, 1981), pp. 20-26.

14. Joel Osler Brende and Erwin Parson, "War: Its Effect on Identity," *Vietnam Veteran* (New York: Plenum Press, 1985), pp. 85-102.

15. Staub, pp. 31-32.

16. Lifton, p. 148.

17. Ibid. pp. 149-53.

18. Howard Thurman, *Disciplines of the Spirit* (Richmond, Ind.: Friends United Press, 1963), pp. 13-26.

25

"The Stones of My Country Are Holy"

A Feminist Theological Reflection on the Intifada

MARY E. HUNT

Women have been involved from the beginning in the development of a Palestinian Christian theology of liberation. Women's concerns have not been tacked on at the end, but are a constitutive part at the outset of the theologizing. This is instructive for all who do liberation theology. We have learned from past omissions how important it is to integrate so-called women's concerns into the liberation process from the beginning because this guarantees women's enthusiastic, capable, and essential participation.

A Palestinian folk song captures the current mood of contemporary Palestinians: "The stones of my country are holy." Young people are losing their lives and limbs in the Intifada, the uprising of Palestinians against their Israeli occupiers. The young people throw stones at well-armed Israeli soldiers and pay a dear price for their liberation.

Yet Palestinians still sing and dance; Palestinians study despite closed universities; and Palestinians dream, confident that one day the stones will give way to land, land to peace, and peace to a new era of history. This is the context in which a Palestinian Christian theology of liberation is being created.

It is a serious effort to confront the meaning of faith, God, and politics in a setting where no established categories fit. Traditional notions of Christian theology are inadequate to construct a world view in which such suffering makes sense. Even the vaunted concepts of liberation theologies, so useful in making social change in Latin America, are cruelly lacking in this context. Promised land, chosen people, and exodus make a mockery of the

Palestinian experience insofar as even their liberation definitions leave aside the role of the vanquished.

As in so many settings, one looks to the women for hope since they who have had so little role in creating the chaos usually find creative ways to survive. This is a setting where traditional female customs are, of necessity, passing away. Dowries are an unaffordable if dubious luxury; large weddings are a thing of the past since such parties are more than most families can handle. Survival is paramount, but family continues to be central. What will replace traditional ways is not clear, but that life goes on in the interim is the remarkable reality.

Women in Black and other Jewish and Palestinian peace groups (many led by women) take a realistic if tough approach to the problems at hand. As a feminist who borders on pacifism, I look to them for insight as I despair of the violence, all of it, as a means for solving problems. At least they keep the conversation going between those who live in what Lois Kirkwood calls "structural enemyhood," that which keeps Israeli Jew from Palestinian Christian. It is an improvement over the stalemated political situation in which each attempt at forming a government seems even more ill-fated than the last. While my own inclination is to repudiate the violence, even the stone throwing, I try to listen without such judgment, trusting that these women too would have it be otherwise if there were any options.

My brief encounter in Israel and Palestine reminded me all too poignantly of living in Argentina under the military dictatorship. The same fear and mistrust, the same shadowy lines between friend and foe, the same murky details with no one assuming responsibility for the dead and disappeared kept occurring. Of course there are deep differences, but the point is that where a certain content to liberation theology works in one setting—oppressed people as the chosen people of God, for example—it is completely inappropriate, not to say unhelpful, in the other.

I began to look for new content, starting with women's experience because I have come to trust that out of the praxis of liberation, in this case out of the need for survival, will come the most adequate theology. I look beyond the presentations and writings of professionals to the daily life of people where the deepest values and richest meaning are lived out.

Hospitality is the hallmark of the Palestinian households I visited. Although war rages, if in some places beneath the surface, hospitality reigns. Food and drink are proffered in abundance. Strangers are made to feel welcome, children are accorded the priority that their dependence demands. Some human dimensions are unaltered by the political landscape, unchanged by the demands of power.

This provides a modicum of hope that a two-state solution might emerge from the same peoples who understand their common needs for land, work, and dignity. Christian women tell of life with their Jewish neighbors, their common concern for their children. Hatred is hard to harbor in the face of children. It is not a naive hope, that one day the political posturing will end and hospitality will win out.

Art continues to play a central role in the cultural life of Palestinians. The stunning tapestries and weavings that adorn homes attest to a human concern for beauty and self-expression, essential parts of any culture. Palestinians are in the process of not only losing their land but their history and culture as well.

It is striking that cooperatives women have founded include traditional handcrafts along with the making of everyday clothes. Displaying the traditional costumes of the various regions, sewing, and weaving the designs that have passed from generation to generation are ways of insisting that what has been lost can be reclaimed, that the spirit of a culture will not be extinguished just because the borders of a country have been erased from the maps.

This persistence cues me to the tenacity of a people whose collective pride and ancestral strength will not be snuffed out. Any political solution must take this human factor into account, honoring the integrity of a people whose preoccupation with the aesthetic reflects a love for the land, a reverence for the past.

Reluctance to use violence characterizes virtually all of the women's conversations on the Intifada. This does not mean that they do not support the efforts, led mostly by young people, to express the collective frustration of decades of occupation. What it means is that they encourage the movement with deep reluctance, aware that other women's children are the targets of their children's wrath.

This reluctance is not to be confused with cowardice or with passivity. It is simply a healthy guard against macho violence that can result in a turning of the tables rather than in a substantively new approach to the problem. Their reluctance is what fuels the endless discussions on strategies, more important, what assures that other less directly risky modes of change will be employed. For example, Palestinians teach in the face of closed colleges; they write letters, proclamations, and strategies that are copied and delivered in a complex clandestine network. Palestinians tend the injured and bury the dead; they bear the babies and nurture the children who will grow into revolutionaries. Their reluctance means that violence, a sometimes necessary strategy, will never be engaged in uncritically. Their reluctance bears witness to the nonviolent future they envision, brought about by some necessary, albeit unfortunate, violence. Rather than being caught in ideological debates about nonviolence, most of the women seem to take a pragmatic but principled stand tempered by this important reluctance.

Finally, the women *provide the services necessary to build a new society*. Palestinian cooperatives are led by strong women who oversee the production of food and clothing, job training, and sewing projects through which they reorganize society and keep a strong link with their tradition. The

Society of In'ash El-Usra under the direction of Sameeha S. Khalil is but one example of an organization whose influence is felt in many corners.

The women of the YWCA conduct educational programs that impart needed educational skills. Religious women's groups aid the sick and provide preventive health care in the absence of such an infrastructure. Craft cooperatives provide an outlet for the work of women who are isolated because of political boundaries.

In each of these efforts the remarkable creativity and courage of the women makes clear where the young people found their inspiration for the Intifada. Likewise, it provides rich resources for the theology that is wrought from the bloodshed of the Intifada. It points toward a day when hospitality and art, a cessation of violence, and the creation of a new, cooperatively based society will mark the new Palestine. The women's efforts make that day seem less distant, thanks to the holy stones.

In my effort to make theological sense in the midst of the Intifada I offer four points from a Western feminist perspective in response to the Palestinian women's insightful and inspiring presentations: 1) women do theology as part of a strategy for creative survival; 2) theology is a communal not an individual activity; 3) so-called women's concerns enhance the historical project of liberation, they do not distract from it; and 4) a veritable "theological Intifada" is occasioned by the entrance of women as full participants in the theological conversation. I offer these ideas with deep thanks for the privilege of participating in the process with Palestinian women. This is global sisterhood at its best.

Survival is the hallmark of womanist theology, the reflection by Afro-American women in the United States. Womanist theology is a black feminist response to both black theology, which is done primarily by men, and feminist theology, which is done primarily by white women. While feminist theology began with a focus on women's rights, and black theology with a focus on mostly male experience, the focus of womanist work is on the very survival of women and their dependent children in a culture that would destroy them. As a white feminist I am indebted to my womanist colleagues whose perspective sheds light on the Palestinian situation.

Survival is the most adequate and meaningful basis for a theology wrought in the Intifada because the deaths and maiming of thousands of people make survival an expensive commodity. It is a useful horizon over against which to measure the value of theological statements, because it is their very survival that is at stake when people are willing to fight to the death over concepts of the divine and interpretations of history. Placed alongside Rosemary Radford Ruether's notion of finding meaning "at the borders of the Bible," the survival of the most deeply affected, namely, women and children, is a critical question for a Palestinian theology of liberation that aims to be a part of the process of liberation. It provides religious motivation for social change.

It is clear in speaking to Palestinian women that survival is more than mere existence. It is a creative, life-enhancing approach to fundamental structural change. How appropriate, then, that poetry, hospitality, attention to beauty through crafts, and concrete acts of solidarity play such an important part in each woman's work. The difference between mere survival and creative, life-affirming struggle is a vision, in this case a religious vision, of what will follow these horrendous years of suffering, a vision of a just future.

A second dimension of a Palestinian theology of liberation that emerges in the women's voices is the fact that *theology is a communal activity*. The model here is one of plenty and not scarcity, with many people engaged in the theological pursuit, not simply professional theologians. Various jobs can be done by various members of the community, and the community is much larger than the local gathering. For example, the question of how to respond to Christian Zionists shifts from the personal question "How do I respond?" to the political question "Who is the most effective respondent?" It may in fact be that non-Palestinians will do the job best, leaving Palestinian energy for other tasks.

The underlying idea is that there are plenty of people to do the work, not just a few, an assumption that international solidarity within larger liberation theology circles assures. Likewise, theology is too important to be left to the theologians; the insights of children and young adults, of laypeople as well as clergy, bear on the issues at hand. This lightens the load for everyone and increases the strategic possibilities. Women learn this technique at home and in neighborhoods, where we are forced to rely on one another for survival, and it works.

A third question which emerges when women focus on concerns seemingly specific to women is *whether such efforts distract from the larger historical project of liberation.* To this I encourage two responses. First, all issues are women's issues, and women's issues are for all to consider. There are no areas of inquiry that do not have an impact on women. At the same time, there are virtually no issues that are specific only to women. Marriage, education of children, the changing role of women in the family and in society, the role of women in ministry and church, all imply cultural shifts that women must name for ourselves. But men must consider them as well.

It is not for Western women to impose mores from our cultures. Rather, our task is to learn from and support the choices of Palestinian women. Likewise, it is not for men to wash their hands of such concerns, to write them off simply as women's issues when in fact each one implies concomitant changes for men in society. The point is that such cultural changes are part of the historical project of liberation; without them no liberation project can be said to be complete.

The second factor is that women's participation is a clear signal of the historical project at hand. The statement issued for International Women's Day (March 8, 1990) by the General Federation of Palestinian Women in the state of Palestine makes this clear:

> Masses of Our Struggling Women, Masses of Our Heroic People:
>
> The memory of March 8 comes upon us this year at a time when our glorious Intifada continues and its achievements and sacrifices increase.
>
> In the name of the women martyrs and prisoners and in the name of the mothers of the martyrs, women and men; prisoners, women and men, expellees and wanted persons in every camp, village and city in the occupied country; in your name, you who wrote the most magnificent verses of glory and heroism, which the whole world witnessed, we salute the memory of March 8 while the Intifada receives its 28th month, with a depth, a brightening and an insistence upon achieving our legitimate rights to return, self-determination and the confirmation of our independent Palestinian state on our national soil, with Arab Jerusalem as its capital . . . under the leadership of our sole legitimate representative, the PLO.

This statement leaves little question about the stance of Palestinian women, little risk of their being distracted by trivial pursuits. Rather, it suggests that Palestinian and non-Palestinian women alike can see the Intifada as one more concrete struggle in which women's work is essential. Women's energy, freed from the constraints of patriarchal expectations, will make a decided difference.

This brings me to the final point, namely, *what the full participation of women in the Intifada means in terms of the churches where women's participation has been limited heretofore.* I want to suggest that women's full participation in churches will occasion a kind of "theological Intifada" within the ranks of Christians. Like the Intifada against Israeli occupation, women's entrance into the theological and ecclesial ranks will be grassroots actions based on critical reflection of the oppression women have suffered. It will be expressed in ritual and celebration, in ministry and education. As more and more Palestinian Christian women study theology and bring insights to bear, the whole Christian church in the Middle East and throughout the world will reap glorious benefits.

It is hard to imagine a society in which women are risking life and limb in the streets, where teen-age girls are being killed as well as teen-age boys, that would not bring that same spirit of dignity and equality to the churches. It is hard to conceive of pulpits and altars where women would be unwelcome given the sacrifices they have made in the streets.

Palestinian Christian women are a sign of great hope to those of us who struggle in our countries for such full humanity. They are religious agents who achieve spiritual integrity by engaging in theology and ministry just as they are moral agents who achieve bodily integrity by fighting for their rights.

As religious agents Palestinian women name their experiences on their own terms; they speak their religious word with confidence. They make decisions based on those experiences, and they form communities of trust and accountability in which they receive the critical support necessary to act courageously. Likewise, their spiritual integrity is the freedom to be faithful to the religious roots of their ancestors. It is their responsibility to bring their faith to bear on the pressing issues of the day, and it is the privilege of passing on to their children the proud faith heritage which has motivated them to give up their lives if necessary that values of justice and equality might reign.

This is how I perceive the struggle of Palestinian women developing liberation theology in the context of the Intifada. As Palestinian poet Nuha Kawar wrote, "Those who give their lives build the future." It is a privilege to accompany them.

26

Returning for the First Time

ANN LOUISE GILLIGAN

Sometimes in life we return to a place and in returning we see it for the first time. This was my experience in returning to Israel/Palestine after an absence of fifteen years. My first visit in the mid-seventies was inspired by the works of Bruno Bettelheim and Elie Weisel. I wanted to work in a kibbutz and judge for myself whether Bettelheim's claims that the communitarian model lived by kibbutzniks was an ideal to be imitated. I also felt judged by the writings of Elie Weisel and was happy to participate in establishing a land for a people much beleaguered by global prejudice. During those months we were quite isolated in a work program that provided little opportunity for critical awareness of our surrounding neighbors—the Palestinian people. In light of what my recent visit unveiled, I wonder how I could have been so blinkered then.

Over recent years, especially since the commencement of the Intifada in December 1987, my eye has often strayed to small columns in our daily newspaper which clearly understate the plight of the Palestinian people. Gradually I had become aware that all was not well in the "Holy" land. So when an opportunity presented itself to accompany an international group of liberation theologians to observe and reflect on the crisis facing the Palestinian people I was deeply grateful. For the fire of anger to energize the struggle against injustice it is often necessary to experience first-hand the nature of oppression suffered.

WOMEN'S STORY AND THE INTIFADA

In all situations that we observe and reflect upon we carry our own interests, our own prejudices, and not to admit these is to be less than honest. As a feminist I live and move with antenna sensitive to the plight of women, ever concerned about their situation, their oppression, ever anxious that the goal of feminism—that lives of mutuality and equality between men and women—be realized. As I moved through the land of Palestine/ Israel for those ten days in March 1990, and as I observed the atrocities suffered by the constant violation of human rights, my persistent question was: How does all this influence the lives of women?

Statistics can be cited coldly; namely, of the nine hundred unarmed Palestinians shot dead since December 1987, 10 percent have been women, or again, of the eighty thousand maimed and disabled, the minority have been women. But behind each of these numbers there is a story. Narrating each story is usually a woman who is left alone to cope with conditions that are inhuman. As we moved from refugee camp to village I was left with images that still startle my sleep. In the Jabaliya Camp we sat under canvas and were served tea with regal dignity by women whose menfolk were either imprisoned or hospitalized. From behind their veiled costumes these Muslim women spoke with a gentle strength of resisting this oppression and pleaded with us to break the silence in the international community. In a nearby village we talked with a woman in front of her recently demolished home. This destruction was undertaken "by court order" because her husband was suspected of being engaged in the resistance movement. Her apparent fragility and youth was soon transformed by her impassioned plea that something be done to address this injustice. Her poignant words were accompanied by the plaintive wail of her babe in arms.

I could ladle out story after story to illustrate the abuse of justice that the Israeli army and settlers are perpetrating against the Palestinian people. But what is more important than endless illustration is that action be undertaken to stop the repetition of stories such as these. It was with this clarity of vision that the women surrounded us in a Palestinian hospital. As they led us from bed to bed, speaking with intensity of the wounds of their loved ones, they begged us to alert public opinion about the atrocities we were seeing.

As we journeyed around this torn land, it struck me that, far from deflating morale and rendering people listless and apathetic through repeated acts of violence, the Palestinian people were ever more energized and determined to resist Israeli oppressiveness. Nowhere is this more evident than among the women. A bonding which transcends class and religious divides is clearly present. This element of the Uprising is *not* peripheral but is central and should be fostered in every way. Our response to injustice must be rooted in communities of solidarity and resistance, something these women know intuitively. Indeed, when Jesus walked the "Holy" land, he did so not as a heroic individual apart and alone, but rather his pilgrimage of confronting injustice was rooted in a community of empowering relationships, often with women.

During our visit many women shared with us the fact that, through the Intifada, Palestinian women are coming to a new identity. As one said, "Intifada has given a voice to women. Before the Intifada I couldn't name myself Palestinian, but since then the movement has given me the strength to name my identity."

Women in Palestine today are active political partners in the struggle against oppression. In affirming their strength, their courage, I hope that the political struggle will remain rooted in a profound awareness of the interrelatedness of all oppressions. Sometimes in the past, and I have seen this in my own country, a nationalist struggle can take precedence over the struggle against sexism or racism. So the liberation of women gained in the political struggle recedes once the present crisis is resolved. Any freedom of women gained in the Intifada must translate into a change of laws governing relationships at every level and sector of society. Gains for nationalism must always mean gains against sexism and racism. Otherwise, true liberation will never be achieved.

TOWARD A PALESTINIAN THEOLOGY OF LIBERATION

Over the last few years, while profoundly influenced by the method of liberation theology, I have been disturbed by the rather naive and exclusivist use of scripture used in this paradigm. As one of my young students recently questioned, citing Exodus 3:17: "If God did give the Israelites the rich and fertile land of the Canaanites, the Hittites, the Amorites, the Perizzites, the Hivites, and the Jebusites, what happened to all these people who were then dispossessed of *their* land?" Returning to Palestine/Israel I was anxiously awaiting answers to this question which, despite the passage of time, remains the central issue.

The conference we attended after walking the land was to reflect on this very question about the land. The attempt was to find a biblical paradigm that would enable a Palestinian theology to be a theology of liberation.

Over the years feminist biblical scholars have alerted us to the evils of an exclusivist reading of scripture. For centuries, an all-male interpretation of the text was given the rating of divine inspiration, despite the fact that many of the resulting teachings contributed to the oppression of women. Today, on the strength of women's authority, we can say that anything that contributes to sexism must be deemed as not redemptive. The shift is a shift in truth-claims. It's a shift that humbly recognizes that none of us has a total handle on the truth. But, to hear the voice of the spirit through the text, we must listen to the voice of those whose lives have been oppressed by the text. In a shared dialogue with their experience, we may come to glimpse the truth. In the land of Palestine/Israel the text has been used as a weapon of oppression by many groups and peoples. To move beyond this impasse we must all humbly recognize that *all* understandings of the text are drawn from interpreted readings of the text.

Therefore, authority for *the* correct reading does not lie in some objective space that we can tap into or that we can persuade others to accept. Rather, it will be in the shared mutual dialogue between all the partners reading the one text that truth will be discerned and solutions suggested. In other words, authority lies with the interpreter. As interpreters, we must recognize our own presuppositions, our own prejudices, and then share our understandings with our sisters and brothers whose vested interests are other than our own. We pray that, in the exchange among the Jew, the Arab Christian, the European Christian, a truth will be glimpsed that will allow the scripture to be part of the solution rather than entrenching the problem. I would hope that *women* and men play a mutual role in this public discussion, as each brings different "interior landscapes to their interpretation." To achieve this I would encourage a growing number of Palestinian women to receive formal academic training in scripture and theology.

Within a feminist theological reflection there is a constant awareness that the way we image God and the language we use have a profound impact on the social reality we create around us. Exclusivist imagery of God and sexist language are sinful because they contribute to a world view that deems women inferior and furthers their oppression. In the birth of a Palestinian theology of liberation I would plead that a profound sensitivity to this issue be brought to all publications and public statements. If we want a solution that is just, we must use language and imagery that is inclusive.

WHERE LIES THE SOLUTION?

Throughout the conference the refrain was oft repeated: How can we move to a new future? Where lies the solution? As international observers and respondents, thankfully none of us proffered a solution. Yet, each of us, from lands as distinct as South Africa, Zimbabwe, Sri Lanka, North America, the Philippines, and Ireland, heard the pain of our Palestinian brothers and sisters and entered it in solidarity and in dialogue with our own struggles.

As one doing theology from the premise of feminism, I heard the debate about "the land" from that perspective. Feminism works out of a framework that seeks to reestablish a mutual partnership between all reality. The hierarchies between heaven and earth, men and women, must be dissolved into patterns of partnership. Creating relationships of mutuality is a political act. The future solution cannot exalt the land, any land, to a position of exaggerated importance that allows one to kill for it or to claim it as one's exclusive right, nor can it be abused, treated with disregard, or destroyed.

During our brief stay in Palestine/Israel, we witnessed both these extremes. Israeli troops were barricading off new slices of the Occupied Territories, which they claimed they needed for security reasons. Given past patterns, these army encampments soon become new civilian settlements on Palestinian land. But we also witnessed destruction of the land.

To date, the Israelis have uprooted 77,698 trees. With our own eyes we witnessed the recent uprooting of citrus trees and olive trees, acts of revenge against the Intifada. Destruction of the earth has always been part of a racist mentality; it can never be part of a solution.

There is an urgent need for the churches to take a strong stance against the oppression of the Palestinian people. Some would hold that in recent times we have witnessed some principled statements by the official church bodies against the oppression of the Palestinian people. These statements must now be coupled with policy enactments, clearly demanding self-determination for the Palestinian people. As one woman clearly stated, "The Church can no longer place itself under house arrest or its faith under curfew." We have had enough of church theology, a theology of pious aspiration; we need the churches to become catalysts in the process of change, working prophetically for the freedom of the oppressed and denouncing the oppressor.

Returning to Ireland from this brief but pain-filled visit to the "Holy" land, I was left with many abiding memories. The pacifism and gentleness of the Palestinian people is something I will always remember. Their extraordinary hospitality made our Irish variety pale in comparison. Their love of learning and pursuit of knowledge, despite the closures of their schools and universities, was heartening, and their culture, which refuses to be squashed despite all attempts to imprison writers, poets, and song writers, was enriching. Yes, this is a people who will survive, but at what cost?

And the question remains: Where lies the solution? I wonder if the solution lies in any of the present remedies on offer. Mary Daly, that great feminist philosopher, suggests that to move to a transformed future, we need a changed consciousness where we must cease looking at life three dimensionally and introduce a fourth dimension. That fourth dimension lies in the world of the imagination. It is that world that we must tap for images and creative processes that will allow all peoples to journey together in a fourth exodus to a liberation for all.

27

An Exposure to the Palestinian Struggle

A Filipina Reflection

MYRNA ARCEO

What I have seen and experienced among the Palestinians reminds me a great deal of my own situation in the Philippines. Though some manifestations may vary, the pains and miseries of the people are much alike.

For the past twenty years my country has been struggling with the problems of militarization and systematic exploitation. Though people around the world congratulate us for our brave nonviolent ousting of a dictator by "people power" in 1986, we continue to bear the same problems as before. The dictatorial rule had created a military structure and a system of exploitation and deprivation far too sophisticated and powerful to dismantle. It has deep roots—United States imperialism. The violence that did not take place in 1986 erupted in the December 1989 coup d'etat. This encounter between two military factions competing for power was devastating. The silent "total war," and the low intensity conflict being waged against insurgents, drags on daily in the countryside. We have learned many lessons about our conflict, survival, and empowerment over the years. The process of liberation goes on.

Over the last fifteen years I have spent my time teaching theology to college students in a progressive school. During martial law years, when most of the schools had been silenced on issues of justice and liberation, my college launched an alternative curriculum, opting for the poor and oppressed. With a vision of building a just community with the marginalized, we experimented with a program of education for justice.

My theology classes spend the first few weeks of their time in "exposure";

that is, in meeting and dialogue with victims of violence, exploitation, and injustice. We visit organized and conscientized communities of the urban poor in squatters' districts, factory workers at the picket lines, political prisoners, peasants in the countryside, women working in the bars outside the United States bases, tribal minorities who have lost their lands, and other such groups. During this visit we try to dialogue with them about their realities. We analyze and reflect with them about the meaning of life, liberation, and community. Together we attempt to make connections in solidarity for a liberated country.

My exposure to the Palestinian communities in the Occupied Territories, my participation in a seminar with them, my dialogue with people who are direct and indirect victims of violence and repression, my reflection and celebration with them about their struggle for liberation deepen my attempt to do the same task of doing reflection with victims in the Philippines. This is my reflection on the Palestinian struggle. What did I find most striking about their situation? Why? What are the roots of this conflict? What are Palestinians' hopes and visions of the future as a people? How do they make them concrete? What is the connection between Palestinian and Philippine experiences of liberation? Where is God in all these events?

First, what did I find most striking? As I moved from place to place and encountered Palestinians, I felt a strong sense of tension and insecurity among the people. It is a mixed feeling of fear and vigilance. "Anything can happen to me now, so I have to be alert and prepared." I observed their suspicious looks, alertness in movements, sensitivity to sounds. I could feel a baleful "hovering spirit" as I moved around. When I gave a talk to a group of students in Jerusalem and described this "sense" in their movements, they started to laugh and affirmed that feeling.

In the Philippines we have lived for twenty years with this feeling of apprehension and tension. This moment reached a peak point during the last months of the Marcos dictatorship and during the December 1989 coup d'etat. This feeling is very close to the tension one feels a few hours before the coming of a strong typhoon or the tension of something about to explode. In a situation of injustice and oppression, it appears to me that, once people unite to defy their unjust conditions, conflict between the victims and the oppressor is heightened. There seems to be no middle ground. You are either with the oppressed or against them. That is a conflict situation. The tighter the conflict, the greater the sense of tension.

The people now confront a life and death situation—collectively and individually. By doing things collectively in mass actions, such as rallies, demonstrations, boycotts, marches, and other similar actions, confrontation can be dealt with more easily. There is greater empowerment in collective action. But quite often, confrontation with violence is not collective but individual, like arrest, torture, beatings, and dying. Hence the readiness to put up with this event takes a great amount of courage, preparation, and commitment. Even the most courageous of the committed people are taken over by fear which results in panic that paralyzes action. I remember my own experience in mass actions in my country. When the military breaks a demonstration, participants who panic are often the victims of beatings and arrest because they are unable to run fast or move at all. Among the rebels in the countryside there is a saying that goes: *Unahan lang ng takot*, "Who gets afraid first gets killed first."

I was invited by a Palestinian woman to a memorial of her relative in Ramallah in the West Bank, part of the Occupied Territories. On our way to Ramallah, our car was stopped at a military checkpoint. Two soldiers ordered Nadja to get out of the car, saying, "We need your car. Please get out." "No, I can't give you my car. We're already late for the funeral," protested Nadja. "Go get a taxi," the soldier insisted, and then he called for a taxi. "I cannot, I am already late," Nadja insisted again. Apparently surprised by such resistance, the soldier demanded her I.D. An I.D. is the soul of a Palestinian. Without it, a person is unable to function in that country. Nadja gave him her I.D. Then we were asked to park at the side of the street to be held there indefinitely. The soldier moved out to stop another car.

Blue-plated cars such as Nadja uses are for Palestinian residents of the West Bank. Occasionally these cars are forcibly taken by Israeli soldiers. Since these cars can easily penetrate refugee camps without suspicion, soldiers use them to abduct young boys manning street checkpoints in the camps. When the boys get close to the car, soldiers grab them and take them to detention centers for interrogation and torture.

"What is the worst scenario for you?" I asked Nadja. She told me that some of her friends were forced to "lend" their cars when the soldiers poked guns at their heads and threatened to shoot them if they refused them. Cars are returned after a few days. The soldiers call the owner to pick the car up at a certain place. But cars are returned in bad condition and often smeared with blood.

"We will just wait and see what happens," Nadja told me, telling me to stay calm and not be afraid. She immediately changed the car keys into a single key and gathered important belongings in one bag. "Just in case I have to give my car later on." We waited for almost an hour until a Red Cross car with two foreign volunteers passed by and interceded for us. In a short while, Nadja's I.D. was returned and we were released.

In a conflict situation people who are victims of oppression have to be prepared for such an event. "My hour may come anytime." Nadja's response to the situation had been foreseen long before it happened. She knew beforehand that one day her car would be stopped and taken by force from her. Her reaction to the situation has to some extent been thought out in moments of reflection. She will resist and stand for her rights. No, she will not give in without a fight.

A few years ago, when I spoke to a North American audience about our struggle for liberation, my audience commented on my strong sense of urgency about my condition. They said I spoke as if the end of time would come soon. During my stay in the United States, I realized the big difference between living in a "peaceful" condition and living in a conflict situation. In my country it is so difficult to make long-range plans. The vision of a peaceful, democratic, and liberated Philippines is about the longest range plan we have. Most of the time we have to deal with our struggle on a day-to-day basis. When asked if I would definitely make it to this conference in Israel, I answered, "It really depends on whether we have another coup d'etat like in December." The airport had to close for several days during the event. Our markets ran out of fresh food because of the blockade. Just like the Palestinians, we are not sure when classes will be interrupted and when they will resume.

And because we do not know what may happen tomorrow, we take each day seriously. Whether we work or play, we give our energy generously, since this may be our last. In fact, our parting greetings in the Philippines end with, "Be careful." Aware that the hour of reckoning may come anytime, I feel the need to maximize my living days. We don't feel so glum about the situation that we walk throughout the day with long faces, only to smile at the final victory of liberation. We are also aware we may not live long enough to participate in the people's liberation march.

Aside from the feeling of tension, I also felt a familiar sense of joy, hope, and celebration among the Palestinians. Like the Filipinos, they are able to celebrate with so much joy and giving. Their cultural shows – dances and songs – express both protest against occupation and at the same time joy and celebration of a people united against injustice. "The sound of Intifada is stronger than occupation." Side by side, with tears of pain and suffering, people who are transforming their situation celebrate life, community, and empowerment.

In the Philippines funeral marches of martyred leaders and community organizers are an occasion for mourning as well as celebration and protest. I remember the funeral of a well-known labor and human rights lawyer who was kidnapped, badly tortured, and killed by a rightist group. His wake, which lasted for almost a week, turned into evenings of cultural shows – songs, poetry readings, and drama. His funeral march extended for several miles, with thousands of people protesting his death. In Gaza I heard how victims of political execution have been denied a period of mourning and the participation of the community in the funeral. This must have caused much pain to the relatives of the victims.

How striking it is to see the contrast between the Occupied Territories and the Jewish Israeli communities. The walls of the West Bank, Gaza, and East Jerusalem are mostly covered with graffiti – signs of protest, like salutes to the PLO, Palestinian flags, and notices of strikes and boycotts. These graffiti are also found on many, many walls of Manila and in other parts of the country. "Land, not bullets." "Land to the tillers." "Dismantle the U.S. bases." "Down with U.S. imperialism."

I heard many stories about the burden Palestinians have to bear for these graffiti. Soldiers order home-owners to clean up their walls, even if they are not responsible for the graffiti. Otherwise, they get fined.

I remember vividly the story of a young activist in Manila who was caught posting protest signs. Jon was an 18-year-old youth organizer in an urban poor community. One evening in March 1987, just a year after the ousting of Marcos, a group of PSG (presidential security guards) patrolling in a jeepney along the main street of the city noticed a group of youngsters pasting posters on the walls, reading "Dismantle the U.S. bases." The event took place just about fifty yards away from where I live. When the military jeep stopped to arrest them, they ran in different directions. But two of them were caught, Jon and Rey. They were blindfolded and taken to a safehouse not too far from the presidential palace.

For three consecutive days they were beaten, forced to eat rotten food, interrogated, and threatened with death. Rey had serious asthma, and Jon, in a separate room, would shout to him, saying, "We're too young to die. We must live." On the third day, blindfolded, arms tied behind their backs with sharp barbed wire used for fencing, mouths stuck with newspaper and covered with tape, Jon and Rey were taken to the "killing field." Jon recalled how a third person, a young girl, was also taken with them in the car. They were to be stabbed to death and dumped in an abandoned factory site beside a mountain of garbage very close to the bay.

The first one dumped and stabbed was the young girl, whom Jon heard moaning. The next one was Rey. Then some hundred yards away Jon was dumped. He felt a blow on his upper back, close to the neck. He felt numbed and blood started to flow down his back. He chewed the newspaper in his mouth until the tape around his mouth loosened, and he was able to shout for help. He shouted for almost an hour before a private security guard from the abandoned factory came to his rescue. "Are you a salvaged victim?" asked the security guard. Jon denied it: "I am a theft and robbery victim."

"Salvaged victim" refers to a person summarily executed for political reasons. Had he admitted he was a salvaged victim, he would have been left to die in the killing field. He survived, a rare victim of salvaging who lived to be able to tell his story. But his spinal column was badly damaged by the blow caused by a long sharp shoe knife stabbed in his back. He is now in exile in a foreign country. His life remains in danger in the Philippines. Rey's body was found later that day. But the young girl's body was never located. Her body must have sunk in with the heap of garbage.

The whole atmosphere of control and terrorism in Israel creates in me the same feeling of anger and apprehension as in the Philippines. The checkpoints all over Israel, particularly before entering and leaving the Occupied Territories, remind me of the number of times when Filipino soldiers opened and searched my bags when entering buildings. The curfew hours remind me also of the number of years we had to be at home between midnight and four in the morning. Our traditional midnight masses during the Christmas season had to be changed during those years. The strikes and boycotts give me the same excitement of protest that we have during *welgang bayan* ("general strike"). When Palestinians told me stories of how their houses get demolished, how their sons get arrested, tortured, and shot, I felt as though I was listening to the mothers and wives of peasants in a refugee camp in southern Philippines, except they were speaking Arabic.

In Negroes, a southern island in the Philippines, we have thousands of so-called internal refugees. The biggest number of refugees must have been during the summer of 1989. About fifty thousand residents of villages close to mountainous areas were ordered by the military to come to two centers. They were housed in schools with practically no facilities for decent living. In a month's time about fifty children died of sickness due to bad sanitary conditions and lack of food. Since most of the refugees were farmers, they were unable to harvest their crops and tend their animals. Those who attempted to return to get some belongings and harvest their crops were shot.

By putting the people in the camp, the military expects to subdue countryside insurgency. The rebels in these areas are generally supported by the community. A great majority of the people have been victims of a long history of land confiscation and exploitation by big landowners. Hence it is not surprising that the support for the rebels here is widespread. As I listened to a woman in Jabaliya camp in Gaza narrate the story of the arrest and torture of her two brothers and her father by Israeli soldiers, a picture of Negro refugee camps came to my mind.

Another striking story I have heard among Palestinians is the security check in crossing the border between Israel and Jordan along the Allenby Bridge. When I heard a woman complain, "I was stripped naked and searched at the border entering Israel," I thought it was a figure of speech—until I met a Palestinian woman who had just gone through such an experience. She was born in Palestine before the occupation, but her family moved and lived in Lebanon when she was a child. At present she is married to an American businessman, so she carries a United States passport. Because of the Intifada, she felt the need to identify with her people and decided to visit her relatives in Haifa. When crossing the border, the security personnel noticed her Palestinian origin stamped on her passport. Her hour had come.

This woman went through two hours of security check. Her bags were thoroughly inspected piece by piece. Her receipts were checked one by one. The receipts with Arabic writing were thrown away. The sleeves of her coat were screened part by part; her cigarettes were unwrapped stick by stick; and then she was stripped naked. She was so angry when I met her. As a United States passport holder, she could not believe that authorities would make her go through the same ordeal as her people. I was told many stories about the Palestinians' ordeal at the border security check. Some spend about half a day, while others are even asked to come back another day.

What bothers me so much about the security check is the attitude of many foreigners. I remember the security check I went through before I departed from the airport. I had to be "interrogated" twice. It was made clear to me that they were doing this for my own security. When the person in charge of inspecting me asked the question, "Are you carrying with you any deadly weapon?" I looked at her and almost laughed at the ridiculousness of the question. She caught my facial expression and smiled. No one with a bomb or deadly weapon will openly admit he or she is carrying one. Certainly not.

What then is the intention of all this tight security? I perceived that the intended goal of this ordeal is to project an image of Palestinians as terrorists. This is why I feel so angry with foreign passengers who do not look beyond security and would say, "I don't mind the tight check-up. In the end I feel good and secure." How could they miss the point of exaggeration and absurdity of the check-up? This is not to mention the fact that, for Palestinians, the intention is to harass and to humiliate them as a people. No wonder the people I met during my visit in Gaza often asked me, "Do we look like terrorists?"

This humiliation as a people at the border provoked my feeling of anger when I passed through Rome on my way to the Philippines. I arrived late in the evening at Leonardo da Vinci airport. My connecting flight was the following evening. My travel agent had arranged for a hotel reservation in advance, so I felt secure about my overnight stay. At the immigration window I was denied entry. I was told that they could not allow me through because I needed a transit visa, which they refused to give me. I pleaded and explained that all I needed was a good night's rest. The police took me to the airport lounge, showed me long stretches of benches, and suggested I sleep there. I noticed some Africans sleeping on benches, so I turned to the police and asked, "Is this the way you treat third-world people?"

Whenever I travel to developed countries, I always fear that my entry will be denied, in spite of my visa. Will they deport me, detain and handcuff me, or will they strip me naked, like so many other Filipinos? The biggest export of the Philippines is labor. We send about half a million workers to different parts of the world every year. Half of these workers are women. About twenty-eight thousand work as entertainers and dancers in Japan, thirty thousand as domestic helpers in Hong Kong, sixteen thousand in Singapore, thirty thousand in Italy, and seventy thousand in the Middle East. The main reason for this mass exodus is poverty. Approximately 60 percent of our people live below the poverty line. This situation is brought about by systematic exploitation by big foreign multinational companies and their local collaborators.

I feel sad that whenever I travel, I meet thousands of homesick Filipinos who are treated as second-class citizens. They are usually in ghettos by themselves, unable to integrate with local citizens. The image of the Filipino as a desperate worker who is willing to do anything just to earn a living is the dominant one I find in most of my travels. The discrimination I endured at the port of entry in Rome and other countries reminds me of the humiliation Palestinians have to deal with in crossing the borders. When are we going to be treated like decent human beings?

Why does this situation in Israel and the Philippines continue to exist despite our protest? When lands and properties of Palestinians were taken in 1948 by the Zionist soldiers, the people were taken by surprise. Palestinians thought the event was a temporary condition. But they were totally powerless, caught unprepared. The massacre in Dier Yasin was so terrifying that it made the people submit to the occupiers without much resistance.

Similarly, in 1972 when Marcos declared martial law, the Filipinos were also taken by surprise. They also thought the situation would return to normal in a short while. In spite of massive student protests before the martial law imposition, the people in general were powerless. In a month's time ten thousand people were arrested. Well-known and powerful personalities were locked up in jail. How could we resist?

The first massive protest took place only in 1983, with the assassination of the famous exiled politician Benigno Aquino. While a gradual build-up of people's organizations was taking place during the years of repression, it took the assassination event for the people collectively to protest the dictatorial rule. The protest actions eventually led to the end of Marcos' dictatorship.

For the Palestinians, the control has almost been total over the past forty years. In spite of the years of organizing and isolated defiance of the people, it took the killings in Gaza to trigger the Intifada. With this event, the protest overcame its fragmentation and isolation; it became a collective action of the people against their occupiers. Like the 1987 Intifada, during the 1986 "people power" the masses shouted, "Enough! We cannot take this any longer." How similar are the patterns of defiance!

The dictatorial rule in the Philippines ended in February 1986. A few months after the "people power" event, we ratified a democratic constitution. It may not be an ideal one that pleases a great majority, but it promises a lot. We were euphoric for a period of one year, until January 1987. That month peasants from all over the country marched to the president's palace to demand genuine land reform. They were not expecting that miracles take place in a year's time, but the peasants and grassroots people were expecting a clear vision and goal of a more humane and democratic life for them. Instead of a clear policy statement, the marchers were met by bullets. The military massacred seventeen peasants and wounded scores of marchers.

How difficult it is to explain to outsiders that our situation has not really changed. How difficult it is to make them understand that a Christian woman president does not guarantee a peaceful, democratic, and liberated country. How difficult it is to explain that military monsters cannot easily be dismantled with the ousting of their creator. How exasperating it is to argue that our enemies and the roots of our oppression go deeper than the dictators.

How long are the Palestinians going to hold out with their strikes, boycotts, mass actions, with the Intifada? How many more lives will be spent before the enemies listen? How are they to deal with their enemies' military strength? My experience of the struggle is beginning to point to a reality about the process of liberation. It appears to me that liberation is a lifetime process. It will go on from one stage to the other. Perhaps there is no such event as a final victory.

When organizing a workers' union in my academic institution, we worked for a prolonged period of time to be legally recognized. When the workers' union finally got certified through an election, we thought we could relax for a while to prepare for the collective bargaining agreement. Yet even before we could sit at the negotiating table, a number of our progressive members were terminated from work and one was arrested. It is beginning to dawn on many of us that once we enter into this form of struggle, we are in for a protracted revolution. We go from one small victory to the next. But there seems to be no great and final victory. This is one reason we do not call our Filipino theology liberation theology, but the theology of struggle. We realize we cannot give false expectations to the people.

Political analysts may give us brilliant analyses and scenarios of our future. Yet deep down I am aware that we do not have a clear end to our struggle. What remains clear and firm is, first, our vision of a liberated society that we hope to achieve, and second, that we will commit our lives to materialize that vision. A Philippine song sums up our aspiration as follows: "I will never allow my freedom to be denied again—never!"

When asked about their future, Palestinians responded similarly. The people's hope and commitment to transform their unjust and oppressive reality provide a clear vision for both Palestinians and Filipinos. How are people transforming their situation? What are the concrete manifestations of their hopes and vision for the future? Who is bringing hope to the people? And where is God in all these events?

During the seminar I often heard Palestinian participants speak about a confusing identity. One clergy said: "I am an Israeli-Arab and an Israeli passport holder. Before the Intifada, when asked who I was, I used to give varying answers, depending who was asking the question. If an Israeli, my answer was, 'I am an Israeli.' If an Arab, I answered, 'I am an Arab-Palestinian.' Then I have to clarify whether I am a Christian or a Muslim. Oh, how I got so confused before. But now I just say, 'I am a Palestinian,' and I take the consequence of that identity."

I have observed that same kind of identity crisis among Filipinos. As a colonized people, many of us felt ashamed of our identity. In fact, many of us speak English better than our Filipino language. Often we prefer to identify with Americans or Spanish—both our colonizers. With the "people power" event Filipinos began to be proud as a people. Hundreds of Filipinos working abroad went out onto the streets after the event to identify themselves with the Filipino people who deposed a dictator.

It appears to me that a people who defy injustice and oppression acquires a new identity. They are no longer oppressed people but a people with a new consciousness. Isn't this what happened to the Israelites when Moses liberated them from slavery? Their defiance of Pharaoh's rule made them a new people of Yahweh, their liberator God. Because they are no longer the same people, they cannot live the same way as before. As awakened and transformed people, they seek out ways to express themselves. They create new structures. These structures are concrete manifestations of their new realities.

Although many committees and organizations had already been formed before the Intifada, the event activated these structures. Practically, the most significant aspects of people's revolutionary life are made concrete in these organizations. Women, health, human rights, press, martyrs, and so forth, these are now the Palestinians' venue for their new reality and actualization of their future as a people. In the Philippines we call them cause-oriented groups and organizations. There is one for almost all sectors of society and for basic issues confronting them—peasants, workers, urban poor, fisherfolks, women, tribal minorities, human rights, religious, cultural, just to mention a few.

Palestinians talked much about the transformation of their women. Now women are actively engaged in politics. Some even are leaders in demonstrations. Traditional restrictions on women are relaxed. They can move around without permission and unescorted by men. Intercultural marriages are accepted. Dowries are more practical. These new realities are translated and materialized in the alternative organizations. In addition, these new structures changed their relationships. A network of new relationships is emerging side by side with these structures.

These organizations and committees and networks of people are the tangible expression of Palestinian hope. Though not yet, it is almost the realization of their vision of a liberated society. With these structures people collectively denounce injustice, fight their oppressors, dismantle their oppressive apparatus and articulate their hope. They empower people. That is why they are continually threatened by closures, raids, and elimination of leaders. They are a serious threat to the state's security because ultimately these structures will replace the oppressive state apparatus. However, in spite of the government's effort to crush them, they continue to grow and get more established. If only the state can kill people's consciousness, then it has nothing to fear.

The Filipinos' protracted struggle reveals the totality of war. No wonder the government's war against Filipino rebels is referred to as "total war."

On the other hand, the United States counter-insurgency approach is called low intensity conflict. Low intensity conflict tends to fragment the conflict, to give it an appearance of smallness and isolation from the ongoing war. Yet the effect is equally devastating. For instance, the military concentrates bombings, strafings, and hamleting (internal refugee camps) in one or two islands. People from other parts of the country are often totally unaware of the ongoing hostilities. By the time fact-finding missions arrive at the scenes of the events, hundreds have already been killed and the people are almost completely controlled by the military. On another level, religion, media, and other cultural forms are used in psychological war to alienate people from the struggle. As a result, people get confused and the struggle gets fragmented.

By contrast, in Israel the war against the Palestinians appears total. Repression is nationwide, terrorizing almost all, rich and poor, those in the Occupied Territories and those outside. The oppressor also uses psychological war to alienate supporters. The tensions of the conflict appear to have reached or are about to reach a peak point. "Something ought to change," is a remark I often heard Palestinians say about their abnormal situation.

I can foresee some changes in the treatment of Palestinians in the next couple of years. The United States may even convince Israel to allow democratic changes in the Occupied Territories. But these changes will only be palliatives and temporary unless the issue of arms and state power is addressed. Whatever response Israel delivers to the Palestinians, or the United States to the Filipinos, unless the roots of imperialism are genuinely confronted, the issue of people's security, sovereignty, and survival will remain.

As people fighting for justice, we need to deal with the state power and its armed might. I am saddened by the passive acceptance of many Christians of a possible nuclear holocaust: "In a nuclear warfare we all die anyway." What a grim picture of the future! What a difference from people committed to justice and liberation. They have great courage and hope in spite of the odds.

We have learned in our conflict in the Philippines that violent and bloody encounters can be lessened and even prevented by the participation of people who have options. Our grassroots Filipinos had long wrestled with the dictatorship before the assassination of Benigno Aquino. When the middle class got involved and participated in the protest, the events turned to a nonviolent confrontation. The world paid attention to our cause. Media covered us. And soldiers were hesitant to shoot the middle-class and upper-class sector of our society. Hence, the miracle of EDSA (*Edsa* is the name of the street where people stopped tanks and military troops in the 1986 "people power" event).

The people's power event took place four years ago, and we are still facing the same problems as before. But, at the same time, we are no longer the same people as before. We have learned much from our struggle for liberation. Gradually a faction of our people is beginning to realize that it was not enough to have blocked the tanks and weapons at Edsa; we should have dismantled them piece by piece and buried them for good. We should have asked the United States soldiers to pack up, leave their bases, and go home to their country. We should have turned their weapons into plowshares and farming tools, since we need food so badly.

We still ask the same questions: How are we to eliminate the war weapons and remove the United States bases in our country? What are our chances of saying no after the attacks on Panama and El Salvador by the United States? How are Palestinians going to deal with the occupation, with Israel's nuclear weapons?

Yet in spite of all the *angst*, the Palestinians and the Filipinos have remained courageous and hopeful. It is as if this is our strongest weapon against our enemies. Hope empowers the people who oppose injustice. And, as we continue to toil and struggle for our liberation, we are deeply comforted by the very process of our conscious participation in the creation of a new reality. We continue to hope for a final end to evil, and a complete new reality. In the words of the Bible,

> Then I saw *a new heaven and a new earth*; the first heaven and the first earth had disappeared now, and there was no longer any sea. I saw the holy city, the new Jerusalem, coming down out of heaven from God, prepared as a bride dressed for her husband. Then I heard a loud voice call from the throne, "Look, here God lives among human beings. He will make *his home among them; they will be his people*, and he will be their God, *God-with-them. He will wipe away all tears from their eyes*; there will be no more death, and no more mourning or sadness or pain. The world of the past has gone. . . .
>
> "Look, I am making the whole of creation new" (Rv 21:1-4, 5).

Contributors

PALESTINIANS

NADIA ABBOUSHI was born in Nablus, Palestine. She studied philosophy and religion at Beirut University College, and piano performance at State University in Potsdam, New York, where she received her B.A. She presently lives and teaches piano in Ramallah.

HANAN ASHRAWI lives in Ramallah and is professor of literature at Bir Zeit University. She is a distinguished writer, poet, and lecturer. A political activist, she is one of the representatives of the Palestinians of the Occupied Territories that met continually with U.S. Secretary of State Baker in 1991 and has taken a leadership role in the Palestinian-Israeli peace negotiations.

CANON RIAH ABU EL-ASSAL is rector of the Anglican Church and also directs the St. Margaret Hospice in Nazareth. A political activist, he has been a candidate with the Progressive List for Peace.

CANON NAIM S. ATEEK is the pastor of the Arabic-speaking congregation at St. George Cathedral in Jerusalem and author of *Justice and Only Justice: A Palestinian Theology of Liberation* (1989).

BASSAM E. BANNOURA was born in Beit Sahour by the Shepherd's Field. He received his Master of Divinity degree from the Associated Mennonite Biblical Seminaries in Elkhart, Indiana, in 1989 and has taught at the Bethlehem Bible College. He is presently director of Overseas Social Services in Jerusalem.

FATHER ELIAS CHACOUR is a Greek Catholic (Melkite) priest who pastors the Melkite Church in the village of Ibillin, Galilee, where he founded the Prophet Elias High School. He was born in the village of Bir'an in the Galilee which was destroyed by the Israelis in 1951. He is author of two books on his experience as an Israeli Palestinian working for peace: *Blood Brothers* (1984) and *We Belong to the Land* (1990).

CEDAR DUAYBIS is a Palestinian Episcopalian who works with the Jerusalem YWCA and is particularly concerned with women's issues in church and society.

MUNIR FASHEH teaches in the faculty of education at Bir Zeit University and is co-founder of the Tamer Institute, which promotes community-based education.

SAMEEH GHNADREH was born in Ramin in 1950. He holds an M.A. in literature, journalism, and philosophy. He currently lives in Nazareth and is the director of the Institute for Management and Vocational Training. Ghnadreh is married and the father of three children.

DR. JAD ISAAC, a native of Beit Sahour, received his higher education in England in plant physiology and biochemistry. He is the Director of the Applied Research Institute in Jerusalem and Associate Professor at Bethlehem University. During the Intifada he became well known for his promotion of backyard farming. He was imprisoned because of this activity.

DR. GERIES KHOURY is a Palestinian theologian from the Greek Orthodox tradition. He directs the Al-Liga Center for Religious Studies in the Holy Land, which focuses particularly on Muslim-Christian dialogue.

SAMIA KHOURY was born in Jaffa and received her B.A. in business administration from Southwestern University, Georgetown, Texas. She is active with women's work and is currently President of the Rawdat el-Zuhur Women's Voluntary Organizations. She is on the YWCA National Council and is a member of the Board of Trustees of Bir Zeit University.

NORA KORT was educated in Jerusalem, Switzerland, and the United States. She is a social worker and is manager of Social Services and Emergency Relief for Catholic Relief Services in Jerusalem. She is also president of the Arab Orthodox Society for the Relief of the Sick and of ATTA Services.

JONATHAN KUTTAB is a Palestinian human rights lawyer who received his J.D. degree from the School of Law of the University of Virginia in 1978. He is cofounder of Al-Haq (Law in the Service of Man) and the Mandela Institute for Political Prisoners. He is a member of both the New York and the Israeli Bar Associations.

DR. MITRI RAHEB did theological studies in Germany, completing a doctoral dissertation on the history of the Evangelical churches in Palestine from 1841 to 1967. Dr. Raheb is pastor of the Evangelical Lutheran Christian Church and teaches theology at area high schools and colleges. He is active in efforts to develop a contextualized Palestinian theology.

SALIM TAMARI is professor of sociology at Bir Zeit University and also edits the social science journal *Afaq*. He is associate editor for the *MERIP Middle East Report*.

SUAD YOUNAN is a Palestinian Lutheran living in Ramallah. She is pursuing a master's degree in English literature at Hebrew University and is also leader of the Women's Circle in Ramallah, in addition to serving as coordinator of women's groups in Lutheran churches throughout the West Bank.

JEAN ZARU is a Palestinian Quaker born in Ramallah. The mother of three children and the grandmother of four children, she has been involved in peace and justice issues both locally and internationally. She has served as a vice-president of the international YWCA and with the dialogue sub-unit of the World Council of Churches, as well as being a teacher of ethics and religion.

ZOUGHBI ELIAS ZOUGHBI is a Palestinian Greek Catholic (Melkite) who was born and raised in Bethlehem. He received his B.A. degree from Bethlehem University and his M.A. in Peace Studies from Notre Dame, Indiana, in 1989. He works with the Middle East Council of Churches and Middle East Witness in Bethlehem and in Jerusalem.

INTERNATIONAL

MYRNA ARCEO is a teacher and political activist in Manila, the Philippines.

MARK CHMIEL received his M.A. from the Maryknoll School of Theology and is presently pursuing doctoral work in theology at the Graduate Theological Union in Berkeley, with a particular concentration on issues in Jewish-Christian and Middle Eastern dialogue.

MARC H. ELLIS is a Jewish theologian who directs the Justice and Peace Studies Program at the Maryknoll School of Theology and is author of numerous books on Jewish liberation theology, most recently *Beyond Innocence and Redemption: Confronting the Holocaust and Israeli Power* (1990).

DR. ANN LOUISE GILLIGAN is an Irish feminist theologian who teaches theology at the Jesuit University in Dublin. She also is co-founder of the "Shanty," a community education project for poor and abused women.

DR. MARY E. HUNT is an American feminist theologian who is co-director of the Women's Alliance for Theology, Ethics and Ritual in the Washington, D.C. area. She is author of *Fierce Tenderness: A Feminist Theology of Friendship* (1991).

DR. ARTHUR PRESSLEY is an Afro-American pastoral psychology professor who teaches in the theological faculty of Drew University in Madison, New Jersey.

DR. ROSEMARY RADFORD RUETHER is an American feminist liberation theologian who has written numerous books, among them *The Wrath of Jonah: The Crisis of Religious Nationalism in the Israeli-Palestinian Conflict* (1989). She is the Georgia Harkness Professor of Theology at Garrett-Evangelical Theological Seminary and member of the Graduate Faculty of Northwestern University in Evanston, Illinois.

DR. MARY H. SCHERTZ is a professor of New Testament at the Associated Mennonite Biblical Seminaries in Elkhart, Indiana.

DON WAGNER is former Director of the Palestine Human Rights Campaign and presently director of Middle East work for Mercy Corp International. He is a Presbyterian minister who lives in Evanston, Illinois.